CAVEMAN LOGIC

HANK DAVIS

CAVEMAN LOGIC

THE PERSISTENCE OF PRIMITIVE THINKING IN A MODERN WORLD

Prometheus Books

59 John Glenn Drive
Amherst, New York 14228-2119

Published 2009 by Prometheus Books

Caveman Logic: The Persistence of Primitive Thinking in a Modern World.
Copyright © 2009 by Hank Davis. All rights reserved. No part of this publication
may be reproduced, stored in a retrieval system, or transmitted in any form or by
any means, digital, electronic, mechanical, photocopying, recording, or otherwise
or conveyed via the Internet or a Web site without prior written permission of the
publisher, except in the case of brief quotations embodied in critical articles and
reviews.

Inquiries should be addressed to
Prometheus Books
59 John Glenn Drive
Amherst, New York 14228–2119
VOICE: 716–691–0133, ext. 210
FAX: 716–691–0137
WWW.PROMETHEUSBOOKS.COM

13 12 11 10 09   5 4 3 2 1

Library of Congress Cataloging-in-Publication Data

Davis, Hank, 1941–
    Caveman logic: the persistence of primitive thinking in a modern world /
    Hank Davis.
      p. cm.
    Includes bibliographical references.
    ISBN 978–1–59102–721–8 (pbk.: alk. paper)
    1. Reasoning. 2. Thought and thinking. 3. Stupidity. 4. Errors. I. Title

BC177.D385 2009
153.4 22   2009010307

Printed in the United States of America on acid-free paper

CONTENTS

 # ACKNOWLEDGMENTS

My parents, Sarah and Al Davis, offered religion as part of my cultural identity. The details were a bit fuzzy and they were never shoved down my throat. My parents and extended family tolerated any manner of questions; in fact, they seemed to enjoy them. I grew up assuming that Jews, indeed people of all religions, loved to discuss and debate their faith. Obviously, I was wrong. My parents wanted and expected me to be a good boy. Being smart and being kind were the two biggest virtues in our home. Both were independent of religious training or pressure of any kind. I was never threatened with God's vengeance or "going to hell." I couldn't even imagine such things. There were other, gentler incentives for "being a mensch."

One way or another, I've been writing this book for over thirty years. That means I have countless students and colleagues to thank, whose influence was indelible. None more so than Harry Hurwitz, as fine a friend and mentor as one can have. I am also thankful to Martin Daly, who in the course of casual conversation informed (or perhaps reminded) me that I was an evolutionary psychologist. He didn't have to tell me twice.

I have many other people to thank. Kataline Trudel spent the past several years reading drafts of this manuscript and discussing ideas with me. She made this project her own, back when she was still an undergraduate, and has remained with it to completion. I can't imagine having done it without her. Holly Franklin became involved more recently and caught up quickly. She contributed encouragement as well as her newspaper background and copy-editing skills. Both were very much appreciated.

Friends and colleagues supplied me with a steady diet of articles about Caveman Logic in its many, sometimes bizarre forms. There seemed no limit to them. Fortunately, these friends were also willing to discuss the ideas they had provoked and critique what I had written about them. I thank Doug Reberg and Scott Parker for their insights. I also thank Kat Bergeron, Chris DiCarlo, Alan Wildeman, Loren Lind, and Colin Escott for their contributions. I am also grateful to Chris Scimmi, a fine artist, for creating the Caveman image that appears throughout this book.

There was also plenty of moral support for what I was doing. I thank Beth Scimmi and Susan Simmons for those simple "How's the book coming?" or "What did you write about today?" queries. I never felt like I was working alone.

Many of us working in this field have been provoked, one way or another, by the scholarship of the late Steven Jay Gould. Gould and I were born in the same year and we both grew up in New York—he in Queens and I in the Bronx and Yonkers. We disagreed strongly about the virtues of evolutionary psychology, but we shared the broader conviction that comfort is a poor substitute for rationality in shaping one's worldview. When Gould and I found ourselves sitting side by side at dinner after his commencement address at my university, we talked nonstop. Almost all of it was about baseball. Not baseball as a metaphor for life or natural selection, but baseball as a game we had both played as children and watched, analyzed, and written about as men.[1]

I think my parents would have been proud of this book. Maybe a little surprised, but proud. Mostly they would have been pleased that I was happy with the result and had thoroughly enjoyed the process of creating it.

 # INTRODUCTION

Diana Duyser saw the face of the Blessed Virgin staring up at her from a grilled cheese sandwich she had begun to eat. The Florida resident sold the remainder of her meal on ebay.com for $37,000. Guadalupe Lopez, the mother of actress Jennifer Lopez, walked into a casino in Atlantic City to play the slot machines. She eyed the huge prize, uttered a few heaven-bound words, then sat down to play. Before the dust cleared, she had won a jackpot of $2.4 million. In the press conference that followed, Ms. Lopez called her winnings "proof of the power of prayer."

Few Americans would disagree with her. A June 2008 survey[1] revealed that about a third of Americans believe they receive answers to "prayer requests" at least once a month. Eighty percent of respondents believe in angels and demons as active forces in their everyday lives. This goes beyond mere belief in God, which clocks in at about 92 percent according to the same poll. No one was doing formal surveys of superstitious belief or religiosity in medieval Europe, but it's hard to imagine the results would have been a whole lot different.

Both Lopez's statement and seeing the image of a religious icon on a piece of fried food are prime examples of what we will refer to as *Caveman Logic*. So is our tendency to utter a reflexive "Thank God!" when something good happens to us, or to blame vengeful deities or spirits when natural disasters occur ("New Orleans must have had it coming!"). Fear, irrationality, and superstition are rapidly moving to the mainstream of American culture. International surveys confirm that the United States has lost its preeminence in education and science. In their stead, we rival Middle Eastern and African nations in measures of religiosity.

Yes, it's true that we can fit more songs than ever on an iPod and we regularly expand the boundaries of medical knowledge. But we also show the sophistication of a Neanderthal in evaluating fragmentary evidence and are still prone to reaching conclusions about ghosts, "signs," and magical powers in the world around us. We can design and repair rocket engines, but most humans are unable to confine that primitive part of their minds to the back burner. Caveman Logic continues to inform the most personal side of our belief systems.

In this book, we have chosen the caveman as a symbol of our less-rational, more-superstitious self. I hate to pick on cavemen and stigmatize them any further. Cavemen have been turned into caricatures in popular culture by everything from cartoons like *The Flintstones*, *B.C.*, *Alley Oop*, and *The Far Side* to a series of highly successful commercials by GEICO Insurance ("So simple, even a caveman can do it").[2] These depictions all convey misinformation for comic effect. But there is one trait we can be pretty sure of: cavemen were not very bright. Few of us would consult a caveman for financial or romantic advice; nor would we want to worship with one. Yet, in a sense, we do all three. That's how much power our Stone Age minds have in everyday affairs.

While we can parody those who worship fried food or bargain with deities to intervene in their everyday affairs, these kinds of activities remain alarmingly widespread. Why are we so illogical and why do we reach similar superstitious conclusions the world over? This book examines both of these questions and finds answers rooted in evolutionary psychology.

Evolutionary psychology is a relatively new field that offers a scientific, indeed a biological approach, to understanding human behavior. Unlike other fields of psychology, an evolutionary approach attempts to understand humans as part of the biological world in which they evolved. Many of those puzzling, irrational behaviors may stem from adaptations made by our ancestors. If so, we are stuck with mental modules that weigh us down in both laughable and dangerous ways. That mental equipment we carry in our modern skulls is over a hundred thousand years out of date. But instead of challenging our limitations and trying to remedy their effects, we create cultural institutions that normalize them. At this rate, we'll remain stuck in the Pleistocene for years to come.

I don't blame our prehistoric ancestors for being who they were. They did their jobs by surviving and reproducing and contributing to the chain of events that led to us. Their world was very different from ours and they understood a lot less about their place in it. Most of what we inherited from them, mentally speaking, is pretty impressive. From an evolutionary point of view, we are the descendants of a long line of successful competitors. But times have changed. The Pleistocene Age, when the bulk of human evolution took place, is over, although it left some deep marks on our minds. Fortunately, they weren't written in indelible ink.

Is this book taking potshots at a few primitive and superstitious individuals? Has magical thinking gone the way of the Middle Ages, if not the Stone Age? Sadly, the answer to both questions is no. Caveman Logic is alive and well in our everyday lives. Our ancestors who made it through the Pleistocene Age did so with brute force and a brain full of "primitive instincts." Most of that brute force is long gone or illegal, but some very primitive forms of mental life are still with us today. Worse yet, those cognitive and perceptual flaws often function unchallenged in our daily lives. Their roots may lie in the Pleistocene Age, but their costs in the modern world are very real. Those winners in the relentless competition that preceded us passed along everything they had. We got the full package, warts and all. At best, we are saddled with too many mistaken beliefs. At worst, we may end up annihilating each other.

We need to see our defective Stone Age minds for what they are if we ever hope to drag ourselves, kicking and screaming, into the twenty-first century. This book advocates a difficult transition from the Pleistocene to the modern age. Our bodies seem to be standing up rather well; it's our minds that are slipping into obsolescence.

Is such a transition possible? Will it require a brain transplant to fix the problems we identify here? I believe we can do it without surgery. The good news is that we actually have something to say about how we use our minds. We may be predisposed to Caveman Logic but we are not bound by it. Biology is not destiny.

Our Stone Age brains will continue to send us hair-triggered perceptions and conclusions that are just plain wrong. What we need more than anything is the will to question those messages as quickly as they occur. It won't be easy. Those autopilot reactions not only feel "right"—they often feel "good." They have been second nature to us for so long that we can't imagine not accepting them at face value.

Caveman logic persists for another reason as well: it receives social support. That's no small incentive when it comes to human behavior. We are arguably the most social species on the planet and consensual validity counts for a lot with us. But we can level the playing field a bit by developing support systems for those coura-geous people who do question their Stone Age reactions. At pre-sent, there is very little of that support available.

If we fail to do any of this, we are relinquishing control to our ancestors. Whether or not we take those first few halting steps out of the Pleistocene night is the agenda of this book. It's time to unlock the manual override portion of our brains, put those primi-tive autopilot settings into storage, and explore the real mental potential of our species.

Chapter 1

THE ROAD TO IMPERFECTION

THE CRADLE OF LIFE

Human beings evolved in a world unlike the one we inhabit today. Our sense of history, as it is taught in high school and portrayed in films, doesn't begin to do justice to what our species has been through.

Going back two hundred years for an entertaining "historical drama" leaves us squarely in modern times, evolutionarily speaking. Other than different hair and clothing styles, that brief journey hasn't begun to move us out of the modern world. Even if we go back to the time of Jesus or, further yet, to Greek civilization, we're still in modern times. Gone are the trains, planes, automobiles, and iPods, but if we could magically visit these times and places, we'd still see recognizable humans acting in recognizable ways. That is why stories set in so-called ancient times still resonate with us today. Their settings are very recent.

Human beings may be a very new species in terms of life on Earth, but we still go back a long time. The hominids that would eventually become humans split away from a common ancestor, leaving the apes behind about 6 million years ago. Those early proto-humans went through a hell of a lot so you could download music and buy airline tickets online. The selection pressure on them to survive and reproduce was tremendous, and living conditions were harsh beyond our imaginations. The physical appearance of these early hominids was also different from what we take for granted today. Physical changes were evolving and accumulating slowly in both the minds and the bodies of our early ancestors.

Natural selection was in no hurry. On one hand, it is a ruthless efficiency expert, heartlessly excluding those features that do not maximize reproductive success. On the other hand, it can only select among existing alternatives. That slows things down. Natural selection can't cause giraffes to grow long necks just because the food supply happens to be located above their heads. But if a relatively long-necked individual does show up, he or she is more likely to experience reproductive success. Because that longer neck is coded in the individual's genetic material, and because that individual may be more successful than its short-necked competitors, long-necked giraffes may gradually become more numerous in the population.

Plainly, evolution through natural selection only works on traits that have a genetic basis. Heredity is the cornerstone of Darwinian theory. Without it, the effects of natural selection would be confined to a single generation. Every generation would be starting from scratch. If some trait (e.g., a snazzy new hairstyle) were acquired during an individual's lifetime, then natural selection could do nothing with it other than conferring some transient rewards (perhaps a few more sexual partners). Here on Earth, almost every important behavioral and physical feature of plant and animal life is transmitted genetically and is directly vulnerable to selection pressure. Thus, traits that lead to greater reproductive success eventually spread and often become standard equipment for a species.

Traits that meet environmental challenges and enhance reproductive success are known as *adaptations*. When the person carrying the genes for these traits reproduces, there is a chance the traits will be carried into the next generation. The final results also depend on the genome of the sexual partner. For all the pleasure it produces, sexual reproduction also carries some disadvantages. The most obvious is that each partner contributes only half of the new genome.

It makes sense that individuals do not mate indiscriminately. No one, whether a Nobel laureate or a tree frog, wants a substandard partner. All forms of animal life have evolved methods for "screening" potential mates in order to select those with the best genomes. Such screening need not be conscious; indeed, it rarely is, even among our own species. Human mating rituals, whether practiced at high school dances or in so-called primitive societies in the Amazon basin, are only one example of this. A zoologist could dazzle us with stories of how other animal species choose or attract partners. One of my favorites involves the gladiator frog (*Hyla rosenbergi*). As in most species, the female is very particular when it comes to choosing the father of her offspring. Since "toughness" is a desirable trait in this pugnacious species, the female practices a very simple screening technique. She approaches her potential mate and literally does her best to knock him off his feet. If she succeeds, that's one Mr. Froggie that won't get lucky with her.

Natural selection is not really a very contentious process despite the uninformed political debate that swirls around it. At its most basic level, natural selection simply means that heritable differences within a species lead to different levels of reproductive success. The most successful adaptations tend to spread in the population. That hardly seems like a difficult or dangerous idea. Dog breeders routinely take advantage of it, substituting their own preferences for the traits that nature might select.

According to most surveys, the majority of Americans do not "believe in" Darwinian evolution. This seems an unfathomable state of affairs in the twenty-first century. Obviously, someone has to understand a viewpoint before deciding whether to accept or reject it. I've talked to enough high school students and teachers to conclude that Darwinian evolution is neither well taught nor well understood. It is entirely possible that the view of Darwin many

Americans reject would also be rejected by most scientists. It is simply wrong. The misunderstanding is so pervasive. Most people can't even tell you the name of Darwin's famous book. Ask someone and, if they know the book at all, they are likely to report *Origin of the Species* rather than *On the Origin of Species*. It is a subtle difference, but quite telling. Even Spencer Tracy, appearing as Clarence Darrow in the award-winning 1960 film *Inherit the Wind*, got it wrong.

At a time when debates over the teaching of evolution are turning neighbor against neighbor and throwing local school districts into chaos, it would seem criminal not to bring combatants to a common understanding. *Then* let them debate. This has plainly not happened and is a glaring fault of the American educational system. When students tell me (as they occasionally do in Introductory Psychology classes) that they do not accept Darwin, I usually ask them what they mean. I cannot recall a single occasion when such a forcefully opinionated student has gotten it right. The most frequent response is, "It means we come from monkeys." Who wouldn't reject that? Whether by incompetence or willful misrepresentation, natural selection is just not getting a good hearing.

Perhaps if people *understood* natural selection, they'd be more likely to *accept* it. The principle does not seem very threatening (although the wrongheaded version can be quite upsetting to many). Moreover, as Richard Dawkins argues, natural selection is inevitable once you accept a few basic premises. Susan Blackmore concludes in her book *The Meme Machine*, "If there is a replicator that makes imperfect copies of itself, only some of which survive, then evolution simply *must* occur. . . . The inevitabilty of evolution is part of what makes Darwin's insight so clever. All you need is the right starting conditions and evolution just has to happen."[1]

So what conditions must be in place for this inevitable process to occur? For one thing, we are all replicators. Human beings replicate sexually. Some anti-Darwinians may be uncomfortable acknowledging that process, but it is nonetheless true. I have never heard an anti-Darwinian debate heredity. Most, if not all, accept that we pass along our genetic information, which is then combined with our partner's contribution to form a new organism. That is not contentious. The fact that our offspring are composed of a mixture of maternal and paternal DNA is also not contentious. Every gene you carry came from either your mother or your father. No one debates that.

So far, so good. We've got the "replicator" part into the acceptance column. What about that "makes imperfect copies" part? This simply means that copying errors occur. They don't occur very frequently (maybe about one in a million), but they do occur. These errors are called *alternative alleles* or, more commonly, *mutations*. They result in some change in the phenotype. Most of the time they are inconsequential. When they do matter, they are usually negative. In other words, the ancestral allele was a better deal than the mutated one. And so the mutation does not spread in the population. But the important point here—and it is indeed a central point to natural selection—is that mutations, those inevitable copying errors, provide variation in the human genome. Variation is *good*. You wouldn't want uniformity or perfection. Those errors are essential to the survival of the species. If there were no errors (i.e., if copying were perfect), there would be no variation among phenotypes and nothing for natural selection to work on.

So far, we have upset no one in the audience, regardless of whether seated on the extreme right or left side. What's next? Those slight variants go forth into their environments and some of them do better than others. You might not like the idea of competition, but it is an inevitable part of life on this planet. Some of those mutations result in greater reproductive success than others, as members of the species compete with each other for precious resources. The environment is a filter, and some traits lead to greater reproductive success than their alternatives.

As Darwin argued in 1859, occasionally animals undergo sufficient change to become reproductively isolated. Geography contributes to this isolation as well. When these noninbreeding populations become sufficiently differentiated, a new species has been formed. Rats and mice are good examples: they remain closely related, but as long as we have known them they have been separate species with a common ancestor. They share physical and behavioral traits, but they also have differences in size and behavior.

And there you have it. An absolutely blind and lawful process without values or agendas. It may not be the stuff of fairy tales or creation myths, but it grinds away in its relentless way, producing outcomes. My colleague Martin Daly has stated it eloquently: "Natural selection doesn't have goals, but it's the reason organisms do."[2] That's a wonderful summary of life on this planet, although the idea is a bit difficult for some people to grasp. It also doesn't help that natural selection moves very slowly, making the concept an even more difficult sell.

True, there is no father figure/deity with agendas we can talk about in human terms. But that isn't Darwin's fault, any more than Newton was responsible for the law of gravity. In any case, natural selection is part of a world full of wonder, willing to reveal itself as we ask the right questions and pool our knowledge. The universe is no less thrilling as we gradually uncover its secrets and confront its mysteries. And we do so using the splendid intelligence our species has evolved. What could be more uplifting than that?

It's worth remembering that part about copying errors. If all individuals were identical (e.g., in a cloned population), selection would be forced to stand still. All it would take is a single parasite or predator to detect a weakness and a whole population would be at risk. The Irish potato famine of the mid-nineteenth century is a widely cited example of such vulnerability. Historians often point to Ireland's dependence on a single crop as the key to the tragedy, but it was more than that. Genetic variation could have saved the Irish potato crop. Without it, a single form of water mold (*Phytophthora infestans*) was able to destroy the crop almost overnight. Genetic variation is an essential building block for the design of well-adapted individuals, and it is also a source of resistance when a species comes into contact with predators, be they four footed or single celled. As many as 1 million people were killed by the Irish potato famine by 1850 and perhaps twice that number were forced to immigrate to the United States, Canada, Australia, and other parts of Great Britain. The expression "Celebrate Diversity" takes on new meaning when you consider how natural selection works.

THROUGH A MICROSCOPE DARKLY

Although molecular biology is well beyond the scope of this book, there are several basic things we need to cover. The collection of genes in an organism, called its *genotype*, is largely responsible for creating (with some help from the environment) the organism's observable traits, collectively called its *phenotype*. Genes are composed of deoxyribonucleic acid (DNA). DNA contains the instructions that specify which proteins should be made. By doing this, the DNA is responsible for shaping the phenotype.

If stretched out for display, every cell in your body contains about six feet of DNA. Every nine hundred cells therefore produce over a mile of DNA. Because the human body contains as many as 100 trillion cells, our bodies house over a billion miles of DNA. That's a pretty large number. The distance to the sun is only 93 million miles, in comparison.

We are still learning about DNA. It seems that every time we look at the human and chimpanzee genomes side by side, the degree of similarity has grown. Other than making glib statements like "Humans and chimps are more related than mice and rats," what do we really know? As I write this in 2008, it seems the less I say about this area of research, the better. Almost anything is likely to become obsolete in short order. Craig Venter has decoded the human genome and made his own diploid genome available on the Web (www.jcvi.org).

We have watched estimates of the "degree of overlap" between human and chimpanzee increase from 97 percent to nearly 99 percent in the span of less than ten years. At the same time, estimates of the number of base pairs in the human genome seem to be dropping at a steady rate. Prior to mapping the human genome in 2000, estimates of the number of human genes were fixed at about 100,000. Shortly thereafter, that number fell to about 25,000, a dramatic drop by any reckoning. Had I written this book a year ago, that number would have stood at about 22,000. By the time you read this, it may lie below 20,000. The estimate keeps shrinking, yet the human genome remains firmly in place. Plainly, the number of genes is not the whole story of what makes us distinctly human.

Somewhere, somehow, there are "switches" in the genome that tell our genes when to turn on and express themselves, thus turning a genotype into a phenotype. The switches that turn genes on and off are not well understood. Some of them lie within the genes themselves. Others are thought to lie within the so-called "junk DNA," poorly understood matter that comprises the large majority of the genome. The picture is even more complicated. In 2006, it was reported that individual differences may result from previously undetected variations in the number of times that certain key genes are copied in the genome. Preliminary findings suggest that entire sequences may be repeated as many as ten times, differing widely between individuals and yielding differences in the overall "copy number" of genes. Perhaps we have ignored material such as this or "junk DNA" for too long, focusing instead on the more obvious proteins that were easier to measure and investigate.[3] In any case, high school genetics books (often called molecular biology texts in universities) are losing their resale value almost as quickly as they are published. It has become that difficult to stay current.

BACK TO THE PLEISTOCENE

Our own ancestors (don't visualize your grandfather here; try to imagine someone who lived two hundred thousand years ago) lived in small nomadic bands. A lot of inbreeding occurred and most of the persons within the band were genetically related. They made a living by hunting together and gathering nuts and fruit that grew locally. These activities were fraught with peril. Animals that were being hunted for food had no interest in being eaten. They had their own concerns about survival and reproduction and vigorously resisted our attempts to turn them into table scraps. Even nuts and berries that were available locally presented difficulties for our ancestors. "Nuts and fruit" may sound like a healthy diet today, but much of that locally grown produce had an agenda of its own that probably did not include traveling through a human digestive system.

In short, food sources were, to quote a vivid description, "scarce and antagonistic." Food acquisition and storage were only a few of the daily problems facing our hominin ancestors. *Hominin* is the term we want here, since we're concerned with only humans and chimps, not with the other great apes. Their survival was also threatened by environmental predators. Some of them were other humans, whose traveling bands were anything but friendly or cooperative. The study of present-day "primitive" people like the Yanomamo of the Amazon rainforest provides some insight into the perils of Pleistocene life, including competition between neighboring social groups and the kind of "spoils" a military victory entitled the winner to claim. Murder rates in contemporary cities like Detroit or Miami have nothing on so-called primitive cultures and, presumably, the Pleistocene world in which our ancestors lived.

In addition to human predators, our ancestors also faced threats from animals that viewed us as potential food sources and enthusiastically hunted us as we did them. But perhaps the greatest peril of all came from the smallest members of the living environment. Microscopic parasites represented, as they do today, a major threat to human health and survival. Imagine facing a predator that is invisible, deadly, and whose ways are beyond your understanding or control. Even if you could defend against it using some poorly understood natural remedy, the predator could mutate quickly to work around whatever paltry defense you could put in its way.

This scenario partially describes the life of our ancestors. For them, the workings of the physical world must have seemed unpredictable, unfathomable, and truly frightening. Perils were almost constant and comprehension was minimal. Keep this in mind when you're trying to imagine the kind of mental processes that would have helped serve survival and reproduction. Understand also that much human evolution took place before there was written or spoken language. (The Sumerians invented written language around 3000 BCE.) If someone could not state his business clearly, it would have helped to be able to read his intentions and trustworthiness using other means. Long before there was spoken language, there was body language. Anyone who could send and receive it fluently was at a considerable advantage.

Something else to consider: there were no external agencies for the enforcement of right and wrong. Social rules and alliances may have been in place, but the notion of codified "laws" or individuals whose job it was to enforce the laws was unknown for much of human history. If anyone were going to detect and punish that cheater, it had better be you. Rule breaking, nonreciprocity, and cheating were major issues for our ancestors and exerted strong selection pressure on the design of their minds. Such mental "circuitry" continues to play a major part in our lives today, long after formalized social rules and legal systems have reduced the need for it.

For well over 3 million years after splitting away from the apes, our species remained largely unchanged socially, cognitively, or physically. These early hominins were not very impressive by today's intellectual standards, although they were the best the Earth had to offer at the time.

Then something happened. Just what that something might have been remains a matter of conjecture. The results were a series of dramatic changes to our ancestors that led to a near doubling in the size of their brains and an exodus from the African continent by *Homo erectus*. Compressing 3 million years of hominin history into a paragraph or two can only trivialize or omit important events, but the bottom line is this: over this period, our species grew in stature, dispersion, and intelligence. It is the last of these that mattered most. Competition for finite resources on the planet has always included species and individuals who were stronger or more numerous than our ancestors. But the competition was never smarter.

By 500,000 years ago, our ancestors were busy defining their dominance. When we think of ourselves as a species, we are usually picturing the anatomically modern version known as *Homo sapiens*. But there is a direct line between the modern *H. sapiens* and earlier hominins like *Australopithecus*, *Homo habilis*, and *Homo erectus*. The physical changes, most notably in stature and relative brain size, occasioned a growing range of intellectual abilities.

That final 500,000 years, composing barely 10 percent of our development, was a time of many crucial changes in our species. Probably the two most important changes, in terms of what our lives have become today, were language and domestication. It is virtually impossible to overstate the importance of language in defining who we are or our range of accomplishments. Communication is widespread within the animal kingdom; language is not. Using labor-intensive procedures, we may train a chimpanzee or a parrot or a gorilla to ask for a tickle or tell us the number of items on a computer screen. But as we know and employ it every day, language remains the sole domain of our species. Indeed, getting a human *not* to learn language is quite a feat. How important is language in other aspects of human accomplishment? Make your own "Top 10" list and try to imagine any of those feats emerging without written or spoken language.

Domestication may seem an odd choice for the second most important milestone in human development but, when it occurred about ten thousand years ago, our species took a giant step forward. To bring plants and animals—essential sources of food and labor—under our control was a turning point for our species. Consider the effects of freeing our ancestors from the daily toils and perils of searching for sustenance. Now they could pursue other matters, perhaps the very things that make our species so noteworthy. Nothing on your "Top 10" list would have been accomplished if our species had been half starved or had its time consumed with hunting, berry picking, and back-breaking labor. Domestication goes well beyond pet dogs and cats.

We were not always the only human species on the planet. Most people know that other humans came *before* us but are surprised to learn that different species of humans lived at the same time. The most conspicuous example is *Homo neanderthalensis*.[4] Neanderthals, who have become figures of almost cartoonlike proportions in popular culture, were actually successful competitors who lived as recently as 28,000 years ago. *H. sapiens* and Neanderthals diverged from a common ancestor about 370,000 years ago, and Neanderthals lived successfully in Eurasia for nearly 200,000 years. They were not mere brutes or scavengers, as occasionally portrayed. Evidence from 60,000 years ago indicates that Neanderthals buried their dead ceremonially with medicinal plants or flowers. Even more important, they carried a version of the FOXP2 gene associated with human language ability. Shorter and stockier than *H. sapiens*, Neanderthals eventually disappeared along with *Cro-Magnons*, our ancestors in western Europe. When we hear stories of elaborate cave paintings and burial sites in France and Spain, it is the Cro-Magnons who were responsible. In their book, *Biology, Evolution and Human Nature*, Timothy Goldsmith and William Zimmerman describe Cro-Magnons as "intellectually and emotionally very much the same as ourselves."[5]

The bottom line is that when you think of ancestors, you're likely to stop the search at the level of great-grandfather. When you think of history, images of George Washington often come into view. Neither is particularly relevant to the issues in this book. The ancestors we have in mind here are shared by you, me, *and* George Washington. We're talking about our *species'* ancestors. Whether we like it or not, the solutions to their numerous struggles are reflected in our genome today. For better or worse, their successes are translated into the mental and physical equipment we carry with us in the modern world. We're talking about far more than eye color or hair texture. These are about basic, species-wide human qualities and predispositions. They are there whether your hair is curly or straight, blond, brunette, or receding fast.

And there you have it. A journey that began its final leg about 6 million years ago, simmering without much change for much of that time, suddenly coming to a boil in the last half a million years and then reaching a frenzy of activity during the past 50,000 to 100,000 years—an era called the Pleistocene. This "history" is plainly very different from the images conveyed by Julius Caesar, Abraham Lincoln, or World War II. It is also ancient and lengthy. And through it all, our species was undergoing physical and mental changes that best adapted it to life under conditions that barely resemble our present world. The genetics that underlie these adaptations were carried forward even after they ceased to be particularly useful. As the expression goes, "Evolutionary wisdom is past wisdom." It is always out of date. It reflects where we came from. The proverbial Cradle of Life is where our minds were formed.

THE ILLUSION GENERATOR

The human mind is an illusion generator. Since you *have* a human mind, that statement probably either feels wrong or like an insult.

It is neither. Patterns are everything to us. We hunger for them. We revel in them. They are the basis for art, literature, music, and much more in our lives. But a perceptual system that is so geared to wrestling patterns out of complex arrays of stimuli is bound to produce some false positives. From time to time we are going to see or hear what is not there, and those cases will seem no less compelling to us. They are the territory of this book.

You have sense organs (we'll focus on the eye and the ear) and an apparatus for interpreting the information those organs provide. That's where your mind comes in. Strictly speaking, we are talking about your brain, which is a modular organ. Our focus here is with the *interpreter function*—the part of your brain that takes all those raw sensory impulses just forwarded by your eyes or ears and does its job by trying to make sense of what it has registered. There are a lot of other jobs your brain does—it regulates your body temperature, controls your arousal level, modulates your response to pain in your left foot, and so on. All of those things and a lot more are beyond the scope of this book. It is that function of the brain we loosely call "the mind" that is our focus.

Technically speaking, our eyes and ears are flawed too. Yes, they are a marvel of engineering that took millions of years to evolve. But they are incomplete: they are not responsive to all the sights and sounds out there. In fact, they are responsive to a very narrow range of what exists around us. Imagine a line stretching for over a mile. It represents all the stimuli, the physical waveforms if you prefer, that you might see or hear. Now imagine going up to that very long line and sticking a pin into it. The head of that pin represents the range of stimuli you can actually see and hear. All the rest in both directions is beyond your capability. For some people, that news alone is startling. They've always assumed they can see and hear everything there is to see and hear. It's true that older folks may need eyeglasses or a hearing aid, but prior to that all the sensory information in the world must have been getting through, right?

Nothing could be further from the truth.

As rich and beautiful as the world may look and sound to us, it is based on a tiny little bandwidth of raw sensory information that we manage to glean. For example, wavelengths longer than those for the color "red" are called "infrared." We cannot see them. Similarly, wavelengths shorter than those for the color "violet" are called "ultraviolet." Again, we are blind to such energy, although it is measurably present all around us. Our ears are similarly insensitive to sound waves that lie above or below the audible part of the spectrum (roughly between 20 and 20,000 Hz or cycles per second). The energy is there. Some of it we might have heard when we were younger or before we attended too many rock concerts. But, even then, we were relatively impoverished. Those other wave frequencies just couldn't get through. Our problem was simply that we are human.

Nevertheless, the information we do see and hear seems enough; it constitutes reality to us and gives us the illusion of a complete world. We may be vaguely aware that other animals see and hear different things than we do. Dogs (and rats and many other mammals) can hear high-frequency sounds we can only imagine. Bees can see polarized light; hawks can see accurately at distances we can approximate only by using high-tech intervention.

But, the truth is, none of these sensory deficits matters as much as the limitations of our mind. We don't *need* to see and hear everything out there. We are getting more than enough raw sensory information to function at a very high level. It is what we make of those raw sensations that creates problems. Those cognitive and perceptual problems are the subject matter of this book. The science of psychology makes the distinction between sensation and perception. Sensation refers to the structure and activity of our sense organs. Again, that is not the focus of this book. Perception, on the other hand, is. How we perceive the world is the story of what our minds do with those raw sensory inputs. Once our minds get involved in the process, we are in for a bumpy ride.

Most Introductory Psychology textbooks contain sections on optical illusions. There are relatively few of them and they are well studied. Most students enjoy reading about them because, like watching magic tricks, they provide some excitement. They violate your expectations and create experiences that you *know* can't be happening in the real world. But even optical illusions are just a hint of the mental distortions that are part of our everyday lives.

Introductory Psychology books also contain sections on common errors in thinking. These come a lot closer to our concerns here. Compared to optical illusions, these cognitive shortcomings are less well studied, although that is starting to change. They go by different names such as "heuristics" and "biases" and often appear in chapters of Introductory Psychology books labeled "cognitive psychology."[6] There is even some controversy over whether they are assets or liabilities. In truth, they are both. The real problem is our failure to recognize them for what they are and take steps to remedy them.

Let's consider a simple example. If you depended strictly on a literal interpretation of your sensory evidence, there would be good reason to believe that (1) Earth is flat, and (2) the sun, moon, and stars rotate around our planet, which remains fixed at the center of the universe. In fact, that is exactly what people believed until fairly recently in human history. They did not question the evidence of their senses and found it both threatening and, in some cases, quite offensive to have these beliefs challenged.

The reason their beliefs were challenged is that scientific advances provided more-sophisticated ways of gathering evidence. This new evidence became more and more difficult to ignore and it bore directly on how we saw our planet and its place in the solar system. As word spread, it became increasingly threatening to certain institutions whose power was vested in the status quo, no matter how wrong it was. The Catholic church, for example, used all the authority at its disposal to suppress the idea that Earth revolved around the sun, and it brought severe penalties (ranging from excommunication to death) to those, such as the astronomer Copernicus, who professed an alternative viewpoint. Institutional resistance is not uncommon in cases where science challenges widely held but outdated viewpoints. Although not as powerful as the Catholic church, there remains to this day a Flat Earth Society.

This is not simply ancient history. It has everything to do with issues facing us today. Ask yourself why flat earth and center of the solar system beliefs were so widely held a thousand years ago. The answer quite simply is that the human mind did the best job it could with the available evidence of its senses, and that the conclusions it reached, however wrong, were socially supported. The person on the street in the year 1242 had essentially the same mind you do. He had far less information than you have, but he was subject to the same perceptual illusions, needs, and social pressures that you are. Arguing about Earth's place in the universe made no sense because, as far as he could tell, the status quo seemed right. Moreover, it felt good, even comforting, to think that he and his family were important enough to be living at the center of the universe. And, speaking of his family, they all seemed to share this view, as did his closest friends and associates. Challenging this view, even if he had some evidence or doubts, would only bring conflict. Life was stressful enough already.

And so for many years Earth remained flat and at the center of the universe, at least according to popular belief. Don't make the mistake of believing that such ignorance or defensiveness was confined to the Middle Ages. Transitional times, as far as ideas are concerned, are often ugly periods in human history. Arguably, such ignorance and resistance are even more egregious during more-enlightened times like the present.

In some ways, we are the lucky ones. Our civilization has never been as knowledgeable as it is today. There has never been as much scientific understanding of the world around us as there is right at this moment. We have put many faulty beliefs behind us. Yet, because our minds are no more evolved than they were a thousand years ago, we are just as vulnerable to illusion, comfort, and social pressure as our ancestors were. Faced with incomplete sensory evidence, we are just as likely to come to wrong conclusions and then fight passionately to maintain those views because of the comfort or stability they provide. We may be less ignorant than our ancestors, but all the hard-won additional information does us no good if we don't let it inform our thinking.

TWO TYPES OF ERRORS

Broadly speaking, there are two ways you can make a perceptual mistake: You can fail to see something that is there, or you can see something that isn't there. Neither is good, but as errors go, these two mistakes may not be equally costly. Imagine that you're in charge of designing the justice system for a new society. If your citizens decide the worst thing that can happen is to let a murderer go free, then you will require a fairly low standard of evidence. In this way, you'll probably catch every murderer in sight. Nobody will escape detection. The problem is, you'll probably also prosecute a few people who weren't actually murderers. Think of these as *Type I errors*. By allowing a few Type I errors (i.e., "false positives") to occur, you worry a lot less about real murderers going free. Those are called *Type II errors*, and you've just about eliminated them in your system.

But imagine that your new justice system has a different set of priorities. What if its primary concern is to never execute an innocent man. In other words, Type I errors are absolutely intolerable. And so you raise the threshold for a conviction so high that you can virtually guarantee that no innocent person will be wrongly executed. Of course, in doing so, it's likely that a few real murderers will get away.

This simple lesson in statistical decision theory makes an important point. The probability of Type I and Type II errors are related. You decide which is more important to you and set the thresholds accordingly. There are always risks of errors occurring when you make decisions based on incomplete information. You simply have to decide which of the two kinds of mistakes will be better tolerated. I have many middle-aged male friends who debate the merits of a PSA test for prostate cancer. The test almost never misses an actual case of the disease, but it is notorious for false positives. As a potential victim of the disease, would you want to be sure that nothing life threatening has slipped by undetected, even if it means worrying needlessly after being told about a condition you actually didn't have?

Natural selection of the human perceptual system faced these issues quite some time ago, and it is clear which approach to the Type I versus Type II errors it took. Imagine the following scenario. One of your ancestors is walking through the forest and sees something on the path ahead. It might be a predator. Then again, it might be a random array of shapes and textures amounting to nothing. If he believes it to be dangerous, he takes the appropriate defensive steps. Perhaps he freezes or arms himself or flees. What's the best that can happen? He survives a lethal encounter and gets to live and function another day. What's the worst? A false positive. He finds himself with heart pounding, pulse racing, hiding behind a tree with a spear drawn for no good reason. It was only a pile of twigs on the path. He's wasted some effort and experienced a baseless fear. But he gets to go home, eat dinner, and snuggle with his mate. Maybe he's even got a good story to tell, if such things were part of hominin social life.

Now consider an alternative scenario. The same individual sees something ahead that might or might not constitute a threat. Rather than assume the worst and squander some autonomic arousal, his perceptual system does not integrate the shapes and register the pattern as a threat. The best that can happen? He saves some calories, does not flee or freeze needlessly, and can boast a perceptual system more finely attuned to physical realities around him. The worst that can happen? A false negative, or Type II error. By not interpreting those stimuli as a threat, he fails to flee. Type II errors in this context are probably fatal. This hypothetical hominin is less likely to become anybody's ancestor.

In short, perceptual accuracy was not an agenda of natural selection. Survival and reproduction were. The worldview of this less successful hominin may have been more realistic than that of his neighbor who scampered away from nearly everything and also saw faces in the clouds. But, again, accuracy wasn't the real concern. Survival and reproduction were. Over time, natural selection probably favored perceptual systems and pattern detectors that were hyperreactive enough to make their share of Type I errors. In a perilous world, Type I errors tend to be less costly. And one of natural selection's mottos has always been, "Better deluded than dead."

STANDING APART

You may find it disturbing to think that something is wrong with your mind. Certainly it is better to learn that our entire species is saddled with a flawed piece of equipment. At least it's nothing personal. But thinking like most people doesn't mean your mind deals in accurate perceptions and analyses. It just means you've got lots of company.

Needless to say, if a lot of flawed minds work together, they are likely to produce cultural institutions that enshrine their flaws.

There will be little support for, and perhaps even active resistance to, questioning our perceptions and beliefs about the world around us. The protagonist of Carl Sagan's book *Contact*,[7] an astronomer named Ellie Arroway, is denied the opportunity to travel into space to meet an alien race because she does not believe in God. She is told in no uncertain terms that 95 percent of the world's population believes in some form of supreme being. She is asked, in effect, "How can you, a nonbeliever, be trusted to represent our species?"

Consensual validity is a very powerful force. In many cases, if those around you believe it, it must be true. It is also a prime example of what are called *heuristics*, or shortcuts that save each member of the group (or species) from having to reevaluate the same evidence. Just accept what your neighbor says and save a few calories of effort. But it is also a dangerous impediment to growth or progress when the belief in question may not be true. It takes considerable courage to stand up, as Ellie Arroway does, and say, "Yes, I want this mission very much and I believe I am highly qualified to accept it. But I do not share the belief of the group. I have examined the same evidence and reached a different conclusion."

This book is about standing apart. It examines the workings of the human mind and identifies some of the areas in which our minds are likely to misfire. The neuroscientists and psychologists who conducted much of the research we discuss deserve great credit. Admittedly, it is easier to hold unconventional views within science, but it still remains difficult for the human mind to analyze itself. Those same limited, highly constrained mental processes we are about to dissect are the very tools we will be using to perform the operation. You've got to be quite logical to find gaps in logic. You have to be highly perceptive to see perceptual illusions. In short, this might have been a far easier task for another species to perform.

IF IT AIN'T BROKE, DON'T FIX IT

"What's wrong with how I use my mind?"

To begin with, you were born with a device that was designed for service at least 50,000 to 100,000 years ago. Are you content to operate it on the same automatic-pilot settings that served your ancestors? Assuming there is some flexibility in the system (and new evidence of "neuroplasticity" seems to suggest there is), why not consider making a few adjustments? Admittedly, we can't change cognitive architecture overnight, but at least we can change our slavish dependence on it. This is not to disparage the original autopilot settings. They were probably a good idea for our hominin ancestors, who understood little about the physical universe around them. But those autopilot settings may have long ago outlived their usefulness.

Consider Steven Pinker's statement, "The mind is what the brain does."[8] In that spirit, I follow the lead of much contemporary scholarship (e.g., Atran and Norenzayan)[9] and make no distinction between the terms *mind* and *brain*. Plainly, in the latter case we are talking about a physical organ, but it is ultimately the mind—that is, what the brain *does*—that is of concern to us and that provides the phenotype on which natural selection operates.

I have a friend who sometimes looks at my wardrobe or record collection and says (lovingly), "The sixties are over! Get over it!" Sometimes I want to say to our species (perhaps not so lovingly), "The Pleistocene era is over. Get over it!" We're living in so-called modern times. A lot of the default settings in the human mind are really showing their age. They are no longer necessary. Continuing the analogy to a physical device, the autopilot mode can be safely turned off in favor of more-enlightened manual settings that reflect thousands of years of human knowledge and civilization. We can safely open the package, reason independently, and move past those fail-safe, one-size-fits-all, safety- and comfort-oriented settings that got our ancestors through the terrifying night. Let's grow up.

But can we or will we? For some of us, the answer, sadly, is no. There are all kinds of reasons for this, rooted in fear, ignorance, and lack of social support. That makes it all the more imperative for those who can entertain such changes to take their first steps toward doing so. Consider that we take similar steps every day. Biological predispositions are overridden regularly. For example, we diet. We resist impulses toward violence or sexual aggression. Even if it doesn't come more naturally to us, there is no reason we cannot also think more clearly and less primitively about the world around us and our place in it. Admittedly, this is difficult work. And it will be more difficult for some than for others, just like dieting or resisting impulses. Changing how we think about the world around us will require effort and force of will.

What makes it so difficult? First, it is important to remember that the mental predispositions we are talking about have their roots in biology. That doesn't mean they can't be changed. It just means there will be work involved, like pushing against something that's been in place for a long time. But it will move.

Second, there is strong social support for much of this faulty mental work. People who share belief systems and perspectives bond together. The sense of belonging within a community feels good. As many have learned, communities do not suffer defections and defectors lightly. You may suffer disdain or worse if you withdraw from a shared belief system.

Third, you will be losing comfort. This particular comfort comes in two flavors. It entails the comfort of familiarity—you may have held these beliefs for a long time. There is also comfort in the beliefs themselves. As we shall see, many widely held mental distortions are geared to keeping the existential demons (like the impermanence of life or our insignificant place in the universe) at bay. They offer the mental equivalent of a thumb to suck or a skirt to hold. Which leads to the fourth reason it can be difficult to change how we think about the world around us: Fear. Alternate views of the world may not only be unfamiliar, they can be downright scary.

There is comfort in the status quo even when it isn't right. Ideas attain a status quo position for a lot of reasons, the majority of which are nothing to be proud of. There was a time in most of our lives when belief in Santa Claus was appropriate.[10] It felt good and it had the social support of your parents and your friends. It doesn't anymore. The Flat Earth Society fought valiantly to maintain its dominance over its upstart rivals. The pre-Copernican view of the universe was not quickly cast aside when a few extremists suggested that, despite the loss of comfort and power to some, Earth was not nestled firmly in the center of the universe.

Many of these ancient shortcuts we've inherited lead to incorrect conclusions about the world around us. Earth is *not* flat. Neither is it five thousand years old. And, in the words of one comedian, Adam and Eve did not ride to Sunday school on the backs of dinosaurs. To borrow Richard Dawkins's humorous (if intemperate) comment, "That is not just wrong. It is catastrophically, utterly, stupefyingly wrong."[11] There are many additional beliefs that are also not true. The spirits of dead ancestors do not swirl around us, influencing the lives of the living. Nor do the living speak with the dead. All of these views, many of which are widely held, constitute factual errors that can result from Caveman Logic.

But there are other reasons to abandon such mental distortions. In addition to a factual argument, there is also a moral one for upgrading our thinking. As we note on several occasions in this book, a strong case has been made by writers like Richard Dawkins and Christopher Hitchens that incorrect supernatural belief systems can and do lead to atrocious acts of violence and destruction. Not all of these are directed at fellow humans. In *How We Know What Isn't So*,[12] Thomas Gilovich offers a distressing list of animal species whose numbers have been needlessly decimated because of erroneous and superstitious belief systems involving medical cures and aphrodisiacs. More widely publicized acts of violence have been directed against fellow humans. In the first quarter of the twenty-first century, this point needs little amplification. But the issue of "violence in the name of religious differences" is hardly unique to the twenty-first century. The real philosophical question is whether we need to wait until more such violence occurs in order to condemn the underlying thinking. If we believe that violence and mistreatment are inevitable consequences of religious distinctions and xenophobia, then encouraging mental upgrades makes sound philosophical sense even before the next terrorist attack rules the headlines.

Another reason for abandoning Caveman Logic is essentially a philosophical argument about human potential. Consider a beautifully constructed automobile or airplane, capable of navigating as no such vehicle has done before. Precision turns, higher altitudes, speed changes: all these possibilities and more lie within the capability of this machine. However, for reasons of practicality, the equipment is delivered with an autopilot setting locked in place. This allows the automobile or plane to navigate in unexceptional and generally competent ways. You'll get to the supermarket safely or fly from Dallas to Denver on time, but the trip will be boring and safe and just like most trips before it.

The thing is, time and effort have been spent on this engine, only for its new owner to fail to use the majority of its potential. In fact, many drivers or pilots have actually forgotten that the autopilot setting is locked in place. They've never experienced the thrill (or the risk) of taking control of all those high-end features that were part of the package. When someone even suggests that an autopilot setting might be limiting his potential as a driver or a pilot, the owners become defensive. Some will argue (getting back to caveman logic), "If we're so primitive and deluded, how come we can . . ." Here they offer a litany of man's technical accomplishments, perhaps including building the Large Hadron Collider (to address questions about how the universe began), or the medical advances of our age, or our daily use of computers and satellite transmission to process data and bridge the miles. Collectively, these works seem to call into question any suggestion that human intelligence is compromised or bounded.

So what do we make of this? How can we be so clever and so primitive at the same time? Are there two separate species of humans? The intellectually gifted and those who grovel at the feet of idols, talk to ghosts, or go to creationist theme parks?

No, there aren't. And that's just the point. If there were two separate species, this book would be wholly unnecessary. Improvement would be out of the question. We'd be facing a real "us versus them" divide: the rocket scientists and the grilled cheese sandwich worshipers. I might as well write a book about the limited intelligence of zebras. All *they* ever do is graze and make more zebras. Why can't they be more like *us* and design spaceships and write books?

That's not the case here. The problems I describe in this book are species-wide. Anatomically, there are not two classes of *Homo sapiens*. The spectacular accomplishments of some of us define the potential of all of us. With training and social support, we can all work around the lure of Caveman Logic. The impulses and perceptions that arise in us all do not have to be honored. Carl Sagan offers a very moving narrative in his book *The Demon-Haunted World*[13] (itself, a forceful polemic against Caveman Logic). Sagan describes how deeply he missed his deceased parents, and how he sometimes veered toward the comfort of widely held beliefs about their souls still being with us, communication with them, and an afterlife in which we are all united. But Sagan recognized these needs for what they were and did not act on them. This book, as well as Sagan's, acknowledges how powerful such impulses can be but encourages you not to follow the well-worn path to delusion and superstition, despite the comfort it offers. In his view, as in mine, the transient benefits are extremely costly in terms of our intellectual integrity.

There is another aspect to the argument against Caveman Logic, and it has to do with wasted human potential. Many people are strongly opposed to feeling they are being "controlled." Notions of "free will," although they may rest on shaky philosophical ground, remain central to pride and self-respect. It is understandable that individuals want to feel in charge of the important decisions they make. They want to believe that they have thought things through clearly before making a decision, that the evidence before them has been weighed carefully, that their highest mental faculties have been brought to bear on their beliefs, perceptions, and actions. Anything less than that would be cause for concern, even embarrassment.

It is precisely for this reason that Caveman Logic and Stone Age thinking should be viewed with disdain. Those Pleistocene default modes with their mental and perceptual shortcuts are the very essence of "being controlled." They amount to nothing less than relinquishing control of your mental equipment to a brutish, clueless, fearful caveman. It may not feel that way, but you have turned over the reins to an inferior being. You simply cannot take pride in being in control of your own destiny at the same time you have handed the strings over to a prehistoric puppeteer.

A MIND IN COMMON

There is no way to overstate how the architecture of the human brain sets limits on the beliefs we generate and share. The strongest reading of this view is offered by Noam Chomsky; it says simply that if we humans did not share brain architecture, culture could not exist. It is those hardwired modular circuits common to the brain of every human, regardless of his or her race, religion, or geographical home, that make culture possible. If we each had unique blank-slate bits of brain tissue in our skulls, allowing all our uniqueness to emerge each day, it is doubtful we would get together long enough to mate, much less form productive social groups.

Occasionally, you'll find a neurological outsider—someone like Albert Einstein—whose inferior parietal lobe was 15 percent wider than normal. The result was an exceptional person, a bit of a social klutz who didn't do well in school but who effortlessly saw connections between mathematical and spatial entities in a way unlike those around him. The result was breakthroughs in theoretical physics or mathematics. Most ordinary people labeled Einstein as a genius, although the case can be made that he wasn't any smarter (whatever that means) than most people. Indeed, he may not have worked any harder than most. He simply "got it." He understood aspects of the universe that few others did. Even when Einstein's ideas and perceptions were expressed in everyday language, it took mental effort for his normal colleagues to grasp those relationships. The standard-issue Pleistocene brain is not geared for such rarified skills. If Einstein's anatomical mutation had been present 100,000 years ago, it's uncertain whether it would have been favored by natural selection. One thing is for sure: if Einstein's mind were the norm, culture as we know it would be quite different.

The culture that emerges from our shared mental equipment is impressively diverse, but even more impressive than its diversity are its similarities. To this day, I have undergraduates who argue that we are what (or who) we are because of culture. Incredibly, they have spent very little time looking at the question of where culture, itself, comes from. To many, it is simply *there*. It predates us and acts to determine our behavior. Such a view tends to de-biologize human beings by turning them into purely social beings, unfazed by the biological imperatives that operate on every other form of life on the planet.

Once we accept that culture—which surely does influence human behavior—is, itself, an outgrowth of the human mind, we begin to see a bigger, more consistent pattern to life on our planet. The human body was designed through a painstaking and value-neutral process of natural selection. All of our organs evolved in this manner, including our brains. The human mind, like the human foot or eye, is common to all members of our species. Several friends of mine joined Doctors Without Borders and traveled to remote portions of the globe, bringing modern medicine to people who had been without it perhaps forever. Consider the obvious: These doctors did not worry about taking special courses in the anatomy of the third world eye or foot or spleen in order to practice in these culturally remote locations. They knew those organs would be the same, even in the most exotic locations.

So, too, with the human brain. It does its job in the same way in remote locations. It provides the same perceptual and logical short-cuts everywhere it works. It also sets the user up for the same perceptual and logical distortions everywhere it goes. The *content* of those irrational conclusions and delusions will probably differ from place to place, but their essential nature and their effects on us will be startlingly similar wherever we go.

DEBATING WITH GRANDMA

You will not find a lot of books touting the flaws of the human mind. On the contrary, there is a market for singing the praises of virtually every organ and structure of our bodies. There are tributes to the nose, the ear, the eye, and the hand. Even the lowly knee draws praise. The human heart? Whether literally or metaphorically, there are books that rhapsodize over its engineering and its resilience. But in all this body boasting, there is no winner greater than the brain. On that one, most authors simply stand back in wonder, listing accomplishments of human ingenuity and drawing comparisons to "lower species" that, despite sharing large portions of chromosomal material with us, seem to hit their peak when they can manage to use a stick as a tool to extract dinner from a termite mound. In most ways, the mental competition out there is pretty shoddy. We are the clear winners. The human mind with its wondrous abilities trumps all pretenders in the known universe. And so we have the spectacle of the human mind singing the praises of the human mind.

Who in their right mind would disagree? Who would criticize the mind? And on what basis? Prepare yourself: We're about to do just that. As my grandmother might have said, "What? We're not smart enough for you?"

I'd like to keep my grandmother in the discussion. I do so with no disrespect intended to grandmothers anywhere, least of all my own. Having this imaginary debate with my grandmother will focus my effort on the "common sense" opposition to what I say, as well as forcing me to think clearly and express myself in a nontechnical manner.

And so . . . no, Nana. It's not that we're not smart enough. That's not the trouble. We are very, very smart. The problem is, some of that "smart" isn't done quite the way you might have imagined. It's done through "shortcuts." Scientists call them *heuristics*. When these heuristics are working the way they were designed to under the conditions they were designed for, they are astoundingly good.

So what's your trouble then? This isn't good enough?

The trouble is that what these heuristics do best isn't just accuracy. It's accuracy with high speed and very low cost.

Cost?

Yes. Everything we do and everything that's part of us has a cost/benefit trade-off. The brain is an expensive thing to run. It takes more energy than any other part of our bodies. Anything our bodies do has got to be efficient. If a particular job isn't really helping, it may get phased out altogether. Remember those TV documentaries about fish that live in the dark and eventually lose their eyes? You just don't need them deep down in the ocean. Even if the job is important but it requires too many calories to do, there's pressure to get it done more efficiently.

And who is this cost cutter? This efficiency expert?

Call it natural selection. The most ruthless efficiency expert that ever was.

So this is why you don't like the human mind? It's too efficient?

No, Nana. I love the human mind. It lets us do what we're doing right now, you and I, which is wonderful. But the mind also has some real problems, and they have a lot to do with all those efficient shortcuts.

Like what, Mister Critic?

Well, think about how shortcuts work. First of all, they aren't 100 percent effective. If they work more often than not, or enough to produce *relative* success, that may be good enough for natural selection.

But not for you?

The thing is, Nana, natural selection and I have different "agendas," if you can use that word. I'm concerned with more than just survival and reproduction and moving genes into the next generation. I'm thinking about "quality of life" issues, like being smart and undeluded and clearheaded and informed. Natural selection is blind to those kinds of qualities, and to a lot more that many people think are important aspects of human life.

Being right or seeing something correctly 70 percent of the time may be good enough to get some software into the next generation, but it still results in a lot of faulty perception. What if some of those mental mistakes start to receive social support? What if people *bond* around those mistakes that their minds frequently make in interpreting the world?

You think that happens?

All the time, Nana. And that's under the best of conditions. Remember that these shortcuts work best under the particular conditions for which they were designed. That's where natural selection did its work. What if the conditions have changed enough so that the shortcut is still triggered, but now the results are even less likely to be correct? Our minds don't deliver a written disclaimer saying, "The conclusion you are about to reach may not be accurate. The image you think you see may actually be something else. In fact, it may be nothing at all. You could end up being entirely wrong. Sorry. I was really not designed to handle *this* situation for you. I'm at my best under slightly different conditions and even then, I do tend to get it wrong from time to time. It's part of why I was chosen. I'm quick and inexpensive."

It sounds like the contract was given to the lowest bidder.

That's not a bad analogy, Nana.

So you're saying maybe people should get a second opinion before they reach conclusions or describe what they're seeing?

That might help, but it's not how most of us conduct our business. Even worse, that second opinion is likely to come from another human who has just received the same faulty information. Now there are two of you and it's even harder to get you to question your conclusions.

So if we humans are so defective how come your efficiency expert hasn't done away with this whole mess?

A few reasons, Nana. First, natural selection moves very slowly and can only choose among alternatives. Second, you have to think about the costs of being wrong under these conditions. Remember, natural selection isn't necessarily looking for "smart" or "accurate" or "nondelusional." It's concerned with survival and reproduction. So what if you see a face in the clouds that isn't there? You still get to have dinner and make babies. If the guy in the next cave sees the same face, maybe you can be friends. Buddies with a shared delusion. He might even help you if you get attacked or if you run out of food for your kids. There's not much to lose by making a whole bunch of mistakes about the world around you.

But consider the alternative. What if we realized there are no faces in the clouds. What if we get it *right* about nothing being there, but as part of the bargain we occasionally miss seeing someone or something that really *was* there? *That* kind of mistake might be fatal. That's not a good recipe for reproductive success. You can see how natural selection would have a very different response toward that kind of perceptual system. It may be less deluded, but it's also less likely to survive.

So you're saying that we're descended from survivors. We got the good with the bad?

That's exactly what I'm saying, Nana. And if you read the rest of this book, I'll try to be fair about the good we got. But I'll also spend more time than usual talking about the bad we got, what it might be costing us, and how we can remedy the situation.

Chapter 2
CATALOGUING IRRATIONALITY

CATALOGUING FOR DUMMIES

t is important to see your mind or, for that matter, your brain, as you do any organ in your body. It has a particular job to do and it has evolved slowly over millions of years to do that job. Your heart pumps blood; your lungs aerate blood; your liver and kidneys filter impurities from the blood; your ears respond to pressure changes in the atmosphere and relay them so your brain can process and interpret them. These are specialized functions and they are in no way interchangeable. In a pinch, your spleen could not stand in for your heart or your lungs. Organs have evolved under strict selection pressure to do highly specific jobs.

Your brain is just one more organ, subject to the same rules and limitations as any other part of your body. Its job, broadly speaking, is to process and store information and instigate bodily movements that are efficient and cost-effective. Given the complexity of what the brain does, that is a barely adequate description. The important thing to remember is that the brain is highly modularized. It is *not* a general-purpose computer that was a blank slate at birth, waiting for your personal experiences and inputs from your culture to write upon its empty pages. That kind of description hasn't passed muster with neuropsychologists for well over a half century.

Each of those modules can boast a long natural history and a lot of selection pressure. When I bought the laptop computer on which I've written much of this book, it came with preinstalled software. Thankfully, I didn't have to create or even install the programs. In fact most new computers are ready to operate right out of the box. You can start downloading music, writing essays, manipulating digital images, and e-mailing friends as soon as you plug in your computer. The human brain, although it too becomes a spectacular information processor and manipulator, takes many years to develop, much like the rest of the body. Granted, it will go through a lot of stages en route to full capacity, but the nature of that software is pretty well determined if not at the moment of conception, then surely by birth.

Those mental modules that we prize so highly served our ancestors well. But because they are so highly specialized they are also capable of some dramatic and often humorous mistakes. This is the price you pay for highly specialized software. It can save you time and calories when environmental conditions match the ones it was designed to handle. But when the match is off or that software gets triggered inappropriately, stand back! You're going to see, do, or believe some pretty outrageous things. Worse yet, you may not have a clue just how off-base those things are. There's also a good chance the person standing beside you will be experiencing a similar cognitive glitch or veering toward the same delusion.

There are several ways that your mind, an otherwise marvelous piece of engineering, can go wrong. To keep this simple, we'll consider only two broad categories. The first stems from the kind of information that was either scarce or absent altogether when our minds evolved. For example, many people acknowledge serious problems in grasping information about quantities. Remember, we're a species who spent a lot of time with number systems no more sophisticated than "1, 2, 3, many." Probabilities are even tougher for many people to handle.

Not surprisingly, this kind of information is "evolutionarily novel," or at least recent enough so that it is unlikely we have evolved any modular systems to deal directly with it. Any success we have will involve pressing some related modules into service. They'll do all they can to help, but they may fall well short of the task. Before you ask, this is *not* like asking the spleen to fill in for the heart while the latter is momentarily off-line. These are all mental modules, any number of which may be activated by a particular stimulus. Normally, there is some kind of mental *triage* that determines whose job it is to respond, namely, which module is the best fit for the task. In cases where no module really fits the bill (e.g., balancing a checkbook), our mind is likely to use a second-best approach that, for some of us, is not very good at all.

The second kind of mental shortcoming that we humans commonly encounter involves the hair-trigger response of a module that might have served us better if it had remained inactivated. We will examine these cases in great detail later, although the general principle is important to grasp early on. The inappropriate activation of a specialized mental module can be just as problematic as its failure to operate. This point is central to the logic of this book. It is also very easy to overlook, especially when most people share the same inappropriately triggered mental software.

Two of the most egregious examples of overactivation of otherwise useful mental modules involve *detection of pattern* and *detection of causality*. As you'll see, both of these mental errors lead to belief systems and elaborate behavioral outputs that, in one sense, define our species, but also waste a lot of its time. It is hard for many people to view such mental errors as errors because there is such elaborate and widespread social support for them. And, like much delusional thinking, there is often some secondary gain. This means that such beliefs may be dead wrong, but there are benefits that come from holding them.

PLEASING THOG

It's hard to imagine a time or place when it wasn't beneficial to have control over the important events—both good and bad—in our lives. We are all hedonists. Like every other animal on the planet, humans share the desire to maximize pleasure and minimize pain. If it's good, you don't just want it happening to you, you want to be able to *make* it happen.

The same applies to bad things. The world is full of unpleasant events, some physical and some psychological. People seek control over the bad things that swirl around them. Behaviors that lead to the reduction or elimination of bad things are quickly learned and remain in our repertoires. This is what psychologists call *negative reinforcement*. We are also quick to learn which behaviors produce unpleasant or painful consequences. Unless we are fools or masochists, those behaviors tend to be suppressed. This is called *punishment* by psychologist and layman alike. The good thing about punishment is that one can simply avoid it by withholding the behavior that produces it. Punishment doesn't just happen to you; it's under your control.

Our ancestors would have learned that not all events, either positive or negative, are directly under our control. Sometimes someone else, maybe a group member or a group leader, is in control of whether or not a desired event occurs. There is widespread belief that good things don't just come from nowhere and drop into our laps. That's certainly a sentiment I've heard expressed from family and friends, not to mention songwriters, movie characters, and complete strangers. The idea runs very deep in human nature. If something good has happened to you, it has probably happened for a reason.

Those are not altogether unreasonable beliefs for a social being—or at least the descendant of social beings. We are, of course, the most social primates who have ever walked the earth. The result of all this social living and breeding is that we are likely to view events within the context of our social existence.

There would be a premium on being able to detect such causal agents, and a special benefit for having the social skills to influence the person in control, whoever he was. Imagine that food resources were scarce and their distribution was controlled by Thog, the group leader. It would behoove you to establish a strong relationship with Thog and, in the process, learn what kinds of entreaties and bargains pleased him. Similarly, if Thog had the power to undermine your efforts, perhaps cause harm to your family or crops, you would learn what kind of social exchange might deter him from visiting such events on you. What does Thog want of me? Everyone has an agenda. What does Thog want in exchange for keeping me from harm, or reducing the severity of the troubles he has brought to me?

Moreover, we cannot imagine withholding thanks when we get what we want, whatever it is. Maybe it was winning the lottery or learning that our loved ones are alive and well, after we had reason to fear the worst. Thanks to whom? Interestingly, it doesn't seem to matter very much. This is what social living means. Somebody is usually in power and that means somebody was responsible for what we've received. Social exchange simply requires that we offer a "Thank you." Remember, good things don't just happen. The alternative to a simple "Thank you" is to appear ungrateful, and perhaps anger the source of the gift or, worse yet, risk having the gift withdrawn. That's too big a chance to take, especially if we can avoid problems simply by saying "Thank you."

A friend of mine, whom I would hardly describe as religious, shared this story with me. His wife developed some physical symptoms that were as puzzling as they were painful. When it became apparent that some of the possible diagnoses were potentially life threatening, she went into the hospital for a series of tests. Both my friend and his wife were understandably anxious and waited helplessly for the verdict. After a period of time, the results came back: she was OK. The condition was treatable. The illness was not life threatening. They were immensely relieved. My friend left her room and walked downstairs to the chapel. He went to the back of the room where a guestbook encouraged visitors to leave a brief message. He wrote, "Thank you," and left.

He did not write "Thank you, God." He did not pray. He simply, as he put it to me, felt an irresistible urge to say "Thank you." Whether to God, the doctors, the nurse's aide—it didn't seem to matter. A gift had been received and some circuitry had been triggered in him. The only logical endpoint was the utterance of "Thank you." Social exchange in action: You give. I receive. I thank. Anything less would be a violation of something very fundamental about human nature.

The oddity here, of course, is that my friend was able to observe and later discuss his own behavior. He engaged in what psychologists call *metacognition*. Thoughts about thoughts. His actions struck him as somewhat odd. He reported them to his wife and was willing to discuss them with me. Most people don't go this far. There are so many rituals to normalize "Thank you" that their occurrence doesn't require comment or analysis: "Thank God that my wife will live." "Amen!" Those "Amens" come from others who share our cognitive architecture. They feel the same urge to give thanks when something good has happened. There must be a causal agent and somebody had better damn well thank him.

Social exchange is embodied so deeply in our thinking and so subtly in our everyday language that many of us are unaware of the beliefs we are expressing. When good things over which we have little control do occur, our statements convey not only our pleasure but also some form of thanks. That "Thank you" can either be non-specific, as in the case of my friend's written words, or directed to some imagined causal agent. Note that the circumstances triggering the need for such social exchange can be far less than life threatening. We can shift the venue from the hospital to the sports bar, and little changes.

Imagine two friends discussing the results of a baseball game in which the home team held on to preserve a small lead:

"Thank God they won!" or "Thank heavens they won!" Sometimes shortened to, "Thankfully, they won!"

But why *thankful*? And thankful to whom? Who is this agent or baseball god who delivers victories? Why isn't it sufficient to say, "I am glad that we won" and be done with it? It's telling just how rare such a reaction is, both in hospitals and in sports bars.

A PRIMER ON CAUSALITY

Sensitivity to causal relationships is high on the list of what a species needs to survive on this planet. Psychologist Henry Plotkin put it elegantly when he argued, "Our literal survival depends on a finely tuned knowledge of the causal texture of the world." This is hardly a new insight. Eighteenth-century philosopher David Hume wrote about what might be termed a psychological compulsion to search out and believe in causal relations. Although it lies beyond Hume's scope of interest, this "compulsion" is hardly unique to humans. In Plotkin's words, "Illusions of causality can be induced in exactly the same way in both humans and rats."[1]

There are actually two types of causal detection errors. One of them involves our own actions. We wrongly believe that some behavior of ours is responsible for a particular environmental occurrence. Humans make these errors of attribution all the time and we are hardly alone in doing so. In 1948, psychologist B. F. Skinner published a now-famous demonstration with pigeons showing that the periodic *nonresponse contingent* delivery of food—in other words, food that occurred independently of what the pigeons did—resulted in repeated, stereotyped patterns of behavior.[2] No two birds did exactly the same thing. Some turned to the left, others to the right; some paced to the rear of the chamber, some bobbed their heads repeatedly. Normally pigeons labor away in Skinner boxes, pecking a response key in order to remain well fed. This behavior truly produces food rewards and the animals have no trouble learning what is required of them. But here there *was* no requirement. The pigeons could do anything or nothing and they would still be fed. And yet, not one of them got the message. None of them chose to do nothing. Every pigeon tested under these conditions came up with some behavioral pattern, as if to say, "I've figured it out! I know what I have to do." It's as if the possibility of *not* being in control of their world never occurs to them. People often laugh at the lowly pigeon's mental mistakes. We scoff at their lack of understanding of the world around them. Sadly, as many psychologists have observed, humans behave almost identically under these same conditions.

Skinner described his results as "superstitious behavior," an odd term to describe the behavior of pigeons. He suggested that, like humans, pigeons were not very good at distinguishing those events they had caused to happen from those that had nothing to do with them or their actions. In 1972, my colleague James Hubbard and I published a similar demonstration involving rats.[3] They were every bit as superstitious as pigeons, showing a nearly comic range of behavior patterns that had been adventitiously reinforced by regular food deliveries. Superstitious behavior in lab animals has become a staple of undergraduate psychology education in "learning laboratory" courses, as well as demonstrations of operant conditioning during community open-house events.

Rats, pigeons, and people are all prone to overestimating the connections between their own behavior and things that happen to them. In all cases, it appears that natural selection has favored a "causality detection" module that overinterprets minimal evidence. If that module is going to make a mistake, it's probably better to *see* causality where it doesn't exist than to miss a case where it really does.

Most of us are familiar with the Serenity Prayer from Alcoholics Anonymous (AA). Although its origins are somewhat cloudy— some credit it to the ancient Greeks, others to Saint Francis—this brief approach to achieving peace of mind contains considerable wisdom. A deeper look at AA doctrine will get you enmeshed in references to a "Higher Power" or other borderline spirituality, but this simple prayer (minus its entreaty to God, which I have pointedly deleted) might as well be a mantra for this book:

> Grant me the serenity to accept the things I cannot change, courage to change the things I can, and the wisdom to know the difference.

Admittedly, AA seems an unlikely place to look for agreement with the theme of this book, and many AA members may be unhappy at seeing their serenity prayer co-opted for the present purpose. But good ideas are good ideas, and this particular one is central to our book: "Stop trying to change or control what isn't under your control." The prayer explicitly notes that there are some things that are not controllable and it encourages you to work very hard to learn the difference.

Most of us don't do a good job at making this distinction. We have mental modules devoted solely to detecting cause-effect relationships. These modules are in place nearly from infancy and are prone to erring in the direction of overestimating our degree of control. Like a rat in a Skinner box, we talk ourselves into believing that all those events are tied directly to what we do. "I'll wear my lucky shirt to the softball game," or "I won't change my socks as long as my team keeps winning." If pressed, most people will tell you it's "just in fun," but for many of us, that kind of fun comes from a pretty deep place.

There is a second type of causality detection problem that doesn't even involve our own behavior. This kind of mental error is extremely widespread and known only among humans. Imagine a situation where a particular outcome is highly desired or strongly feared. Now, further assume that its occurrence is truly beyond our control. A parent sits vigil in a hospital waiting to hear the fate of her injured child. A farmer faces financial ruin if it doesn't rain. In situations like these, the person begins by exhausting his or her meager behavioral repertoire until it becomes clear that we have no control over the situation.

Or do we? Most people do not deal well with such lack of control. Since direct intervention is not an option, we default to Plan B. This calls for us to presume that, although we ourselves do not have control over the outcome, there is some agent who does. Now if we can just exert some degree of control over the agent, then all is not lost. Perhaps "control" is too strong a word. What usually happens is that the powerless person will attempt to influence the agent through some sort of cajoling or bargaining or social exchange. "Please let my child live. If you do, I promise to be good. I'll quit smoking. I'll stop drinking. I'll start going to church." *I'll do something for you if you'll do this for me.*

The farmer facing the loss of his crops? "I'll sacrifice a goat. I'll give up something of value if you deliver this desired outcome to me." *I cannot make it rain, but surely you can.* Causal agents are not unknown in real life, and you'd better maintain a good working relationship with them. Usually, these agents have a knowable agenda. Learn it, and you're on the road to success. Children learn to please their parents. Workers learn to satisfy their bosses. Spouses learn how to please (or displease) their partners who control resources within a marriage. In all these cases we have accurately detected the power of another in order to retain some control over the world in which we live.

Some baseball players, and perhaps athletes in general, are prone to attributing aspects of their performance to external agencies. "I want to thank the Lord Jesus Christ for letting me hit that home run to win the game in the bottom of the ninth inning." Such statements, which minimize the player's responsibility for the accomplishment, sound like the very soul of humility, not to mention piety. However, they are viewed a lot more favorably in positive rather than negative cases. If the batter wants to credit his performance to a deity, that's his business. The run still counts, as does his team's victory. However, if the pitcher who gave up that ninth-inning home run shrugs and says, "It was God's will, don't blame me," he may find himself praising the Lord from some minor-league town.

Such superstitious belief systems aren't confined to players. Most loyal fans I know who watch games on television report that they believe, at some level, that their actions (such as getting up to make a sandwich) have a bearing on the results of the game. It is a rare fan who regularly watches his team, cares passionately about the outcome, and believes, "I'm just a spectator. What I say, think, or do will have no bearing on the results."

Imagine that your team is winning 3–0 and you walk away to take a phone call or attend to some biological needs. When you return to the game, the other team has tied the score or gone ahead. Even intelligent, rational fans find it difficult not to feel somehow responsible for the sudden reversal of fortune. They may joke about such Caveman Logic, but many take pains to avoid "jinxing" their team in the future.

Here is an even more extreme example of such superstition, reported on the Philadelphia Phillies Internet discussion group in August 2008. In this case, the fan had TiVo'd (recorded) a game previously. When he sat down to watch it, he quickly turned the sound to mute when the home team took a 5–1 lead. He had learned on previous occasions that not doing so could "cost them the game." As soon as he hit the mute button, he reports, "I realized the absurdity of what I had done. I was watching the recording; the game was already over. Yet I didn't want to change anything for fear of somehow mystically affecting the outcome of a game that had already been played."

Causal agents are usually easy to discover—what parent, boss, or spouse keeps herself hidden? In some situations, however, there is little indication that such an agent exists. These are the cases in which our overactive agency detectors spring into action to fill in the blanks. And we don't just invent causal agents to fill that void; we create powerful, often supernatural, agents who are usually willing to listen. They almost always seem to be within our sphere of influence. Otherwise, what would be the point of creating them?

And so the detection of causality runs the gamut. Sometimes it's as simple as "I press the lever, I get the food." However, this causal agency detector—crucial to survival—is probably a bit too highly tuned in most of us. And so, we enter the realm of superstitious behavior. "If I circle to the left and scratch my head, I will get the food." If I'm in a room full of people who are busy scratching and circling, I'm probably unlikely to discover that the food would have arrived anyway. The bottom line is that we all eat regularly. We survive, we reproduce, and we teach our children to circle and scratch.

Can the human mind simply accept delivery of an important event—be it positive or negative—without seeing it as a *consequence*, either of something we have done, or as the bestowal of an external agent? The realistic answer seems to be, "Not easily." A friend of mine who managed to get into two road mishaps with deer stood out in the road next to her car the second time, crying, "Why me? What did I do wrong?" She wasn't talking about her driving. An educated and rational person, she found it difficult not to see the accident as punishment for some misdeed, as if the universe (read, God) were monitoring her every thought and action and doling out consequences.

There is a popular bumper sticker that addresses this problem directly. It says SHIT HAPPENS. Those two words are all but incomprehensible to the majority of people. The sticker does not say I CAUSED SHIT TO HAPPEN. It does not say SHIT WAS DONE TO ME BY A VENGEFUL GOD. It says simply that nonresponse contingent SHIT does happen from time to time. There is no sense looking for what I did to cause it. By excluding any reference to control, that two-word bumper sticker conveys considerable wisdom. But can our cognitive architecture comprehend the message? Again, the most charitable answer is, "Not easily."

How might such profound distortions around cause and effect have evolved in our ancestors? You'll recognize this as the same issue we tackled in chapter 1 when we first considered Type I and Type II errors. Here are the key points:

1. The perception of cause-effect is crucial to our well-being in the world. This is as true today as it was in the Pleistocene Age.
2. Cause-effect relationships are invisible. You cannot see a logical (for example, *if-then*) connection; you can only infer it from what happens.
3. Our ancestors who were adept at detecting such causal links were at a reproductive advantage over those who were less skilled at doing so. And better to overestimate than underestimate.
4. Such a perceptual/cognitive ability would have been part of their brain architecture and available for genetic transmission to the next generation.

That's all it takes. And it is reasonable to remind ourselves that errors involving cause and effect do not reflect willful stupidity. They reflect how our minds are predisposed to process information. But more than that, they reflect the fact that there is virtually no incentive to correct these mistakes. Your friends and neighbors also make them.

One more observation: the causal agents most people manufacture are supernatural. They do not correct our errors of attribution by saying, "I do not exist." Whether spirits, gods, demons, or dead ancestors, these agents operate on us, the living, by controlling the very things we wish we could control. But there's a catch: we've left a very large and embarrassing clue to the fact that these agents are of our own design. Although they are certifiably supernatural, most of them seem to have the same petty agendas and motives as any human in the village or on the street. "You angered me by doing such-and-such, and so I'm going to get you back." Our gods and demons and ancestor spirits seem not to be very highly evolved entities. In fact, they are as petty and vindictive as any of us. Perhaps this should surprise nobody since, arguably, we created them out of our own limited imaginations.

INTRODUCING HEURISTICS

Psychologists use the term *heuristics* to describe mental shortcuts. Like any shortcut, heuristics can provide great benefits and save lots of time. When they work, it is hard not to admire their elegance. But they do not always work. Often, when they don't, they look *very* bad. Heuristics and the cognitive architecture that supports them have evolved because *on balance* they provided our ancestors with a reproductive advantage. Those who had them and used them tended to do better than those who did not. Natural selection does not demand perfection or a 100 percent success rate. A small net benefit is enough to entrench a trait in a population. In addition, most heuristics are highly situation specific. They work very well under certain conditions. When those conditions are not exactly met, the same heuristic can be triggered and lead to a lot of trouble. Whether the individual sees the error and adjusts his or her approach or continues to hammer away, producing faulty or even disastrous results in the bargain, is anybody's guess. Too often, the latter occurs. Such events can reduce individual welfare or compromise the foreign policy of a nation.

Arguably, heuristics are a form of intellectual laziness. The irony is that our species got to be what it is today by being intellectually lazy. We've already noted that there is no greater efficiency expert than natural selection. Had our ancestors spent their full intellectual resources on every problem they faced, it would have been a recipe for disaster. The winners in the race to survival and reproduction were the intellectually lazy among us who could fall back on the heuristics they carried.

The range of situations in which these shortcuts are brought into play—not always successfully—is staggering. There is almost no area of human function where we do not call upon a social, intellectual, or perceptual heuristic to do the bulk of our work. Worse yet, we are rarely aware that we are using them, so ingrained are they in how we function. We look at a sea of colors and textures and decide it is a roomful of friends; we hear a sequence of auditory stimuli of particular pitch, phrasing, and timbre and recognize it as a song from our teenage years. We meet a stranger and decide that he or she is someone we would rather avoid than seek further contact with. We shop for a place to live and know instantly that this is The One. In each case we have chosen to devalue or ignore most of the information available to us. Our nervous systems are programmed to zero in on a tiny number of salient features and discount almost everything else.

Heuristics have a checkered history within psychology. Do they represent the best of our minds, maximizing information and minimizing effort, or are they examples of mental sloppiness? If Introductory Psychology textbooks are any indication, the answer is mostly the latter. Virtually every textbook published in the past twenty years contains a section that paints heuristics not as commendable shortcuts, but rather as lamentable laziness. The most commonly criticized examples are called the *availability* heuristic and the *representativeness* heuristic. Both are typically treated with contempt for the errors they lead to when the real world is turned upside down in the unnatural conditions of the psychology lab. Imagine yourself encountering an unkempt individual wearing a tattered and torn jacket and smelling rather ripe. Would you have trouble identifying him as a bank president? You bet you would. Why? Because in your experience bank presidents don't look (or smell) that way. Is this evidence of defective processing on your part? Yes, according to some, because the dreaded representativeness heuristic has gotten in the way of your ability to gather and evaluate evidence more fully.

I want to be clear that I am not arguing for the abandonment of heuristics. Even if it were possible, it would be ill advised. Gigerenzer and Todd's book called *Simple Heuristics That Make Us Smart*[4] is at the forefront of an emerging literature praising that head full of shortcuts. Many readers celebrate the idea that we can be smart and effective without being strictly rational. Gerd Gigerenzer's book *Gut Feelings* is another example; so is Malcolm Gladwell's *Blink*. Gladwell introduces the concept of "thin slicing" to describe the cognitive strategy we use to evaluate new information. But he waits seventy-five pages before raising the problems associated with hair-triggered heuristics. Gladwell calls this section "The Dark Side of Thin Slicing." Caveman Logic is also focused on the "dark side" of heuristics. Although I share Gladwell's admiration for these mental shortcuts, I worry even more about their inappropriate application. Sometimes they leave us wallowing in ignorance and misinformation. One hundred thousand years ago, knowledge was in shorter supply and there were few ways to validate what we knew. Today, many of our fellow humans still inhabit an uninformed universe of magical thinking. Certainly, religion is born of and nurtured by the very kind of hardwired, uncritical, autopilot circuitry I am criticizing. But the problems are more widespread than religion. Politically correct or not, it's time to call these beliefs and their consequences into question.

CREATIONISTS IN THE CRADLE

Caveman Logic and prehistoric thinking are not simply written onto the blank-slate minds of uneducated people. It would be a big mistake to view these mental defects as the result of bad information that might have been replaced by alternative facts, if only they had been taught. It was never that simple.

Two of our species' foibles—the embracing of superstition and the wariness of science—do not stem directly from a lack of formal education. As we have already argued, the human mind is not an equal-opportunity consumer that will openly embrace rational thought, the scientific method, magical thinking, or religiosity, depending solely on which of these messages happens to cross our path.

The mental predispositions to Caveman Logic are now being studied directly—not in adult humans, where their presence is well documented, but in young children. Perhaps not surprisingly, this research documents that the precursors to Caveman Logic are well entrenched in each of us long before we became educated, even before we acquired language. Certainly, our adult experiences, such as the lack of scientific education, may contribute to the problem. But, much as we may wish to blame ignorant politicians, conservative preachers, and poor teachers for the problem, the fundamental damage was done long before any of these blameworthy individuals came along. The mental circuitry we have inherited from our unnamed ancestors over the past 500,000 years has far more to do with the state of our species today.

In addition to evolutionary psychology and cognitive neuroscience, another branch of human research has begun to contribute to our understanding of these issues. Within the past decade, the field of developmental psychology (once known simply as "child psychology") has looked directly at the cognitive processes we discuss in this book. We tend to think of "human nature" as what ails your sister-in-law or the annoying guy sitting next to you at the movies. As old-time radio star Fibber McGee observed, "The trouble with human nature is that too many people have got it." But "human nature" also describes how humans thought and behaved long before they became adults; indeed, long before they had a chance to learn much of anything from the world around them. Recent research shows that Caveman Logic and prehistoric thinking are part of what it means to be human—from our very earliest days of life.

Writing in the journal *Science*, Paul Bloom and Deena Skolnick Weisberg[5] argue that the predispositions to the basest, most delusional, error-prone thinking are firmly in place in children so young that testing them cannot always involve language. The authors begin by noting that children as young as one year old are not blank slates. They possess both a "naive physics" and a "naive psychology." These hardwired *intuitions* (Bloom and Weisberg's term) provide children with a "head start when it comes to understanding and learning about objects and people." The authors note, however, that these intuitions may also sometimes conflict with the subject matter of science. In this regard, the authors cite Susan Carey, whose research with children suggests that widespread difficulty encountered in teaching science "is not with what the student lacks, but what the student (already) has." In Carey's words, that "something" is an "alternative conceptual framework for understanding the phenomena we are trying to teach."

Just what are these intuitions that are central to how a child understands the world? A good example is the belief that unsupported objects fall downward. This intuition makes it easy to learn some things about science, such as the theory of gravity (a form of science education few people resist). But that same intuitive knowledge about unsupported things falling down actually makes it difficult to learn other things. For example, children often find it difficult to view the world as a sphere, giving rise to a Flat Earth Society mentality. At the level of childhood intuition, a flat Earth seems quite reasonable. In fact, normal children typically resist the idea of a spherical world until the age of eight or nine. Indeed, if major religious leaders offered public support for the notion of a flat Earth, and the president of the United States publicly stated, "The jury is still out on the Flat Earth theory," it might well enjoy wider public acceptance among adults.

Bloom and Weisberg argue that children's *intuitive psychology*—like their intuitions about the physical world—can also interfere with some forms of science education. For example, children appear to hold deep intuitive beliefs about causal agency, design, and purpose. It is difficult for them to imagine something existing without a *reason for being*. (Lions exist "to go in a zoo" is one example cited by Deborah Kelemen.) Not surprisingly, these mental predispositions conspire against an acceptance of evolution. Bloom and Weisberg suggest that such strong intuitive resistance is then coupled with an unbeatable pair of allies: an alternative position (creationism) that is rooted in widespread childhood intuitions (causal agency, design, and purpose), and a network of strong social support. While the social support is important for acceptance, the authors are clear that it is not sufficient in and of itself. Indiscriminate public sanctioning by trustworthy adults may not do the trick on its own. It is also essential that the belief itself be intuitively appealing. In the case of creationism, that requirement is more than met. The doctrine is rooted in assumptions about the world that go to the very core of what it means to think like a human—even a very young one. Bloom and Weisberg cite research by Evans showing that "when asked about the origins of animals and plants, children spontaneously tend to *provide* and *prefer* Creationist explanations" (italics mine). It is notable that these creationist accounts are coming from children, considerably before religious indoctrination by the adult world has taken its toll.

In summary, Bloom and Weisberg conclude that resistance to certain aspects of science stems from two sources: (1) the "unnatural," counterintuitive properties of some of its claims, and (2) the degree to which more intuitively appealing, alternative viewpoints are supported by seemingly trustworthy individuals. There is little we can do about the first problem. It is simply a fact that species-wide qualities of the human mind render certain kinds of facts and explanations a lot more difficult to grasp, *regardless of their accuracy*. The second problem accounts for well-documented differences in scientific literacy both within and between cultures. In this regard, it is surprising that everyone is not a creationist. How did anyone escape the childhood appeal of creationism and give evolution a chance? It must have taken effort to resist teachers, preachers, and presidents selling a viewpoint that resonates so deeply with Stone Age thinking.

A deeper understanding of the intuitive biases held by human children is essential to addressing the problem of Caveman Logic. If nothing else, it allows us to anticipate where the difficulties will lie, both in acceptance of fact and gullibility to fiction. The intuitions and predispositions of the human mind may be immutable, but they are not iron-clad predictors of adult belief and behavior. That they appear in young children merely tells us something about the natural history of our species. We can acknowledge the untutored appeal of these intuitions at the same time that we elect as a society not to nurture them.

LUNACY WITHIN LIMITS

There is a fascinating and revealing line between what is considered delusional (i.e., certifiable mental illness) and what lies within the bounds of acceptable human behavior. The line is neither straight nor written in permanent ink. Clearly some cultures and subcultures are more tolerant of extreme belief systems than others. Opinions voiced (and behaviors engaged in) within a Pentecostal church on Wednesday night might cause you to be ostracized or worse at your place of employment on Thursday morning. Try speaking in tongues in a boardroom.

A recent series of episodes broadcast during the final season of *The Practice*, a television show about lawyers, illustrates the point. A brilliant attorney, played by actress Sharon Stone, was fired from a large law firm because she professed to have an active relationship with God. She did not simply *believe* in God and confine her activities to polite rituals shared on Sunday mornings. Rather, she claimed to have an ongoing, two-way conversational relationship with God that she brought unashamedly into the workplace. Despite her success in the courtroom, she had become an embarrassment to the firm. Her brilliant legal/analytical mind and successful record as a litigator were not sufficient to offset the negative perception of her. Both clients and colleagues felt that she was "acting crazy," although her belief system appeared to differ only in degree from those around her.

She defended her position by arguing that her colleagues, the presiding judge, and members of the jury had all—at various socially acceptable times—turned to the same deity and engaged in some of the same behavior that had gotten her fired. The brilliance of the episode lay in contrasting Stone's unapologetic and over-the-top behavior with the socially acceptable religiosity of those around her. It became clear that there was little difference in the underlying beliefs: there was enough supernatural agency to go around. A pretrial or pre–football game prayer is socially acceptable. Asking God for wisdom, courage, strength, or insight prior to a contest is somehow a sign of strength of character. However, formally acknowledging the deity as the source of a courtroom strategy or an insight into a witness, as Stone's character did, was grounds for dismissal.

When President Harry Truman asked God (in the name of Jesus Christ) to bless America as it went off to war against the Communists in Korea, this was considered acceptable behavior. Sixty years later, George Bush invoked the same blessing (without the explicit reference to Jesus Christ) and no one cried out for his impeachment, even in a country whose constitution enshrines the separation between church and state. Parents of a sick child routinely pray to their deity of choice to bring their child back to health while at the same time they are transporting her to the hospital. But let those same parents skip the medical help part, trusting only the deity, and they are likely to end up in a court of law, charged with reckless endangerment or criminally negligent homicide. Even then, there is no guarantee they will be convicted. Speaking out against what he describes as "Jonestown in slow motion," emergency room physician Seth Asser[6] documents countless preventable deaths by parents who literally would vaccinate their dogs but not their children. Asser notes that "religious exemption laws," many of which were passed during the Christian Science–oriented Nixon administration, interfere with successful prosecutions, even when the evidence is overwhelming.

A case of this nature made the headlines and was the topic of a special two-hour episode of the NBC show *Dateline*, broadcast on May 16, 2004. The segment, titled "A Twist of Faith," dealt with the case of "a zealous little Bible study group that was transformed to something more deadly." A patriarch named Roland, along with his son Jacques, his wife, Karen, and several dozen extended family and friends, lived and worshiped in a small town in Massachusetts. Gradually, their practices became more and more extreme until they believed they were the chosen people of God. At this point, they began to receive messages from God commanding them to do various things. One of the messages from God commanded them to stop feeding the young son of Karen and Jacques anything but breast milk. After fifty-one days of slow starvation, the child died. He was buried by several cult members who later denied any wrongdoing when questioned by police.

Eventually, the crime was uncovered. (Testimony by cult defectors was critical in finding the body.) However, the state discovered that prosecuting those involved was far from easy. To begin with, there were no applicable statutes to prosecute the cult leader, Roland. The child's mother and father were charged with various counts of murder in two separate trials. Despite a passionate prosecution (the district attorney claimed that this crime, involving fifty-one days of torture, was the worst he had ever seen), it was far from certain that either defendant would be convicted. Appearing in court, the entire group appeared to be decent, well meaning, albeit slightly nuts. Jacques appeared unemotional during his testimony (probably a bad mistake). He truly seemed to be a kind and decent man struggling with a dilemma. He told the jury, in essence, "I am a normal everyday person like you. I, too, love God and love my family. I have come to believe that God talks directly to me. He told me to kill my child so what was I to do?" What he didn't say but might have, is, "You understand because you are like me at the core. You know how my mind works because yours works the same way. I am just as consumed by Caveman Logic as any of you. If you believed God talked to you, would you not listen?"

It turns out Jacques was right, although the jury did find him guilty of first-degree murder. After the trial, members of the jury were interviewed by *Dateline*. Incredibly, they revealed that they held Jacques responsible for his child's death because *they did not believe that God would have wanted the child to die*. They did not question or doubt either that there was a supernatural agent at work or that a deity might speak directly to Jacques or his wife or the cult members. What was at issue for them was the *content* of the message that God was supposedly sending. "We, too, know God," explained the jury, in essence, "but we also think we know His agenda. We do not believe that the message to kill the child could have come from God. It is inconsistent with what we think God is likely to say. Therefore, either you misheard the message or it was coming from someone else. Either way this distortion is your doing, and the murder is on you, not God."

When Jacques's wife, Karen, took the stand, she broke down and cried, expressing genuine remorse that her child had died of starvation. She also expressed that she figured God had it in for her since she was "a whore" (her child had been conceived out of wedlock). Karen was convicted of the lesser crime of assault and battery and immediately released for time already served in jail waiting for the trial to begin.

The phrase "a jury of your peers" takes on new meaning here. These twelve men and women drawn from the local community truly shared the cult's fundamental beliefs. In that sense, Jacques could not have received a fairer hearing. Consider that the jury did not say, "We think you are a delusional nut bar. The very thought that there is a supernatural being hovering over your cult and sending you secret messages, *regardless of what they say*, is just flat-out nonsense. Shame on you for allowing such deluded thinking to infect your lives. And, oh, by the way, you killed your kid in a cruel and unnecessary act and for that we're finding you guilty." In that sense Jacques was lucky: he had a Pleistocene jury evaluate his Pleistocene belief system and, scary as it seems, he almost got away with murder.

The jury, indeed the community where these cult members live, walked away wagging their tongues and shaking their heads. The cult continues to function in their midst, although the children have been taken away from them and adopted out to noncult families and relatives. The noncult community probably takes pride and comfort in the fact that this could not happen to them. They are decent and normal Christians, practicing polite, everyday religion as opposed to this extreme and dangerous nonsense. They are unlikely to kill their children at God's behest, but they will continue to pray to Him and accept as fact His miraculous conception and resurrection from the dead.

THANK GOD FOR ATHEISTS!

I was discussing the basic premise of this book with a friend who listened attentively and supportively. She seemed genuinely concerned about the spread of uncritical spiritual thinking and religiosity. I concluded with a ray of hope by noting the spread of atheist books and secular humanist associations.

"Thank God!" she exclaimed.

And then we looked at each other and started to laugh. Her reaction had been absolutely genuine. Feeling relief at an unexpected, positive outcome, she turned to a common linguistic phrase triggered by such feelings. In doing so, she revealed just how deeply

Caveman Logic is ingrained in our language. Indeed, her two-word exclamation conveys a wealth of information with admirable economy. We have already identified two underpinnings of religion: an overactive causal agency detector and social exchange. Her comment revealed both in action. Although she would not consciously process information in this manner, when told of a desirable circumstance (the presence of atheist books and secular humanist associations), she wrongly attributed their existence to a supernatural agent and felt compelled to thank that agent for his efforts.

As pioneering feminists argued forty years ago, the existence of sexist language does more than reflect problematic attitudes that are ingrained in our culture. It actually contributes to the problem by normalizing these attitudes and practices. As a result, many institutions became zealous about using politically correct, nonsexist language whenever possible. The philosopher Ludwig Wittgenstein argued that language is perhaps the most sensitive indicator of a culture's deepest attitudes and beliefs. The feminists were arguing from this perspective when they lobbied for us to clean up our linguistic act to encourage sexual equality. When someone sympathetic to the views in this book defaults to a "Thank God!" to express her support, it is clear that our culture is rife with unquestioned presumptions about a supernatural world all around us.

The vestiges of former superstitions often lie within the language of polite society. I commonly say "Bless you" when my friends sneeze. I am certainly not entreating a deity to prohibit their souls from escaping in a violent gust of wind through their nasal passages. For me, at any rate, the statement is simply a way of acknowledging a friend's presence, or filling a social void after a rather primitive biological moment. In some ways it feels like a bonding experience. I know of no one who associates any supernatural connotations with a postsneeze "Bless you!"

I am not above saying "Good luck!" to a friend who is about to compete in some way. Since I do not believe in "luck" as a spiritual force that causes things to happen, my intention is social rather than supernatural. "I hope things go well," is all I'm saying. A local real estate agent has blanketed our town with advertising posters saying, "Lisa Smith Makes Miracles Happen!" It's unlikely that anyone expects Ms. Smith to walk on water or turn a bottle of Perrier into wine. The word "miracle" has come to mean "low-probability event," which, in Ms. Smith's case, probably implies that she'll sell your house for more money than you dreamed possible. Granted, language is a constantly evolving thing, but does this linguistic change reflect an underlying mental sloppiness? If getting a few thousand bucks extra for your house is a miracle, then what term do we reserve for someone who actually walks on water?

Admittedly, Caveman Logic won't disappear overnight if our everyday language moves away from supernatural references. But it won't hurt the cause if we stop normalizing religiosity in casual speech.

A VISIT TO THE BOOKSTORE

That old saying, "Nobody ever lost money underestimating the intelligence of the American public," is nowhere truer than in bookstores. If the sheer number of books on the supernatural and paranormal are any indication, then America might be taken for a nation of uncritical fools who are in desperate pain. At the least, we are a people looking for meaning beyond the tedium of our everyday lives, but beyond that we seem to have very low standards. Book buyers appear ready to suspend their critical faculties in search of a quick fix. The quest for spiritual comfort has made millionaires of charlatans, confidence men and women, and their business associates. It's a jungle out there and the foliage is getting thicker by the minute.

A visit to several local bookstores whose large inventory includes everything from best sellers to specialized niche-market publications reveals our penchant for the supernatural. Sections on religion and spirituality have been expanded to include finer distinctions such as aliens and UFOs, ADC (After Death Communication), Wicca and witchcraft, Tarot, numerology, palmistry, and controversial knowledge. Their shelves groan under the weight of an ever-expanding product selection, and the expansion of supernatural titles is encroaching on territory once claimed by such mundane topics as computers and history.

And what do we find on these shelves? Best sellers, to be sure. Indeed, a surprising number of authors who work this territory are described (usually on their front covers) as a *"New York Times best-selling author."* Twenty years ago much of this was considered niche product, consigned to New Age shops and herbal remedy emporiums. Today, the market for paranormal products has expanded into the mainstream. Supernatural or "alternative" belief systems, as they are politely called, are no longer the exclusive domain of freaks, oddballs, and outsiders. They have found legitimacy. Listen to some of the delusional belief systems of mental patients in back wards—how different are some of these from the material on sale in the spirituality sections of large bookstores and Wal-Marts? Consider the following books, along with their helpful subtitles: *The Psychic in You: Understand and Harness Your Natural Psychic Power* by Jeffrey Wands; *Lily Dale: The True Story of a Town That Talks to the Dead* by Christine Wicker; *Spells Dictionary: Everything You Need to Know about Spells and Enchantments to Bring Magic into Your Life* by Antonia Beattie.

Many of these books, such as Rosemary Altea's *You Own the Power: Exercises to Inspire the Force Within* and Doreen Virtue's *Angel Therapy*, cross over into the self-help section. So do titles by David Staume, such as *The Beginner's Guide for the Recently Deceased* and *Sex in the Afterlife*. Communication with the dead has become a growth industry in publishing with titles like *Hello from Heaven* and *Speak with the Dead: 7 Methods for Spirit Communication*.

Books by John Edward and Sylvia Browne are displayed in the same general area. Both have become highly successful franchises (warranting their own sections) of similar-sounding titles that work their audience's seemingly insatiable appetite for material on communication with the dead and past lives. Edward's appeal is further amplified by his television show, *Crossing Over*. But Edward and Browne are pikers compared to Australian TV producer Rhonda Byrne, whose book (and DVD) *The Secret* became an international success story in 2006. Taking the notion of "positive thinking" to outrageous new depths, the book glibly argues (with full support from TV host Oprah Winfrey) that our thoughts actually change the molecular structure of the universe. This, in turn, causes us to "attract" events, both good and bad, into our lives. In short, nothing happens outside of our control.

If all of this is too much for you, there is no shortage of books on more-traditional Eastern and Western religions. However, few of these titles will be confused with serious theological scholarship. Instead, most have a sort of "Christianity meets Hallmark cards" appeal with titles such as *A Travel Guide to Heaven* by Anthony DeStefano and *The Miracle Detective* by Randall Sullivan. If you like your Christianity served with a few threats, there's Rev. Earl Wright's *Why Over 99 Percent of All People Who Have a Religious Belief Are on Their Way to Hell*. The title of Wright's book may be unwieldy but the message isn't: you're not religious *enough*.

For those who still need to take it down a notch, the *Books for Dummies* approach has found a home in this corner of the book-store as well. You'll find *Astrology for Dummies*, and not far from it *Spirituality for Dummies*. These books are not parodies, although their titles bring a welcome note of levity to the somber tone of most paranormal fodder. And, yes, in case you were wondering, there is also a book in the series called *The Bible for Dummies*. That title might offend the more humorless elements of the religious Right, but it is so successful that it has spawned an equally successful imitator called *The Complete Idiot's The Bible*. Whether a dummy or a complete idiot, you will not want in your search for supernatural comfort.

MEN, WOMEN, AND WEIRDNESS

As long as people have surveyed each other about belief in super-natural or paranormal agents, their results have suggested differences between men and women. Finding sex differences in cognitive functions is fairly common, which makes their presence in the spiritual arena not altogether surprising. We will steer well clear of obsolete and unsupported claims about sex differences in intelligence. However, there is a consistent pattern of data showing that women's acceptance of various categories of supernatural agency is higher than men's. For example, a 2003 Canadian survey[7] reported a significantly higher proportion of women believing in God (70 percent) than men (57 percent), as well as 69 percent of women believing in angels, in contrast to 53 percent of men. Blackmore has reported a similar sex difference among US adults,[8] as has Lewis in a 2002 survey of university students.[9] Are women simply more open to supernatural experience?

It appears as if the answer is no, at least not in any general sense. Rather, there is evidence that women and men embrace different *kinds* of supernatural experiences.[10] As Sofka, Bix, and Wolszon have noted, certain types of extreme beliefs (e.g., UFO societies, conspiracy theories, dowsing) consistently draw far more men than women.[11] Similarly, Lewis reports that in his survey of university students, significantly more men held positive beliefs about UFOs, aliens, Bigfoot, and the Loch Ness Monster. Women, on the other hand, were more likely to believe in angels and near-death experiences. Even when they share a supernatural belief, it is not clear that men and women see the object of their affection in quite the same terms. Women, for example, frequently describe God in very different ways than men do. Men and women may check the same yes box on the questionnaire and may kneel together in prayer, but the God to whom women pray has many of the qualities associated with a traditional mother figure—loving, understanding, approachable, compassionate, forgiving, a good listener. The God to whom many men pray is often described by them in terms one associates with a traditional father figure: tough but fair, knows right from wrong, somewhat aloof, solid, strong. The belief may look the same from a distance, but a closer look suggests that men and women construct their personal version of God very differently.

CROSS-CULTURAL DIFFERENCES

There are no studies examining cultural differences in the degree of paranormal beliefs, per se, although there are plenty of cultural comparisons in the degree of religiosity. The problem, of course, is that what might loosely be considered "paranormal" in one culture (e.g., ghosts, communication with the dead) qualifies as religion in another. For our purposes, we can broadly consider belief in supernatural events as a single category.

There is no doubt that cultures differ markedly in the extent to which their members are involved in supernatural belief systems. What is most important from our point of view, however, is this: *nowhere* on Earth do we find a culture that does not embrace some form of superstition, pseudoscience, or supernatural beliefs. Whether you're living in Nigeria or Australia, in Norway or Cambodia, in Canada, Mexico, or the United States, you're likely to find some consensually acceptable form of irrational belief.

Robert Park, the author of *Voodoo Science*,[12] notes, "If you ask people if they are superstitious, they will deny it indignantly. They have been persuaded that there is real scientific evidence for their ideas." Park's book is primarily about pseudoscience, which he believes is the new safe haven for superstition. He might have extended the sweep of his indictment to include spirituality, which has become another justification for superstitious nonsense.

Obviously, lack of scientific support for the pseudoscience that Park decries has done nothing to diminish its appeal. The US government could come out and report in categorical terms that parapsychological phenomena do not exist. In fact, they did: the National Academy of Sciences issued a report in 1987 stating categorically that, having surveyed 130 years of research and reports, there was "no scientific justification" for any such phenomena. That includes reading minds, foretelling the future, influencing physical objects with thoughts, and so on. It mattered not. Belief continues to grow. Talk to a "believer" and he will tell you that the government either looked at the wrong evidence or is part of a massive conspiracy to keep paranormal abilities secret so they can be put to some malignant use. Belief in alien visitations and abductions follows the same pattern. Either the real data weren't examined or the government continues to maintain a massive cover-up operation out in the New Mexican desert somewhere, as it has since 1947.

If you are reading this book in the United States, you are living in one of the most religious nations on earth. The United States is one of the few places where a political candidate can announce that he asked God what to do with his life and God told him to run for president. Indeed, a PBS *Frontline* feature on April 29, 2004, reported that on the day he was inaugurated as the governor of Texas, George W. Bush announced, "I believe that God wants me to be president." Such statements about personal dialogue with a deity might be grounds for commitment to a mental institution in some places. To any but a born-again Christian, such presumptions about knowing the mind of God might seem arrogant, at the least, especially when they are so nakedly self-aggrandizing. In the United States, where nearly half of the US Congress received 80–100 percent approval ratings from the three most influential Christian Rights groups in 2004, they are a way to broaden one's political appeal.

A 2004 survey commissioned by the BBC[13] reports that Great Britain is among the most secular nations on earth. In fact, more than a quarter of persons surveyed believed that the world would be a more peaceful place if nobody believed in God. Nevertheless, 67 percent of Britons reported that they believed in God or a higher power. Depending on your point of view, that number may appear particularly high or extremely low. To add perspective, the comparable figure for Nigerians was 100 percent. Indeed, the study revealed that the highest levels of supernatural belief are found in "the world's poorer nations," such as Nigeria, India, and Indonesia. However, any attempts at drawing simple correlations with wealth, education, or standard of living have to contend with the United States, which excels in all three categories and yet reports a belief score of 91 percent. In fact, as we shall see, this estimate of American belief may be unduly conservative. Indeed, a further measure of the *depth* of belief in supernatural agency is reflected in the question of whether the informant was willing to die or kill for their God or their beliefs. Seventy-one percent of Americans said they were, placing them in a tie with respondents in Lebanon.

Belief in the active role of dead ancestors or supernatural entities in guiding our daily lives is common to many, if not most of the world's religions. The May 23, 2006, issue of *Time* magazine reported on an outbreak of avian flu in a village in Sumatra. The public health official on the scene asked the villagers if it was avian flu. "No," they responded uniformly. The cause was ancestor spirits. When a massive earthquake measuring 7.6 on the Richter scale flattened parts of India, Pakistan, and Afghanistan in October 2005, *Time* quoted the imam at the Illahi Bagh Mosque in Srinagar, India, as saying, "Whatever the scientists say, our Prophet said that when this Earth is replete with sin, this would happen."

Even atheism gets a black eye from the BBC study, which reports that 30 percent of atheists, regardless of nationality, admitted to praying occasionally. A 2008 Pew Trust poll[14] reports that 21 percent of self-described atheists express "a belief in God or a universal spirit." The figure exceeds 50 percent for self-professed agnostics. If nothing else, these findings underscore the difficulty of keeping prehistoric thinking at bay. Like a dieter trying to resist the lure of French fries or chocolate cake, will power and social support may not always be enough. It is hard work to keep thoughts and actions from occasionally slipping under the control of Pleistocene default settings.

The BBC study revealed that it was a rare nation (such as Great Britain), indeed, that didn't report at least an 80 percent belief rate. Other surveys paint an even more extreme picture of American belief in supernatural agency. A Gallup poll conducted in May 2004[15] reports that 90 percent of Americans believe in God (4 percent declare that they do not; the balance are undecided); 81 percent believe in heaven (only 8 percent are willing to report that they do not); 78 percent believe in angels as actual beings (10 percent do not); and 70 percent report belief in the devil and hell as real (17 percent and 19 percent, respectively, do not). These beliefs come at a price. On August 28, 2006, *Time* magazine reported that 77 percent of Americans could name two of Snow White's dwarves, but only 24 percent could name two Supreme Court justices. According to the *New York Times*, the United States once ranked first in the world in the rate of high school graduation. By 2004, it had slipped to 17th. The United States also ranked 49th in the world in literacy rate, and 28th of 40 countries in mathematical literacy.

An ABC News poll from February 2004[16] reports that between 60 and 64 percent of Americans hold a literal interpretation of the Bible (the rate differs for different stories, with Moses parting the Red Sea receiving the highest marks, owing perhaps to Charlton Heston's impact on American culture). These data would suggest that nearly two-thirds of the American population qualify as religious funda-mentalists. A Fox News poll from September 2003[17] provides essen-tially the same portrait of American supernatural belief, with slightly higher estimates (92 percent belief in God; 85 percent belief in heaven; and 74 percent in hell). According to this same survey, just over one-third of Americans also believe in UFOs and ghosts, and one-quarter of the population believes in reincarnation.

In 2006, the journal *Science* published a cross-cultural compar-ison of public acceptance of evolution.[18] Testing samples from 34 countries, the acceptance levels ranged from nearly 90 percent (Iceland), through values in the 80 percent range (Denmark, Sweden, France, Japan), to the 70 percent range (Spain, Germany, Italy, Holland). Poland, Austria, and Croatia lay slightly below in the 60 percent range. At the very bottom of the 34 nations tested were the United States and Turkey. Allowing for sampling error, it may well be that more than half of Americans reject evolution.

Indeed, a more detailed Pew Trust poll conducted in 2005 reports that nearly half of Americans reject Darwinian natural selection as a basic biological principle.[19] They answer yes when asked if species have always existed exactly as we see them today. Such a view goes well beyond creationism or intelligent design, which confines its disdain for evolution to cases of complex designs such as human beings. There is no such distinction here. This is a magical, unchanging world, a still photograph of life taken the day it was willed into existence (about 5,000–10,000 years ago). Such a view literally denies centuries of observations by naturalists and painstaking research by paleontologists and biologists of all nations and faiths. That is a lot of ignorance to profess.

One might assume that such scientific illiteracy would be accompanied by a greater reliance on the Bible as a source of infor-mation about the world. In his book *Religious Literacy*,[20] author Stephen Prothero cites a recent Gallup poll showing that close to two-thirds of Americans believe that the Bible contains the answers to "all or most of life's basic questions." This would suggest that bib-lical literacy has replaced scientific literacy in America. But it hasn't.

Data reported by pollster George Gallup suggest that while they may cite the Bible as an important resource in their lives, Americans are generally as ignorant of its content as they are about science. In fact, Gallup concludes that America is "a nation of Biblical illiterates."[21] The trend appears as dramatically among the families of Evangelicals as it does for the non-Bible-toting person on the street. Americans appear to be a nation of equal-opportunity illiterates.

Compared to the United States, the picture in Canada is a little more reassuring, although by no means cause for celebration. According to a November 2003 survey in *Reader's Digest*,[22] 64 percent of Canadians in general believe in God. Twenty-seven percent of those surveyed weren't sure, and 10 percent did not believe in God. Seventy-seven percent of Canadians believed God to be an "impersonal spiritual force," whereas 17 percent described God as "a person." Thirteen percent believed God was "punishing." Fifty-five percent of Canadians professed to believe in an afterlife. When asked about spirituality in general, the numbers are considerably higher. Ninety-five percent of Canadians expressed belief in at least one spiritual or supernatural entity or process. Nearly as many believe in angels (61 percent) as believe in God (64 percent). In addition, 59 percent of Canadians believe in "synchronicity" (the "meaningfulness" of coincidences); 55 percent believe in destiny or karma; 45 percent believe in personal auras; 43 percent in out-of-body experiences; 37 percent in ghosts; 29 percent in past-life regression; and 27 percent in communicating with the dead. These numbers are surprisingly high, given the relatively low percentages associated with ordinary measures of religiosity. In a country where "only" 64 percent of the people believe in God, it seems odd that virtually half the population accepts as part of their day-to-day reality the existence of everything from angels to auras to out-of-body-experiences, with more than a third accepting the existence of ghosts.

NONBELIEVERS

The old adage "There are no atheists in foxholes," may not be true. Just who are these exceptions? Even if there aren't many of them out there, just *who* is it that does not embrace the supernatural, and how did they get this way?

The headline of an article in the prestigious journal *Nature* in 1998 offers some insight: "Leading Scientists Still Reject God."[23] The two key words here turn out to be "leading" and "still." The latter term refers to the fact that the present study, by Larson and Witham, is a replication of a landmark study performed by James Leuba in 1914. In that work, Leuba reported that 58 percent of US scientists expressed disbelief or doubt in the existence of God. The word "leading" is important because Leuba actually distinguished between competent, everyday scientists and what he took to be the elite subgroup among them. Among that rarified sample of "Greater Scientists," the disbelief number increased to 70 percent. When Leuba replicated his own study twenty years later, he found those numbers had increased to 67 percent and 85 percent, respectively. In other words, by 1934, only 15 percent of America's leading scientists professed a belief in God. Moreover, belief in their own personal immortality barely nudged 18 percent.

The purpose of Larson and Witham's modern replication was to see whether the ensuing sixty-four years had nurtured further supernatural belief in this elite group. Distinguishing between scientists in general and members of the National Academy of Scientists (NAS), Larson and Witham reported that, if anything, the degree of atheism and rejection of the supernatural had grown even more pronounced. By 1998, only 7 percent of "leading scientists" reported believing in God. The number actually dropped to 5.5 percent in biological scientists, with physicists and astronomers slightly higher at 7.5 percent—the same belief rate they held for personal immortality. There are distinctions within the category of "scientist." The *New York Times* reported in 2008[24] that mathematicians were more likely to believe in God than biologists (14.6 percent vs. 5.5 percent), although both fell considerably below the national rate, which exceeds 90 percent.

Commenting on these data, Oxford University scientist Peter Atkins observed, "You clearly can be a scientist and have religious beliefs. But I don't think you can be a real scientist in the deepest sense of the word (and believe in supernatural or paranormal agents) because they are such alien categories of knowledge."[25] This is an interesting distinction. In essence, it suggests that one can be a high school chemistry teacher or perhaps teach first-year physics in a college or university and still believe in God, your immortal soul, angels, heaven, hell, and communication with the dead. There is no reason to believe you won't do a bang-up job at work. But, as Atkins suggests, if you want to be a "real scientist," to use his term in its deepest sense, you can't embrace all that supernatural or paranormal agency into your worldview. It's not about apples and oranges. It's about consuming orange juice when you have a life-threatening intolerance to citrus.

In debates, my theist opponents often mention Einstein's name as evidence that a scientist can also be a "spiritual" person. That's unfortunate. Einstein is probably not a good example of what my opponents want to celebrate. To be sure, Einstein believed in God, but the nature of that God is frequently misunderstood. Albert Einstein viewed the universe with awe and pondered how a divine spirit might be involved in such lawful goings-on. But he dismissed, often with considerable disdain, the very kind of God that is central to much conservative Christian faith in America today. He was opposed to the notion of a God who became personally involved in the events of our daily lives; a God who answers prayer by altering lottery results, romantic conflicts, health problems, workplace promotions, and the outcomes of athletic contests. Pregame prayers in locker rooms were not the stuff of Einstein's beliefs. On those matters, Einstein left no room for doubt. He did not believe in a powerful deity whose favors could be curried with a few well-aimed prayers and entreaties.

There is probably no single group of Americans whose belief in the supernatural is less evident than elite scientists. This tells us several things. The lure of the paranormal can be resisted. It *is* possible, and seems to pose no obvious perils; that is, no one has ever suggested that elite scientists are less moral or live shorter lives than others. And although we cannot be certain as to *how* such dismissal of the supernatural emerged, it is clear that the more strongly one holds a belief in *natural* causal agents, the less likely it is that widespread supernatural views will find a receptive home in these elite minds.

INTELLIGENCE AND IMMUNITY

It is sometimes held that irrational and supernatural belief systems are a form of intellectual inferiority. This may be an unfair judgment, but the psychological literature contains both recent and historical studies comparing the intelligence of believers versus nonbelievers. By far, the majority of these studies (e.g., by Alcock, and Gray and Mill)[26] conclude that those professing supernatural belief systems are simply not as bright—or are less willing to *use* their mental equipment—than those whose views are more rooted in the natural world.

For example, in 1985 Wierzbiki concluded that "believers" made more errors while taking a cognitive reasoning test than "nonbelievers." In 1986 Burnham Beckwith surveyed historical studies of the correlation between intelligence and religious faith. His findings have been summarized on the Web site www.objectivethought .com. Beginning with early studies of students by Howells (in 1927) and Carlson (in 1933), the pattern is unmistakable. In both university and high school students, there is a strong negative correlation between the degree of religiosity and scores on standardized IQ tests. In simple English, the more religious you are, the less intelligent you are likely to be.

It may not be a pretty picture or a politically correct one, but the data are quite clear. Even within church groups, the more liberal thinkers tended to have higher IQ scores (see Symington's 1935 study). Just what do these differences in IQ mean? If we assume that the average IQ score is 100 (with a standard deviation [SD] of 15), then scores of both 85 and 115 are considered normal (±1 SD). An extended conversation between individuals with scores of 85 and 115, however, might lead both to conclude that they were dealing with someone a bit peculiar. Are individuals with 85 (and lower) IQs more vulnerable to supernatural thinking? If so, why? At the least, is it not possible that people with 85 IQs are more likely to socialize with similar individuals, thus normalizing irrational belief systems?

In 1958, Argyle concluded, "Although intelligent children grasp religious concepts earlier, they are also the first to doubt the truth of religion, and intelligent students are much less likely to accept orthodox beliefs." In 1975, Polythress compared the average SAT scores of self-described religious students with those self-identifying as strongly antireligious and found a significant difference (1022 vs. 1148). Confining his analysis to a group of highly intelligent subjects (IQ > 140), Terman reported in 1959 that only 10 percent of men and 18 percent of women held "strong religious beliefs"—figures well below the national average. These results were confirmed in 1968 by Southern and Plant, who studied members of the elite intellectual society Mensa. They concluded that members were far less religious than the average university alumni or adult. This correlation is not a uniquely American result. In 2007, an Angus Reid poll revealed that Canadians younger than thirty-four with a yearly income above $50,000 and a university education are significantly more likely than other segments of the population to accept evolution as part of their natural world.[27]

In 2002, Richard Miller addressed the American Psychological Association (APA) conference and decried the broadening base of undergraduate acceptance for the irrational.[28] Arguing that 99 percent of American undergraduates now accept some aspect of the paranormal such as angels, ghosts, devils, UFOs, and communication with the dead, he identified educational strategies to counteract this trend. Why is this happening among our brightest and best? he wondered. Miller's question had barely stopped echoing before dissent was upon him. Writing in the APA's journal, *Monitor*, Daniel Fuselier and Rob Neiss[29] lambasted Miller for his arrogance in assuming that there was anything defective about belief in the paranormal. Why do we have to take formal steps to guard against something that may ultimately turn out to be correct? they argued.

There is a more important problem with Miller's view of student irrationality. His attempt to uncover its origins trotted out the time-worn clichés about the "functions" of supernatural belief. Miller argues that students embrace supernatural beliefs "because they help reduce uncertainty. These beliefs tend to rise in turbulent times." Obviously, these qualify as turbulent times (post-9/11), and so we should expect a groundswell of more than passing interest in angels, gods, demons, and ghosts.

This view, which is hardly unique to Miller, assumes that any secondary gain provided by such beliefs is also an explanation for their occurrence. The student's belief system has ultimately been reduced to the rat's lever press in a Skinner box. What remains unanswered is why such beliefs are so readily acquired in the first place, and why they feel so "natural." Putting the question another way, why, given the vast number of comforting beliefs the student might embrace, does this same narrow range of possibilities keep emerging? This sounds less and less like normal, "unprepared" operant behavior such as the rat's lever press and more and more like specialized, biologically prepared learning. As work by Martin Seligman, Robert Bolles, and John Garcia reveals, certain types of learning occur much more readily than others and are correspondingly more difficult to dislodge once they take hold.[30] Despite Miller's worst fears, it would seem that something can be done about this descent into the supernatural maelstrom. With all due respect to Fuselier and Neiss, as well as those who view widespread irrationality with no concern, it appears that there may be some sort of immunity to this cultural virus. Whether it is a natural immunity or one acquired through persistent training, there is encouraging evidence of pockets of critical, logical thinking among us.

Chapter 3

SOME REAL-LIFE EXAMPLES

THE ROPE BRIDGE SNAPS

A primitive rope bridge stretches across a section of the Andes Mountains in Peru. The year is 1714. Travelers use the bridge every day, never questioning its structural integrity or the fact that they are taking some risk by crossing. They are probably as unconcerned as commuters who travel across the Golden Gate or George Washington bridges on their way to and from work each day in California and New York.

One day, the rope bridge snaps, killing all five persons who happen to be crossing it at the time. The tragedy is witnessed by a Franciscan monk named Brother Juniper, who is beset by questions such as, Why did it happen? Why now? Why these people? The scholarly monk is convinced that a deeper understanding of this event will provide a window into the workings of God in our lives. Some of you will recognize these events and questions as the theme of Thornton Wilder's 1927 novel, *The Bridge of San Luis Rey*. It is also the theme of the more recent book and film called *The Great Hereafter*, in which a school bus crash on an icy road claims the lives of several children in a small Canadian community.

Faced with events such as these, what kinds of questions do people ask? How are our minds predisposed to handle such tragedy? In some ways, these occurrences are perfectly geared to trigger the worst kind of Caveman Logic. Perhaps our response depends on how close we were to those directly affected, or the degree of empathy we feel with the victims. But ultimately the circumstances reduce to the following: A sudden, unpredictable event has occurred. Its effects are devastating and irreversible. How do we cope with and understand what has happened?

One possibility is to view the circumstances strictly in terms of the natural world. Using the Peruvian example, we can say things like, "Rope bridges are made of biodegradable material. They have a relatively short and limited life span. This may have been, in Wilder's words, 'the finest bridge in all of Peru,' but the year is 1714. The competition for 'fine bridges' is not that impressive. In the absence of a trained city corps of engineers making regular examinations and repairs, it is just a matter of time until the structure gives way. This is most likely to occur when the bridge is bearing weight. In other words, people will be using it when it collapses. Thus, it may not be a question of *why* as much as *when*."

To many people, this account, which focuses on the physical realities of the world around us, may seem bloodless or incomplete. That is unfortunate and in some ways it is the central problem of this book. We are drawn to Stone Age thinking as if it were some kind of gravitational force. Somehow, unexpected events beg a deeper understanding. The supernatural world starts to look mighty tempting. That is part of the reason Wilder's novel was a popular success. His book won the Pulitzer Prize for fiction, was filmed almost immediately, and again in 1944. Sixty years later, in 2004, the novel was again filmed in a big-budget extravaganza featuring Robert De Niro. Obviously, the underlying questions remain timely. Most people are still not satisfied with a physical account of the tragedy. Caveman Logic is alive and well in the twenty-first century. There must be a *reason* for these events, and we're not talking about gravity or rotting sisal. We're talking about a causal *agent*, and who better than a supernatural one? Nearly three hundred years after the rope bridge fell apart, most contemporary readers and viewers agree with the Franciscan monk who witnessed it. Everything we've learned in three centuries goes for naught.

At the core of this descent into spirituality lies the nearly intolerable possibility that some things, especially important ones, are beyond our prediction or control. Thus, the simple equation showing that rotting rope plus weight equals damage and death is insufficient. If we can conjure up a causal agent, we gain several advantages. By understanding the *agenda* of this agent, which was Brother Juniper's avowed purpose as narrator of the book, we might be able to predict, avoid, or understand the events. Thus, for example, it might help to learn that one of the persons on the bridge at the time was a thief or an adulterer. If we then presume that the causal agent (God, in this case) was opposed to theft or adultery, then the whole tragedy makes better sense to us. We gain some understanding. A seemingly random event may not have been so random. The universe is less frightening. Too bad about those other four travelers, but that adulterer just had to be crushed. No wiggle room on this if you're talking about a vengeful deity.

Such understanding can also be used to predict or, perhaps, even control circumstances in the future. Certainly, nobody in his right mind would cross such a bridge knowing that a convicted felon or an adulterer was also using it. And if we had just stolen a chicken or spent the afternoon with a neighbor's wife, we'd be less likely to use the bridge going home that day. Or maybe even that week. This understanding might go a long way to keeping us alive.

Of course, a better grade of rope or more-frequent examinations of the bridge might also not hurt, although these strategies are far less spiritual. At the least, however, our anxiety is reduced because we have taken a seemingly random event and dragged it into a realm that makes sense to us. The account may be utterly bogus, but at some level it feels right. Even if we can't formally predict or control such tragedies, at least we are now able to understand them, post hoc. And that is no small benefit. Needless to say, this approach made a good deal more sense 100,000 years ago when our database about the physical universe was relatively small. But here we are, projected well into the future, living in a society that effortlessly designs and builds bridges across great distances and sends exploratory projectiles into outer space. Yet the same minds that design such devices readily default into their caveman roots. They still seek "spiritual" accounts when some piece of modern hardware malfunctions.

In fact, there is another benefit that comes from inventing a causal agent with some serious agenda issues. (Keep in mind that Thornton Wilder claimed that his prize-winning novel stemmed from arguments with his father, "a strict Calvinist who all too easily imagined God as a petty school master who minutely weighed guilt against merit.") Because of our tendency toward social exchange, we can also beseech this agent each time we or our loved ones are about to cross the bridge. That's one additional way to stack the cards in our favor and gain some apparent measure of control. The occasional sacrificial lamb won't hurt as well. (It won't do a lot for the lamb's health, but it will allow *us* to sleep more soundly.) Of course, every successful journey across this bridge (remembering that most of them *are* successful, or the bridge would have been abandoned years ago) further reinforces the notion of a causal agent who can be successfully bribed. *Oravi, transivi, vixi.* "I prayed, I crossed, I lived."

And so the search begins for some indication of *why* God, the causal agent, would have found fault with some or all of the five people in question. It's likely that any of our lives would have yielded up more than a few glimpses of things that might displease a vengeful deity, but that is irrelevant here. We are not on trial, so to speak. It is our poor, deceased Peruvian friends in 1714 who have presumably brought this on themselves, thus reaffirming our belief that cause and effect or control are always there, if you look hard enough for them.

Two additional points about *The Bridge of San Luis Rey*: First, Brother Juniper never did determine what it was about the five victims that might have brought about God's wrath. They all, including two children, had their share of foibles, but nothing particularly noteworthy. Worse yet, for his trouble, Brother Juniper and his document were burned as sacrilegious by the Spanish Inquisition.

The second point is worth considering the next time you hear somebody making prospiritual arguments. Despite his Pulitzer Prize, Wilder is a bit of a cheat in the way he frames his case. Quoting directly from the book, "Either we live by accident and die by accident, or we live by plan and die by plan." That's just not so. There is *at least* one additional possibility with more to recommend it than either of Wilder's two extremes. Setting aside the question of whether there is any real comfort in living one's life in lockstep with a divine plan (which amounts to predestination), the larger problem stems from how the alternative is phrased. The word "accident" has such negative connotations to most people that it would send them screaming into the arms of God. Accidents are bad things. What do we think of when we hear the word "accident"? A wreck on the highway. A child whose birth was unplanned and, often, unwanted. The negative connotations pile up as we dwell on the word. Does anyone really want to believe that the events of our lives and deaths are "accidental"?

So what's the real alternative? I prefer to see the events of my life as unfolding in a lawful, orderly universe. While it's true that I don't have ultimate control over all of the things that befall me, and I can't predict many of them, I have enough mastery to feel some degree of competence in my day-to-day affairs. The presence of laws, whether the laws of physics or laws made by my fellow humans to regulate our treatment of each other, gives me a sense of mastery over what happens around me. Plainly it is not perfect mastery, but I am not arrogant enough to think I'll be any safer if I invent a few supernatural agents for the things that are truly beyond my control.

Forget accidents. This is a world full of regularities. It provides us with enough information to make informed choices that will maximize the probability of our successes and pleasures and minimize the probabilities of our failures and pain. Most of the time, the bridges work and do not send you plummeting into a Peruvian gorge or San Francisco Bay or the Hudson River. If I were magically transported back to Peru in 1714, things might have been different.

I might have had one look at the material and construction of that bridge and decided to stay home. But that's not about God's plan. It has to do with bringing greater sophistication about the natural world around me to the decisions I make.

Even though Brother Juniper's spiritual quest continues to appeal to many people in the twenty-first century, there are actually exceptions to this descent into Caveman Logic. On February 1, 2003, the space shuttle *Columbia* blew up unexpectedly, killing all its crew and scattering debris over the state of Texas. The nation was in shock and looked for answers. Surprisingly, much of the quest remained focused on the natural world. For months after the tragedy, the nightly news brought details of the physical decomposition of the spacecraft. Headlines detailed the search for defective parts or design, along with who was responsible for such oversights. Certainly, there were passing references to "God's will" and the heroic crew "finding peace in the hereafter." But basically, the nation remained focused on the physical/logical world in its attempt to make sense of the tragedy. Apparently, there was enough comfort in the ultimate message to satisfy our need for prediction and control. The verdict was simply, "You can't cut corners indefinitely in the design and construction of spacecraft. At some point, you or someone else will pay the price."

In all likelihood, some of the loved ones of the crew may have found these physical accounts of the tragedy incomplete and still wanted deeper, more spiritual answers. The question "Why my son?" requires a different explanatory logic than "Why that craft?" Nevertheless, it is heartening that the majority of the American public were satisfied to remain rational in the face of a tragedy of this magnitude.

The destruction of spacecraft, like rope bridges, does not always bring out the best in our mental skills. On January 28, 1986, the space shuttle *Challenger* was similarly destroyed in a sudden and horrifying explosion, killing all aboard. I attended the Ebenezer West Baptist Church in Athens, Georgia, the following Sunday and was treated to a sermon explaining the reason for the tragedy. We were told, "The hand of God had reached down and smacked the craft out of the sky. It was meant to put man back in his place and teach him to stay here on earth where he belonged and not to try to sneak into the kingdom of heaven." Talk about causal agency! Prediction, control, and understanding all wrapped up in one vengeful deity. Just stay here on earth wallowing in ignorance and the Lord will be well pleased with you.

TSUNAMI THEOLOGY

Given the devastation of New Orleans by Hurricane Katrina coupled with New Orleans's reputation as a sinful city, it was just a matter of time before Bible-thumping preachers got on the bandwagon about the wrath of God. They did not disappoint. And such pronouncements were not confined to more extreme regions of the Bible Belt. Indeed, the fall 2005 issue of the admirably even-handed *Religion in the News* publication from Trinity College featured a lead editorial titled, "Was New Orleans Asking for It?"[1] Author Mark Silk surveyed extensive coverage of the disaster and concluded that the inclination to blame the events on a vengeful God provoked beyond endurance was indeed widespread across the United States. There were exceptions such as the *New York Times* and the *Philadelphia Inquirer*, which cautioned against confusing natural occurrences with theology. The *Inquirer* went so far as to label as "blasphemy" any attempt to view Katrina as divine retribution. But these attempts at reason and restraint were an almost inaudible minority view compared to the bleating of conservative and fundamentalist Christian leaders.

How does one dispute such statements? Most critics of the right wing simply said, as the *Inquirer* had, "Don't do that. It isn't right to exploit the tragedy for your own social agenda." In a refreshing bit of contrast, however, New Orleans–based commentator Harry Anderson took a different approach to the events. Anderson did not dispute their relevance to theological matters at all. In fact, he welcomed it. However, he pointed out that we had drawn the wrong conclusion about God from the city's devastation. Appearing on the March 4, 2006, edition of HBO's *Real Time with Bill Maher*, Anderson pointed out that the French Quarter, the presumed hub of evil in New Orleans, was still standing after the flood. Anderson concluded, "If God was trying to destroy evil, He has very bad aim."

In another example of logic turned on its ear, some have used stories about prayer to question rather than affirm the power and omniscience of God. Carl Sagan[2] offers the example of a bishop in the American West who prays for God to intervene and end a devastating dry spell. "Why is the prayer needed?" Sagan asks. "Didn't God know about the drought?" It is indeed perplexing why an omniscient God would routinely require such special alerts or briefings about pain, suffering, and natural disasters. Sagan then questions why the bishop asks his followers to join him in prayer. "Is God more likely to intervene when many pray for mercy or justice than when only a few do?" Sagan goes on to cite an item from a 1994 issue of the *Prayer and Action Weekly News* of Des Moines, Iowa. The issue includes a call to local Christians to join in prayer, asking God to burn down the Planned Parenthood building in Des Moines. The prayer specifies that the destruction of the building should be of such magnitude that "no one can mistake it for any human torching."

What is God to do in this situation? Does he blindly grant requests, especially those coming in large numbers from his devoted followers? Or does God use a moral compass to determine whether such requests are worthy of granting? If so, does he send a sign to his disappointed followers, explaining why he chose not to grant their wish? Will anything be learned by the makers of such unanswered prayers? Might God's silence cause some reflection about the content of their requests, or is the notion that God moves in "mysterious ways" a buffer against having to examine one's social agenda?

I have always wondered what God does in the case of major league baseball. He is often inundated with requests from players on opposing teams. How does he decide which prayers to answer? A French Canadian pitcher on the Philadelphia Phillies steps off the pitcher's mound prior to the start of the inning and appears to be absorbed in prayer. He then crosses himself and goes into his warm-up before pitching to a Dominican player on the New York Mets, who has been busy praying at home plate. In fact, the two players have crossed themselves at approximately the same moment. When the game resumes, the batter strikes out. The pitcher thanks Jesus silently for granting his prayer. But what of the batter? Why was his prayer not answered? Was there a flaw in his life that swayed God to choose the pitcher's wishes over the batter's? They were both Catholic, so that can't be it. Is God more attuned to the wishes of Quebec than the Dominican Republic? Or does God simply not care about professional baseball games and does nothing to meddle in their outcomes? Which, in turn, leads me to wonder why so many players continue to ask for his intervention. Do they not see after so long that such prayers and displays are not tipping the balance in their favor?

There is, I suppose, another possibility to account for the game situation I have described. Perhaps God is a Phillies fan. If he is, we may be forced once again to conclude that God has pretty poor aim.

IF ONLY THEY WERE EDUCATED

In his book *The Demon-Haunted World,* Carl Sagan warns about the dangers of scientific illiteracy. I agree with almost everything in Sagan's book and celebrate his compelling style. But there is one point on which he and I disagree. Sagan, like many critics of religion and pseudoscience, seems to believe that it is ignorance of science, per se, that paves the way for the spread of superstition or belief systems that masquerade as *real* science. There is undoubtedly some truth in that, but it is not the whole story.

Sagan argues, and he has much company on this point, that people seek out belief systems for the comfort they bring and then embrace them uncritically. This suggests that the average person is an unconstrained, if somewhat gullible, consumer who samples many available products (in this case, belief systems) and then chooses the one that provides maximum comfort. Comfort may consist of peace of mind, freedom from doubt, or social support. The important thing is our view of a shopper who is merely evaluating alternatives in a rather hedonistic, scientifically uncritical manner. If people were only better educated, the argument goes, our species wouldn't be in this pickle. Again, I agree that better (or, for that matter, *any*) scientific training might provide some immunity, but it would not address the deeper issue. The so-called open-minded consumer who considers all belief systems as if they were equal contenders is an illusion. Our species has too many mental predispositions to treat alternative explanations as if they were equal contenders on a level playing field. Indeed, to pursue the athletics analogy, the very belief systems that Sagan disdains have an almost overwhelming "home field advantage."

Sagan seems aware of the problem but fails to make the case explicit. For example, he notes that belief in superstition and pseudoscience is not confined to the "ignorant villager" stereotype. He cites modern examples, such as transcendental meditation and the Japanese sect Aum Shinrikyo, both of which attract educated and upscale membership, and make claims of levitation, faith healing, and walking through walls. As Sagan concludes, "These are not doctrines for nitwits. Something else is going on." Sagan quotes revolutionary theorist Leon Trotsky, who noted that the problem was far more widespread than some marginalized illiterates living on the fringes of society and power. In Trotsky's words, "Not only in peasant homes, but also in city skyscrapers there lives alongside the twentieth century, the thirteenth. A hundred million people use electricity and still believe in the magic power of signs and exorcisms. . . . Aviators who pilot miraculous mechanisms created by man's genius wear amulets on their sweaters. What inexhaustible reserves they possess of darkness and ignorance."

Sagan speaks about the "powerful emotional needs" that science "often leaves unfulfilled." But he then suggests that in the quest for such fulfillment, we shop until we find something that fills that emotional void left wanting by science. Again, this suggests an open-minded consumer and a level playing field among alternatives.

If only this were true. A little more scientific literacy, perhaps some glitzy PR work to make *real* science sound sexier, *et voilà!*— an end to superstition, religious fundamentalism, false gods, or, for that matter, *any* gods. And once the solution is under way, it continues to gather momentum. To the extent that unscientific beliefs are given additional appeal by their ubiquity, they would lose even that edge as fewer practitioners were visible on the scene. Sagan suggests that 95 percent of Americans are scientifically illiterate, a pattern consistent with Gilovich's observation that more Americans believe in ESP than evolution.

Even if scientific education were the antidote, there would still be an uphill battle to get science back into the classrooms and textbooks. It is not alarmist to suggest that it is science and not superstition that is marginalized in American society. It is unlikely that Americans will tolerate anytime soon the unapologetic teaching of evolution by natural selection side by side in the science class with other "theories" such as gravity.

Science is *not* an equal competitor in the marketplace of ideas. The *methods* of science may be the stuff of common sense, but the *conclusions* of science are often unappealing. They deal in distances or time periods that are too large to grasp. The distance between Earth and Saturn can be specified in miles, but it has little resonance to the average person who thinks in terms of distance to the nearest Wal-Mart. Our understanding of time is also constrained. The Keck telescope located atop Hawaii's Mauna Kea volcano probes the universe and helped confirm its age at 13.7 billion years. If we think in terms of the human life span, what does 13.7 billion years mean? Can we grasp time moving so slowly and for so long? In a measured piece of reporting, the September 4, 2006, issue of *Time* magazine described the age of the universe as an "unimaginable" time period.

Sometimes an accurate understanding requires us to move beyond familiar time or distance scales. We are plainly not very good at doing it. In their place we are likely to grasp at accounts that almost always are rooted in frames of reference we can understand. I often find it difficult to explain the notion of geological time to my students. You can tell them Earth is 5 billion years old and they can write down the number. Whether or not they have any sense of how large a number it is, or how long a time natural selection has been at work, is another matter. Many textbooks in sciences like biology have taken to using analogies to make such time periods "graspable."[3] For example, the period of human evolution (roughly 5 million years) is likened to a single calendar year, such that the domestication of plants and animals does not occur until dawn of December 31. The growth of cities begins at 3 PM on the last day of the year, and the Industrial Age occurs at approximately twenty minutes to midnight. Virtually everything that is familiar to us appears a second or two before the end of the last day.

Many of the unadulterated conclusions of science suggest processes that lie beyond our understanding and comfort. They offer little or perhaps nothing in the way of egocentric conclusions. We, our planet, our solar system, indeed our galaxy are infinitesimally small and—do we dare use the word—inconsequential. How do you sell those conclusions to a species with a remarkably restricted sense of itself or the universe? With a powerful resistance to perceiving its own place in "the big picture"? Such tunnel vision may have served our ancestors well, but it predisposes us *not* to understand just who we are or where we came from. True, there may be more cultural resistance to these findings on a farm in Kansas or a truck stop in Mississippi, but the problem is found in urban centers as well. Caveman Logic is not that easy to caricature. The real problem is species-wide. The same cognitive architecture that makes it difficult to shake our ignorance in the "red states" is present even in the skulls of educated liberals who worry about growing theocracy in America.

KISS MY SPIRIT

Spirituality is a loaded word. The dictionary defines it several ways. The adjective *spiritual* can mean "of or relating to sacred matters" or "ecclesiastical rather than lay." That's probably a little too close to organized religion to please many people who embrace spirituality. The key definition appears further down the list: "of or relating to ghosts or other supernatural beings." Think about that one.

It's a safe bet that most people who consider themselves "spiritual" would not want to be associated with *spiritualism*, which is "the belief that departed spirits hold intercourse with the living, usually through rapping or trances." Rapping in this context presumably has less to do with Snoop Dogg, Puff Daddy, or Tupac than it does banging on tables.

Spirituality is on the brink of becoming a sacred cow, along with apple pie and motherhood. "He's a very spiritual person" is not a way to tell us, "The jerk believes in ghosts." It is more likely to mean, "He's a beautiful person, attuned to higher, more blissful realities. He's good and decent beyond the rest of us mere mortals, who just seek good food, good sex, and good music in our lives."

If spirituality means a better, more devoted friend or lover or parent or child, then count me in. Someone more likely to accept an outsiders for who they are, without needing to judge, convert, or condemn? I'm all for it. But I'm not sure that's what it means at all. According to many, Osama bin Laden is viewed as being a highly spiritual man. So is George W. Bush. Holy wars are typically fought by spiritual men. Spiritual isn't always good.

There is another reading of "spiritual" that is quite negative and actually more central to the point of this book. Spiritual people may be those who are less likely to embrace physical reality and rational logic. By becoming more spiritual, they may simply be defaulting into a world that emphasizes ghosts, demons, angels, and ancestor worship. It would be a pity for a twenty-first-century Western nation to return itself to the Dark Ages in a misguided quest for "spirituality."

SYNCHRONICITY STRIKES!

Carl Gustav Jung (1875–1961) can rightly be considered the father of the term *synchronicity*. Even by the rather loose standards of his day (Jung was a contemporary of Freud), Jung could arguably be classified as a flake. To be sure, his writings set the stage for and gave legitimacy to a whole new generation of magical thinkers who see patterns where there is only noise, and who are only too glad to wring "meaning" from the blips in the flow of random events. It is possible that even Jung would have raised an eyebrow or two over the sappy and uncritical way his work has been co-opted by the New Age spirituality movement. That's a lot of parental responsibility to shoulder.

Jung observed, rightly so, that life was full of coincidences.

Some of them, like your flipping a switch and a light coming on, are causally related. But others, he argued, are still "meaningful," even though they are not formally linked by causality. This is where the concept of synchronicity comes into play.[4] Jung defined it as "a psychically conditioned relativity of space and time." Admittedly, that definition stops a few meters short of clarity, although Jung argued that synchronicity was equal to causality as an explanatory principle. What this tells you, if nothing else, is that Jung, and likeminded individuals, think they are living in a very different universe than the one most of us inhabit.

The idea of the "importance" of synchronicity is where most people bring their least critical, most flawed thinking into play. Books have been written—although apparently not enough of them—to dispel this kind of delusional thinking. The temptation to "see something" (be it a pattern or a connection) is just too great. It benefits from how our minds are predisposed, as well as from a burgeoning amount of social support, of which Jung is just the tip of the iceberg.

Let's look at one of Jung's own examples of what I like to think of as "Shirley MacLaine thinking." This former actress-turned-philosopher could have been the poster girl for *not* changing careers midlife, especially when the change involves moving into a domain where one has minimal expertise. In general, rock stars do not become nuclear physicists for a good reason. But Shirley MacLaine decided to become a guru of the New Age movement, specializing in past lives. She wrote books like *Out on a Limb* (1994), toured, and gave interviews in support of her beliefs, which were grounded in logical errors so egregious you had to suspend all common sense. Undoubtedly, audiences were drawn to her because of her celebrity and, quite likely, because of her views on reincarnation, which were shared by many. It was the other part— the gathering and evaluating of evidence—where MacLaine and her followers came up short. Had she brought the same wretchedly inadequate standards to her work as an actress, she would have been laughed or booed off the stage. Which all goes to suggest that most people are far more critical of performers than gurus.

But back to Jung, who in many ways anticipated Shirley MacLaine–style thinking by fifty years. Jung writes all about his recurrent encounters with fish over the course of a day or two: dead ones on his dinner plate or lying on the beach, live ones in the sea, linguistic ones in sentences spoken by those around him (or by Jung himself). It's quite an effective narrative and almost makes you wonder just what is going on with this embarrassment of fishes. Treasure the moment: you are experiencing a taste of your own Caveman Logic. But does this string of coincidences deserve serious consideration as an explanation of how the universe works? What specifically is wrong with Jung's growing mound of evidence? Largely, it suffers from what logicians call "multiple endpoints." Multiple endpoints are a seductive and nasty little trick used by all kinds of debaters to "prove" their points to an uncritical audience. They are a staple of religious tracts, sermons, and unsound polemics of all kinds. In a nutshell, they work because there is an almost endless supply of evidence that will serve as "proof" of whatever is in question. The question is usually stated in what sounds like highly specific terms—the sign of a good, rigorous, scientific test. It isn't until we begin the "test" that it becomes clear that just about anything qualifies as "proof."

The believer in despair turns to God and says, "Please, God, if you *really* are out there, send me a sign." It sounds like a fair test, until you realize that just about *anything* can qualify as a "sign" and that there really is no possible outcome that would qualify as negative evidence. Imagine a believer who has lost faith, reporting to his friends, "I asked God for a sign so I might clarify my belief and He sent me none. So I took this as evidence that He doesn't exist and I stopped believing in him." No, you haven't heard that and you aren't likely to.

Shirley MacLaine started with a premise—that humans had past lives—and went looking for evidence to support it. What did not support her belief, she simply ignored. That may be human nature, but it is not science. Nor is it logical. Well-known physicist and commentator Robert Park uses the term "Texas sharpshooter fallacy" to describe it. As statisticians describe it, it is like firing all your bullets into the side of a barn and then walking over to the bullet-riddled wall and drawing a bull's eye where it looks best. That little trick is no more evidence of sharpshooting than Shirley's claims were scientific proof of previous lives.

Jung started with a premise about the recurrent presence of fish and found evidence galore, confirming his views about synchronicity. Using multiple endpoints, I can continue, more than half a century later, on Jung's magical foray into the cosmic world of fish, and what will I have learned? As I sit here writing this book, I gaze out at my backyard. Beneath my indoor perch (pun intended) is the yard that contains a pond. In it are seven goldfish! Earlier today, I took a break and watched some television. As I surfed through various channels, I passed reruns of the classic TV show *Barney Miller*. You might recall that one of the central characters was a cop named "Fish," who was on screen as I watched. One of the commercials that followed was for the restaurant chain Red Lobster, whose ad depicted several appealing-looking seafood dishes. I came downstairs and made myself a tuna fish sandwich before getting back to work. Then a colleague from Montreal called from his office at McGill University. (Get it? Mc*Gill*?) Last night I watched an old 1940s gangster movie and one of the characters, who wanted to borrow five dollars, asked the other one for a *fin*.

Where does it end? Does this seem far-fetched (or *fishy*) to you? Why is my example any sillier than what Jung or any of a dozen New Age gurus teach their wide-eyed followers? Here is another example, drawn entirely from archival sources. Nothing is made up or exaggerated.

In the late 1970s, I published two papers[5] on how a person's name often appeared ironic in light of what he or she did for a living. My first paper dealt exclusively with animal behaviorists. I surveyed about a hundred scientists who worked with various species and who, themselves, had surnames like Tiger, Fox, Wolf, Herring, Trout, Fish, and Bird. After the paper was published, I received hundreds of responses from readers who had more examples to offer. Some pushed the boundaries of my original search even further. For example, there was a paper on abnormal behavior in dogs by Freak, a paper on vision in frogs by Gaze, a book called *The Life of Insects* by Wigglesworth, and a paper on historical attempts to prevent masturbation in stallions by Mountjoy. And once I went beyond the realm of animal behavior, the floodgates opened up. I found a paper on vasectomies by Gillette. My favorite was a paper on urinary tract infections by Smellie and Leakey. The point is, had my quest been—by any stretch of the imagination—serious or *spiritual*, there is no telling what would have been made of my findings. Thankfully, it was all in fun. But even so, the whole thing got taken way too seriously. My work *seemed* to offer a test of a specific premise—that there is some correspondence between one's name and one's work. But because of multiple endpoints (almost anything we found fit the bill) and no serious attempt to look for disconfirming evidence, the paper held no value whatsoever other than as entertainment. Nevertheless, it continues to be cited. In fact, shortly after the second paper was published, I received a call from the *National Enquirer*. The reporter said they were considering doing a feature on it, but only if I believed it *meant* something and could fuel that viewpoint. Humor (which had been my only goal) was not enough.

FOREVER JUNG

Now, you might ask, how would Jung have handled this same issue? In his book *Synchronicity: An Acausal Connecting Principle*,[6] he sorts through exactly the same kind of evidence I did and reaches a somewhat different conclusion. Commenting on Wilhelm Stekel's book *The Compulsion of the Name*, Jung cites the following examples of what for him was compelling evidence of the universe telling us something: Herr Gross (which Jung translates as Mr. Grand) has delusions of grandeur, Herr Kleiner (translated as Mr. Small) has an inferiority complex, the Altmann (old man) sisters each marry men twenty years older than themselves, Herr Feist (Mr. Stout) works as the food minister, Herr Rosstauscher (Mr. Horsetrader) is a lawyer, Herr Kalberer (Mr. Calver) is an obstetrician, Herr Freud (Mr. Joy) champions the pleasure principle, and Herr Jung (Mr. Young) champions rebirth. Jung then asks, "Are these whimsicalities of chance, or are they meaningful coincidences?"

Again, the idea of multiple endpoints looms large here. It appears that a singular piece of evidence has, against all odds, managed to come forth to confirm a meaningful coincidence. A closer look, which disciples of synchronicity no doubt prefer you do not take, suggests otherwise. If Mr. Grand had been six feet tall, that would also have confirmed Jung's point. If Mr. Small had not had an inferiority complex but had been small in stature or generosity, Jung would have again claimed victory. If the Altmann sisters were eighteen when they married, were their thirty-eight-year-old husbands really "old men"? Mr. Stout, the food minister, seems a roundabout way to confirmation. The case would have been stronger had he been overweight, but then how many middle-aged German men of his vintage were not? If that number approaches 50 percent, the notion of a meaningful coincidence pales. Concerning Mr. Horsetrader, the case might have been a bit more striking if he made his living buying and selling equines. The coincidence between his name and his work as a lawyer seems a bit contrived. Similarly, chalking up as another "hit" the fact that Mr. Calver was an obstetrician takes a backseat to the possibility that he might have been a veterinarian. As to Drs. Freud and Jung, contrivance again seems the order of the day. Had Freud just been a happy-go-lucky fellow and Jung a pediatrician, I would be a lot more impressed. But none of these examples holds a candle to my own discoveries of Smellie and Leakey or Gillette. Since those were my own citations, my interpretation must count for something. So here it is: I don't think they matter a hill of beans. I also learned in my research that the head of the Canadian Dairy Association was named Cheeseman. Undoubtedly worth a chuckle but, with all due apologies to Professor Jung, it's useless information. Until someone is willing to enumerate all the dairymen named Smith and Jones, we don't really have a handle on the situation. And how about all the Mr. Smalls and Mr. Grands who are of average height and weight? They are of interest to nobody and don't go into Jung's equation, although they should. This is a really important point, and we will return to it in some detail. For now, consider that if such a study were made and the results documented tens of millions of individuals whose names bore no logical connection to their employment or identity, what would we have learned? What constitutes negative evidence here, Dr. Jung? In retrospect, it's too bad the reporter from the *National Enquirer* couldn't have talked to Jung himself. I'm sure they would have made each other's day.

The odd thing about all of this is that Jung was by no means an ignorant man. In fact, he seems quite aware of the use of statistics and their role in discounting chance as an account of seemingly odd occurrences. Unfortunately, his passing acquaintance with statistics did not immunize him well enough. For one thing, Jung seems totally unaware of the idea of multiple endpoints, accepting virtually *anything* in support of his hypothesis (a true role model for Shirley MacLaine). His is a flexible standard of evidence that cannot fail its master. Moreover, although Jung seems passingly aware of the notion of control groups as points of comparison, he seems to stop short of selecting the most relevant ones. In addition, Jung has a strange view of chance. To most people (and almost all scientists), chance refers to events that happen randomly, with no design or purpose. It offers a neutral explanation that's just about as far from the *Twilight Zone* as you can get. Jung has a different view. He champions a universe in which chance itself is fraught with meaning. It is trying to tell us something. Remember, all things happen for a "reason," and if we are too limited to see the connections in the physical world around us, the shortcoming lies in us, not in the universe. You can see why Jung is a hero to purveyors of Caveman Logic.

Jung saw many things. Some of them—like dinner tables and puppy dogs and attractive women—were perfectly accurate perceptions and allowed him to function in a successful and socially acceptable manner. But Jung also saw other things that, for all intents and purposes, weren't there. He saw patterns of events, odd clusters of circumstances that he wrongly interpreted as exceptional. Jung never questioned these perceptions, any more than he questioned his perceptions of furniture, dogs, and women. He assumed these things were out there in the world and went about acting on the information flashing across his brain. Worse yet, he wrote and lectured about his perceptions, infecting other minds in the process.

It never occurred to him that the odd coincidences or patterns or clusters he "saw" originated in his own mind rather than in the outside world. He trusted his perceptions (and his conclusions about them) implicitly and went about trying to explain them. Because he was an educated man, he drew upon sources as varied as sixteenth-century philosophy and the I Ching. In the long run, he needn't have bothered. There was essentially nothing to explain. All of those bizarre "coincidences" involving scarab beetles flying into rooms and fish of various types crossing his path were actually products of his own imagination. He would have been better advised to spend his time and considerable intellect studying the misguided workings of his own mind rather than supposedly magical forces in the outside world. But, for all his education, Jung's mind did not work any differently from the minds of most humans on the planet. Thus, when he began to describe those mysterious patterns he had observed, people around him shook their heads and said, "I've seen things like that too. I always wondered why they happened." And so the uncritical contagion began.

Here is a Jungian-type tale I sometimes tell my students to underscore how attractive synchronicity can be. In fact, this story is conflated from two famous case histories reported by Jung—one involving a scarab beetle and one involving a bird. The species itself doesn't really matter. For the record, both birds and beetles are well represented in the Jungian world of archetypes, which lies beyond the realm of this book.

Here's the story: A therapist was faced with a chronic depressive patient who seemed resistant to any sort of therapy. Since this tale takes place nearly eighty years ago, the therapist was working in an age without the easy benefits of Prozac, Zoloft, and other commonly prescribed antidepressant drugs. Nothing in the therapist's skills seemed to work on his patient. The problem came to a head on a particularly sunny spring day. The grass was green and the breezes were warm but, despite the splendors of nature, the patient sat morosely on his bed, unable or unwilling to respond to anything.

Realizing he was all but out of therapeutic ammunition, the therapist announced that he could do no more. "What would it take to cure you?" he asked in frustration.

"If only there were some kind of sign," the patient replied.

At this point, a dove flew into the open window. The patient and the therapist were both shocked. Just the sign they both needed. The patient was cured and the therapist knew he had an anecdote, if not a publication, in his future.

Neither the patient nor the therapist was particularly religious, but both knew when the universe was trying to send them a message. Was it possible that this had just "happened," that is, that there was no deeper "meaning"? To the patient, who had wallowed in despair and misery for years, the sudden and dramatic event seemed too large not to be the sign for which he was looking. To the therapist, the events happened when all hope seemed lost. Neither was sure whether it was the dove, itself a creature rich in symbolism, or the coincidental timing of the event.

Although the tale has a happy ending, the actual sequence of events was not quite a Hollywood movie. The patient was not immediately healed, although he did eventually rejoin the world as a functioning individual. The episode with the dove jolted him from his depression so that he was able to respond to treatment, although he did experience periodic bouts of depression later in life.

What did it all mean? The hopeless patient asking for a sign, the flight of the bird, the shock of both patient and therapist, and the eventual cure? To begin with, some might argue that the need to "explain" these events may itself be a sign of our faulty mental apparatus. What is there to explain? Things happen, and sometimes their couplings or coincidences are intriguing. Nothing more. Still, it is a rare person who doesn't find such tales memorable, even inspirational. The question is, do they really suggest anything deeper than coincidence? If you can feel your mental circuits starting to twitch, try to rein them in for a moment while you look at things in a less Jungian way. Consider that birds have been flying into houses (and cars and airplanes) as long as there have been houses (and cars and airplanes). Their appearance is rarely cause for spiritual awakening. Why now? Because the patient asked for "a sign" just before the appearance? That seems a pretty slim basis for raising this episode to the level of myth. I live in the country and field mice often find their way into my house, especially during the fall when the weather starts to turn cold. I happen to like small animals, although I don't want my house overrun by them. Imagine that I were having a particularly bad day keeping up with the property, and I wondered whether to move into town. Perhaps I asked for a "sign"—from whom, I am not sure—that would help me make my decision.

This seems a pretty open-ended business. Just what constitutes a sign? Are certain types of events sign-worthy and others not? If so, what is the criterion? Is it their nature—say, natural versus man-made objects? For example, a bird flying through the window is a sign, but a baseball is not? Is it the relative probability of the event? Perhaps "rare" is good but "commonplace" is not. On second thought, maybe we should steer clear of probability since most people are very poor estimators of it. But, like it or not, probability counts.

Our poor estimates of probabilities have a lot to do with our belief systems. Things that *appear* to be singular and salient events may often, on closer examination, turn out to be quite ordinary or regularly occurring. But by then, of course, we may have already processed them as unique and already assigned meaning to their occurrence. And once we begin to share our reports with other malfunctioning and uncritical minds, we have derived such social support and attention that it is even less likely we will invest energy in correcting our beliefs.

Let's go back to the bird who flew into the patient's room. Just how rare was that event? To begin with, many people spend a lot of time on the lookout for signs in order to lead their lives. Whether checking the astrology column in their morning newspaper or watching the skies, their "locus of control," to borrow some psychological jargon, is largely external. So the stage for belief has already been set by someone looking or asking for a sign in order to move on. As to what happened next, this was hardly the first bird that flew into an open window, even at this elite private sanitarium. Consider your own experience with birds and windows. Sometimes the windows are open and the bird ends up fluttering about the room until it is dispatched by an exasperated homeowner or prompted to fly back out the way it came in. In fact, such events are apparently common enough for there to be superstitions in numerous cultures about what it means (i.e., good or bad luck) to have a bird in your house. Living in the woods, I can vouch for that. Unfortunately, windows aren't always open when birds fly into them. These episodes usually don't end so well for the bird.

Is it rare that a bird in a house coincides with the cure of a persistent ailment, as in the case of our patient? Perhaps we only know of this episode because it happened to be a warm day. Would the therapist have reported the events if the weather had been chilly, the window had been closed, or the same plea for a sign had been followed by a bird crashing into a window and fluttering three stories to his doom? What if the patient, witnessing all this, had lapsed into a suicidal depression, claiming, "See? Everything is hopeless and ends in death." Somehow, it seems unlikely that these alternative events would have been the stuff of great anecdotes, regardless of how frequently they occurred.

The point is that we are apt to lose sight of the fact that most bird-entry cases go unreported, which is why we don't know how rare they are. This is no small issue since rarity is an implicit part of the "meaningfulness" processor, whether we like it or not. If local birds fly through or into windows a thousand or more times a day, which they very well might, the synchronicity in the therapist's story would be far less compelling. After all, do airline pilots fall to their knees and wonder about deeper meaning every time a seagull is sucked into one of their jet engines?

Carl Gustav Jung simply could not accept the possibility that anything, and certainly not a coincidence, was meaningless. To attribute coincident events to "chance" was to diminish their cosmic importance. He *wanted* them to have meaning. Jung argued that if we are foolish enough to dismiss the bird in the window or the fact that Mr. Gross was a fat man, that would put us in conflict with J. B. Rhine's ESP discoveries.[7] Jung goes on to detail these discoveries with obvious admiration and relief, since they offer considerable support for the supernatural universe he inhabits. The great majority of psychologists and psychiatrists, he laments, seems to be completely ignorant of all the carefully verified case studies on synchronicity. Jung goes on to argue that both ESP and psychokinesis have both been verified by solid empirical research.

With the wisdom of half a century's hindsight, we can caution Jungians everywhere that to build one's dream house on a foundation of Rhine's data is to invite architectural disaster. When Jung rhapsodizes, "There are very few experiments in the field of the natural sciences whose results come anywhere near so high a degree of certainty," he has shed any semblance of credibility. He might as well be arguing for the solid evidence behind phrenology or a flat Earth. Jung argues that continued skepticism about ESP is really without a shred of justification. The landmark studies to which he specifically refers include work by Soal and Goldney,[8] which have long ago been disproved and in some cases were the result of outright cheating. In short, rather than serve as the cornerstone for Jung or his doctrine of synchronicity, these ESP experiments are, in fact, a source of considerable embarrassment to the field of psychic research, which itself is no source of pride to the broader field of psychology. We can forgive Jung for not knowing better. But those who today build their empires on Jung's work cannot be so easily excused.

EVERYTHING HAPPENS FOR A REASON

The other day, I sat down for what I assumed would be a casual conversation, only to find myself listening to a very distressing story of broken marriage, infidelity with a younger, tattooed woman, and the challenges of raising a young child alone. I was nodding sympathetically when the tale ended with the words, "But I guess everything happens for a reason. Don't you think so?"

No, I don't. At least not in the way she meant "reason." I do believe in causality. But not divine purpose, which is what she was getting at. I do not believe that events like broken marriages are doled out by someone or something according to a master plan that anticipates their ultimate purpose in the life of the survivor. For example, if my friend were to meet a new partner in the next several months, would she be tempted to conclude that her husband leaving her for his tattooed girlfriend happened so that she, the jilted wife, would meet her new partner—the *real* love of her life?

I believe in a different kind of causality that doesn't include a purpose. I agree that her husband left her for a reason, but I would be inclined to look for it in the known universe: things like lack of commitment on his part, interpersonal conflict, perhaps an unsatisfying sexual relationship, his attraction to younger women, and so on. I believe in those kind of reasons. This husband did not simply wake up one morning in the arms of a tattooed woman, his wife and infant left safely behind. You can bet there were reasons, and they lie well within the fabric of a deterministic universe. In this case, they can be found in our understanding of human nature. There is no reason to turn to the supernatural or the purpose these tragedies might someday serve as lives continue to unfold.

Students of philosophy will recognize my friend's view as an example of *teleology*—the idea that things are determined or caused by their ultimate purpose, rather than their antecedent conditions. If you believe that the *purpose* of this painful breakup was to let her find her next boyfriend, there's no point in trying to understand why it happened in the here and now. The biggest problems with a teleological account of human behavior are that it is ultimately supernatural and that it keeps one from examining the real causes that might allow us to adapt and improve our lot. For example, could the wife recognize aspects of her husband's character that, in retrospect, might have allowed her to predict his infidelity and choose more wisely next time?

On a less tragic note, I've heard people who recently lost their jobs but landed on their feet several months later with "better" jobs conclude that the whole thing was "meant to be." This, again, is teleology at work. Any question of why that first job was really lost (e.g., poor performance in the workplace) is too trivial to consider. There is no personal responsibility within this philosophical universe. We are all leaves in the wind, being swept along by divine plans that are out of our control.

Why do we turn so quickly from Human Behavior 101 into the arms of cosmic spirituality? Plainly, such accounts are very appealing and they benefit from a winning combination: a good fit with how our minds work plus widespread social support. Re-education against those odds is difficult. The woman whose husband left her was shocked at my failure to share her "Everything happens for a reason" belief. She was also none too pleased at the here-and-now approach I took to understanding her circumstances. It offered little comfort, too much responsibility, and almost no social support.

A SMORGASBORD OF ERRORS

Here are some everyday examples of commonly made mental errors. It is likely that you've experienced some of them yourself. In fact, you may still be persuaded by a number of them. These are not hypothetical; I've collected them from encounters with family, friends, and students.

1. The odds of any particular person winning the lottery are extremely small—perhaps a million to one. Thus, if you buy a ticket, it is highly unlikely that *you* will win. But *somebody* will. That is a certainty.

We often confuse these two probabilities, leading us to ask inappropriate questions. A student of mine bought a lottery ticket and lost. She was not particularly surprised although she had prayed long and hard to win. But then she became interested in the winners. Why did *they* win? What was it about *them* that caused them to win? she wondered. I told her I didn't understand her question. She persisted, explaining that if she met and interviewed the winners, it would become obvious (to her) why they had been chosen. "Somebody will always win," I pointed out. "Will there always be a *reason*?" That gave her pause, but she finally replied in the affirmative. I suggested she read *The Bridge of San Luis Rey*.

2. A student of mine came to me and said, "I know you don't believe in this stuff, but I predicted the future today. I was driving to school from Toronto and I suddenly got this feeling that I was going to see a terrible car accident. Just after we got off the 401 (a large east-west highway running between Toronto and Guelph) we passed this awful crash. The cops had the highway blocked and we had to wait about twenty minutes until they let us use the road. I was actually late for school. How do you explain that? I bet you don't believe that it happened."

She was surprised to learn that I believed all of it. Didn't this then compel me to accept her "psychic" account? No, it didn't. Instead I asked her how frequently she had made similar predictions about highway accidents. The question surprised her and she confessed that such morbid thoughts often cross her mind as she makes the daily one-hour drive on a crowded, high-speed highway. "And most of the time when nothing happens, what do you do about your prediction?"

"Nothing," she admitted. "I just forget about it."

"So you might be making upwards of two hundred predictions a year?"

"I guess so," she conceded, aware of where the discussion was headed.

"And roughly how many accidents happen on either the 401 or the Guelph Highway each year? How uncommon are they?"

"Not *that* rare," she admitted.

I pointed out to her that what may look like a singular event is often the numerator in a fraction. On closer inspection, the outcome may have been a lot more probable (and less supernatural) than assumed.

3. A student of mine showed up for class sporting a pair of crutches and a large cast on her leg. "What happened?" I asked.

"I slipped on the ice and broke my leg," she replied. And then she added, "I know why it happened."

"What do you mean?" I inquired. "It's the middle of winter; the ground is covered with ice; you lost your footing and fell; you broke your leg. Isn't that why it happened?"

"Yeah, but it's not really *why*," she explained.

"What's the real reason, then?" I asked.

She looked pained. "Two days ago, I had a fight with my mother on the phone. I was very mean to her. I should never have said those things. I just knew something would happen. And now look."

"So you think you were being punished?" I asked.

She looked down at her cast and shrugged her shoulders. "What does it look like to you?" she replied.

4. On August 27, 2008, station KLTV, an ABC affiliate, reported that a local resident of Pittsburgh, Texas, had found a moth with the face of Jesus on its back. The moth, described as "an amazing

thing," was removed from an RV trailer, where it had settled, and taken to the local church, where residents hoped to sell it. Pastor James Jordan commented, "If God can do that on a little moth, He can do mighty things in our lives."

Why the face of Jesus? We have already considered how our overactive pattern detectors can extract faces from minimal, even random arrays of stimuli. Why Jesus and why not, say, Oskar Kokoschka, the great Viennese Expressionist painter, probably tells us more about the culture of this East Texas town than anything else. In any case, what the residents of Pittsburgh, Texas, actually had on their hands was a male *Eacles imperialis*, the imperial moth. With a wingspan that can reach nearly six inches, there's no doubt that these moths are both beautiful and impressive specimens. But they are not supernatural. The facelike patterns on their backs is characteristic of the species. Sightings are most common between June and August, the very time this individual was found. Images of (as well as information about) imperial moths are readily available online (e.g., www.davesgarden.com).

It is unfortunate that so many of us know so little about the natural world around us and default so easily to the supernatural when faced with uncommon events. Ignorance is truly the handmaiden of Caveman Logic.

5. Professional baseball players—a superstitious lot, to be sure—often become obsessive about numbers. Sometimes the focus is on uniform numbers. Players often believe they have to wear (or avoid) certain numbers on their backs and will go to considerable lengths to make sure their needs are met. When traded to a new team, there is often a scramble to see that uniform numbers are assigned in a way that yields peaceful coexistence.

Philadelphia Inquirer columnist Todd Zolecki concluded the following about uniform numbers: "If they were just numbers, nobody would retire them or put them on walls. If they were just numbers, players wouldn't buy them from teammates. Kids wouldn't fight other kids on their Little League team to wear the ones they want. And adults wouldn't be able to memorize their PIN codes by repeating [the names and uniform numbers of their

Phillies heroes] over and over: Mike Schmidt and Steve Carlton. Mike Schmidt and Steve Carlton . . . 20–32."9

Zolecki notes that obsessing over numbers does not confine itself to uniforms. He reports that Philadelphia pitcher Brett Myers, who suffered a freak injury to his shoulder in a game against the Florida Marlins in May 2007, had been apprehensive about pitching in that particular game. It seemed to him that the number 23 had been appearing everywhere. As explained in a 2007 popular film called *The Number 23*, that number is "cursed and evil" because two divided by three equals .666, which some people believe is a sign of the devil. Myers observed, albeit somewhat jokingly, that that ill-fated number kept appearing. The game took place on May 23. It was the Phillies' twenty-third road game and the Marlin's twenty-third home game. The Phillies' record at the end of the game was 23–23. Myers checked to see if the injury had occurred on the twenty-third pitch he threw but learned it had been the twenty-seventh. Nevertheless, Myers, who does not view himself as particularly superstitious, described the events as "kind of weird." The film went further, promoting itself with the words: "All patterns contain a message. All messages reveal a destiny."

6. A friend of mine tells me that he looks for signs in the momentary coincidences and events of his everyday life. He considers himself "sensitive" to these minimal cues and their meanings. The examples he has shared with me include finding seven cents on the sidewalk. "Not a nickle or a dime," he points out. "Seven cents. The number seven." He remains vigilant for the remainder of the day to events that might be better understood or solved using the number seven.

He is also sensitive to license plates and possible meanings conveyed by the three-letter clusters they contain. "If I bend down to tie my shoe while walking, I might see a car drive by or parking near me. I look at the license plate and might see CYM 106. I think about it and realize it might be telling me to 'Call Your Mother.' Maybe the 106 is a time. If it's a noontime walk, I might try to call her that day at 1:06."

He laughs after he tells me these things, realizing that they make him sound "odd." But he concludes, "There are all kinds of little messages out there. I probably miss a lot of them every day, but I try not to miss them all. Some of them have turned out to be very helpful."

7. You may have seen the following joke page about the exasperations of everyday life. Called "Laws for Twenty-first Century Life," it made its way across the Internet in 2006. To the extent that any of these "laws" induce a smile, they are tapping into the kind of scorekeeping errors most of us make every day.

Law of the Workshop: Any tool, when dropped, will roll to the least accessible corner.

Law of Changing Lanes: If you change traffic lanes (or supermarket lines) the one you were in will start to move faster than the one you are in now.

Law of Audiences: At any event, the people whose seats are furthest from the aisle will arrive last.

Law of Product Change: As soon as you find a product that you really like, they will stop making it or change it for the worse.

Law of Mechanical Repair: As soon as your hands become coated with grease, your nose will itch or you will have to pee.

The original Internet list contained about a dozen more examples, all of them revealing our deficits as scorekeepers or data analysts. The cognitive distortions that contribute to this humor are harmless. But the mechanism that drives them is anything but. Obviously, it is important to notice and recall salient events. But the lack of attention to related negative instances can lead us to profound misperceptions and faulty beliefs about the world around us. From an evolutionary point of view, it is clear why selection pressure would favor overemphasizing the occurrence of salient events. Never mind that the conclusions we reach about their generality will be erroneous. The trouble is that our species has moved from the "staying alive" phase of our development to the information age.

Isn't it time to address the mental distortions that innocently piggy-backed their way into our minds along with the "staying alive" package?

I know each of the above people well enough (with the exception of pitcher Brett Myers and the Texas moth-people) to conclude that they are relatively normal, reasonably bright individuals. They all function within society. Neither they nor these beliefs are particularly unusual. The conclusions or beliefs I have reported all feel "right" to these individuals, although they can each take a step back and observe their own irrationality.

How do we immunize ourselves or others against the effects of this kind of thinking? Is it possible to change such thinking after a history of well-socialized cognitive distortions? I believe the answer is yes. Is it possible to raise one's consciousness and wean ourselves off these examples of Caveman Logic? Many persons have moved beyond the racism or sexism of their earlier lives. In some cases it wasn't easy and it certainly required a lot of self-monitoring and social support. But it is doable. Likewise, many of us learn a second language later in life, long after the sensitive period for language acquisition in our youths. Again, it takes dedicated work but the results more than justify the effort. It's true that you'll always speak with an accent (language learning later in life typically transfers the phonemes of our first language), but the spoken results are still intelligible and worthy of pride. So, too, are the results of weaning ourselves away from the cognitive distortions we've unquestionably used for much of our adult lives: we may have to stop ourselves consciously from slipping into the old default modes, but we can do it. It's a bit like speaking with an accent. It isn't perfect, but we've pushed ourselves beyond reflexive comfort levels in order to accomplish something.

I'll offer two examples of clear thinking in the face of circumstances that might have easily triggered some socially supported superstitious distortions. The first is from my own life, so I am privy to the internal struggle it presented.

Several summers ago I was scheduled to present a talk at an international conference on cognition and religion.[10] My talk was decidedly of the nondevout kind. I was going to be in a public forum making many of the arguments against superstition that I make in this book. A colleague jokingly said to me, "You better hope God doesn't strike you dead on the podium."

I was recovering from surgery at the time and as the date of the conference neared, it became obvious that I would not be recovered enough to travel. Neither I nor the conference organizers wanted me to cancel so we put our heads together about how we might make this work. Several days before the conference we hit upon a solution. The organizers would wire the hall for sound. I would call a special line and deliver my talk over the telephone that would be broadcast for all in the room to hear. A colleague of mine who was attending the conference would carry my PowerPoint slide show and run it while I gave my talk over the phone. Everything seemed to be under control.

The afternoon before the talk, the skies grew dark. It started to rain heavily. By 7 PM the trees around my house were being whipped by strong winds. Shortly after, an electrical storm moved in. Lightning began to strike. I watched a tree come down within a hundred feet of my back deck. It was getting rather scary out there. Finally, the storm let up enough for me to take a deep breath. I picked up the phone to call a friend and share my adventure. The line was dead, knocked out by lightning. I wasn't going to be calling anybody.

And then the realization hit. Not only was I not calling my friend, but I wouldn't be calling the conference tomorrow morning at this rate. I checked all the other phones in the house. They were also dead. It began to grow dark and I sat there considering my options. A thought crossed my mind, although I worked hard not to indulge it: Here I was, about to deliver an antitheological talk at a conference. I would be outlining how defects in our mental processing predisposed us to religious and other supernatural belief systems. No doubt I had some social support for championing such enlightened attitudes. But in a largely comical vision, I imagined a vengeful deity sitting somewhere watching all of this happen: "Who is this heathen who plans to get up on stage and bad-mouth me and my believers? What if this infidel manages to convince these mortals that they don't really need me? That I am just a product of their defective minds? I'll show him!"

And then I replayed the whole sequence. My original plans to travel to the conference had been cancelled due to illness. Perhaps that was the deity's first attempt to block my evil intentions. When I decided to do an end run around that obstacle and give my talk over the phone, the vengeful deity turned up the ante a bit: "Use the phone, will you? Let me teach you a thing or two about puny human devices. Take this!" And with that the rains fell and the lightning struck. It was quite a show. And truth to tell, it did its work. I no longer had a phone. But would I let this little display of supernatural power stop me? Not on your life. I gathered up my papers and drove ten miles to a friend's house. The weather was no better where he lived, but fortunately he had been spared the lightning and the damaged phone lines. After all, he wasn't planning on using his telephone to criticize anybody's theology.

I used his phone to notify the repair service, who promised to try to have someone fix the problem before the time of my talk, although they weren't sure they could accommodate me. I borrowed my friend's cell phone just in case. He observed wryly, "It sounds like someone doesn't want you to give this talk." I told him the thought had crossed my mind but that I was using those moments as a source of insight into the kind of thinking I was asking people to give up.

I got back into my car and headed for home. Almost immediately it started to rain again. This storm made the earlier one look like a summer shower. The rain was torrential and lightning began to strike visibly around my car. The road appeared to be deserted and I was tempted to pull on to the shoulder and let the worst of the storm pass. I kept driving, though. When I was within a mile of my house I noticed something on the road ahead of me. My headlights didn't quite illuminate it so I stopped my car and waited for the next lightning strike. When it came, the entire sky lit up, and there, about twenty feet in front of my car, lay a baby raccoon. He had been hit by a car and was writhing in pain. I closed my eyes, wishing the image would go away. It didn't. I got out of my car and walked through the pelting rain toward him. I stood over his body and looked down at him. We made eye contact. I looked carefully at him and realized the damage was too severe; there was nothing I could do to help him.

I've always been a sucker for baby animals and have taken in countless stray and wounded creatures, from birds and turtles to red squirrels. My lab once adopted a baby raccoon whose mother had been hit by a car. But this one was too far gone. I got back into my car. "Mess with me?" the vengeful deity screamed in my head. "I know you! I know where you live! What else would you like me to show you before you back down and cancel this sacrilegious talk?" I shook my head, fighting back tears of anger. This wasn't easy, but I'd be damned if I caved into the very thoughts I was arguing against so passionately.

"Take your best shot," I screamed to the skies. But I knew what lay ahead. I had to do something about the raccoon and it wouldn't be easy. What I really wanted most to do was move him to the side of the road, out of the rain and further harm. Then I wanted to rush home and not think about him. By far, that was the easiest path, but I couldn't talk myself into it. It seemed like all of a sudden I was being confronted with easy versus difficult choices. A part of my mind I had no trouble discovering, one that used to be second nature to me, wanted me to "apologize to God," give up this athe-istic foolishness, cancel my paper, and lead a decent God-fearing life like any normal person. Just how much peril did I need to put myself (and neighboring animals) into?

Maybe if I were somebody else or perhaps at another time in my life, I would have made the easy choice. Cancel the talk. Move the raccoon off the road, convincing myself I had "helped" while leaving him there to suffer and die. Drive home to my warm, dry house and pour myself a drink. It all seemed so easy.

I backed my car up and ran over the raccoon, terminating what-ever remained of his life and his misery with two thousand pounds of metal. I went home and experienced the full force of emotional horror at what I had done. I had chosen what was toughest for me and best for him. The next day the telephone repair crew completed their work about thirty minutes before I was scheduled to begin, replacing wires seared by lightning. I gave my talk as scheduled and it went well. When I describe this episode to colleagues or students, I tell them that I believe I took the high road, but I know firsthand about the lure of the low road. When I ask people to make difficult choices around these issues, I feel I have come some small distance toward earning that right.

In contrast to my travails, let me tell you briefly about a friend and former professional colleague. He recently visited Prague to transact some business. He was scheduled to stay for about ten days, during which he had a schedule tightly packed with business meetings and events to attend. On his third day, he went for a stroll following a leisurely dinner in the old part of the city. The streets are made of cobblestones, some of which are not in the best of repair. With his mind on something else, my friend took what should have been a normal step and instead found himself flying through the air into a substantial pothole. When he recovered from the shock he found that his leg was injured severely enough to require medical attention. He could not walk. He was able to hail a taxi, which took him back to his residence. Somehow he made it up to the fourth floor and entered his apartment. For some reason he bolted the door before dragging himself to bed.

As he lay there, the pain grew worse. He began to scream for help but no one came. He managed to reach a phone and called an associate who immediately phoned for an ambulance. However, the ambulance crew could not reach him because the door was locked. By this time, he was unable to move enough to reach the door and open the bolt. His last memory was seeing the fire crew standing on a ladder outside his fourth-floor window, about to break their way in to rescue him. He spent the next ten days in considerable pain in a public hospital that left much to be desired by North American standards.

What did he make of all of this? Was he beset by "Why did this happen?" questions? Did he wonder whom he had angered to land in a spot such as this? He paused to listen to my question and announced simply, "No. Why would I do that?"

"Millions would," I observed.

"I suppose so," he replied, "but I don't think like that."

"What gives you the immunity to those kind of magic, superstitious thoughts?"

"That I can tell you easily," he replied. "My mother. No one lived in our house and entertained that kind of thinking. It would have been viewed as barbaric. My mother was a totally enlightened person, straight out of Goethe. She believed man is a moral animal. The deity has no role in it."

It may well be the case that, like language acquisition, magical thinking about causal agency has a sensitive period for acquisition. The software is there. Given the right inputs, the program will do its job. As in the case of language, those inputs can be pretty minimal or degraded and the end result will still be recognizable. On the other hand—and here the analogy to language breaks down—if the inputs are negative, that is, if the critically timed inputs work against magical thinking, they may provide immunity for the remainder of one's lifetime. That seems to be what happened in my friend's case.

There is no doubt that most people would prefer to live in a world where the important events in their lives are under their control, or at least under the control of an agent whom they can influence through social exchange (praying, deal making, cajoling). But I do not believe that individuals, because of this preference, consciously talk themselves into cognitive distortions or overactive agency detectors. That's simply giving them too much credit.

Sure, most of us want a modicum of mastery over our lives, but in its absence we don't go around creating more comforting alternate belief systems out of whole cloth. The simple truth is that these cognitive distortions—the faulty cause-effect detector, the overactive agency detector, the scramble to social exchange with supernatural agents—are far too similar. The neurosurgeon in New York, the cleaning lady in Kansas, the delivery boy in Denver—they all do the same type of things. Their religion, if they have one, may change a few of the nouns or rituals, but the basic program is identical. In fact, it is identical all over the world, in tribes and cultures that most of us can barely pronounce. What we are looking at here is undoubtedly the result of species-wide inherited brain architecture. It may not *feel* like that while it's happening to you; I can guarantee you that from personal experience. But your mind is just doing its job, humming along on autopilot. If you don't question it, it's doubtful anyone else will.

ACADEMIC FREEDOM

The incidence of supernatural belief systems and uncritical thinking is disturbingly high among university undergraduates. For one thing, they are just kids, not fundamentally different from their peers who took jobs after high school and opted out of more formal education. They are still engulfed by all the idiocy and peer pressure of popular culture. It is a rare undergraduate who is not as attuned to so-called reality TV, corporate popular music, and diet fads as her less-educated counterpart. University students are no more or less likely to be critical of the astrology column in the morning newspaper. For another thing, they are rarely specifically taught to think critically, much less how to think critically. Few of their professors want to take on the icons of their student's world or call their cherished beliefs into question. And so they are more likely to learn *facts* than to learn how to think critically and reach (or reject) their own conclusions.

When you face large undergraduate sections (e.g., five hundred to six hundred students) in introductory courses, you can pretty well assume that at least 5 percent of the class have been preindoctrinated into belief systems that are inimical to the methods and values you are trying to instill. Even if 4 of that 5 percent remain silent, that still leaves 1 percent—five or six students—to formally complain to someone within the university administration. The higher up the hierarchy you go, the more conservative the administrator tends to be. These people, regardless of their own political leanings, simply do not want trouble on their watch. A single complaint (even from a class of five hundred) that a professor has been culturally or "spiritually" insensitive can produce unwanted repercussions. Most institutions talk a good game about academic freedom but are surprisingly weak-kneed in the trenches. The recent firing of Harvard president Lawrence Summers is a high-profile case in point.[11]

If you find that instance unhelpful, here is another one: A colleague of mine at another university was teaching a course in the Philosophy Department called Critical Thinking. He repeatedly made his goals clear to the class: "I am trying to teach you *how* to think, not *what* to think." Courses like this often use contentious issues as a springboard to debate. The presumption is that when people are emotionally triggered, they are less likely to argue cogently or reason critically. Such moments provide grist for the mill. One of the topics up for debate was the question of human origin. My colleague presented an evolutionary account, including detailed evidence from molecular biology that suggested a common origin for all humans. In this context, he introduced the idea that "we are all Africans."

One of his students was an Aboriginal woman who asserted that her Ojibway background made it clear that her people had "always been here" (North America) and had not "come from" anywhere. She resented his suggesting otherwise. My colleague's position was that there should be some give and take when tribal mythology conflicted with scientific data. He proposed that her tribe's assertion of a "First Nation" claim could mean that they "got here first," but he resisted the claim of separate ancestry since the case was simply not supported by modern genetic evidence. In any case, my colleague did what a good academic should do under the circumstances and attempted to use the difference of opinion as a teaching tool. He welcomed further discussion with her in a public forum where the entire class could benefit from the exchange.

The woman wanted no part of an exchange. She was not prepared to debate the accuracy of tribal mythology and thought it inappropriate that she should have to endure such a critical experience as part of her university education. And so she went to the dean to complain about both him and his class. For good measure, she joined forces with two other students who also took exception to what they were hearing. These were fundamentalist Christians who also objected to hearing a public challenge to their belief system. My colleague, who did not have tenure at the time, was dismissed. At first, he defended himself vigorously, arguing that if the free exchange of ideas could not occur within a university course in critical thinking, where could it occur? The dean rejected his argument. It was simply easier to terminate an untenured professor than to deal with a Christian and Aboriginal backlash. Unlike many in his circumstances, my colleague hired a lawyer and took the university to court for wrongful dismissal. In a refreshing turn of events, he won his case and is now considering how to translate his victory in court into some kind of redress for the disruption of his academic career.

SPIRITUAL JUNK FOOD

In his 1971 treatise, *The Occult*,[12] Colin Wilson argues that if we are to grow toward our potential as a species, we must reclaim our connection to the supernatural. In Wilson's view, there is no shortage of it out there.

Wilson begins by arguing, "Primitive man believed the world was full of unseen forces." He goes on to assert that "the Age of Reason said that these forces had only ever existed in man's imagination," and that "only reason could show man the truth about the universe." That's a bit glib, but as a whirlwind tour through the history of human events, I can accept it as a general summary. Beyond this point, however, Wilson and I seem to have been watching two different movies. In Wilson's view, the Age of Reason succeeded. Man abandoned his universe of supernatural forces and became a rational creature. Reality became the boring place it has because active involvement from the spirit world has been banished. Sadly, Wilson concludes, man became a "thinking pygmy," giving up on the "supernatural world of broader significance that stretches around him." His book is a nearly eight-hundred-page tome urging man to rediscover his "Power X" and reclaim this world. If only Wilson's conclusions were true.

Since we're talking in broad generalities here, let me propose an alternative to Wilson's view. I'll begin on common ground. Primitive man was indeed awash in a world of spirits. And I will concede that the Age of Reason attempted to replace superstition with science and supernatural causal agents with rational understanding of our limited role in the universe.

But it failed. Intelligent thinkers are always conspicuous—we remember names like Newton, Galileo, and da Vinci hundreds of years later. But it's a common mistake to assume they are representative of the average member of our species and his or her deepest, most intransigent thought processes. These towering figures who valued science and reason over superstition and magic never became a dominant force within the culture. If we fast-forward to modern man, we find a curious blend of technosophisticates whose worlds contain DVD players, iPods, SUVs, and wireless networking; their kids download music and movies off the Web and use Google to do their term papers, but at the core (and this is where Wilson and I disagree) they are not far removed from those "primitive men" whose loss Wilson laments. Give them one of those basic questionnaires we're always reading about in *Time* magazine or *Reader's Digest*, and you'll learn that nearly half of them believe in some sort of supernatural agent, and at least half of them believe in ghosts, angels, predestination, and communication with the dead. And collectively, they support the growth industry in creationist museums and amusement parks that has emerged in the past few years. It's hard not to share Richard Dawkins's belief that "human minds are ripe for malignant infection."[13] Wilson would be proud. And these aren't even the more extreme cases. Any sociologist worth her salt can find you subcultures where the role of the supernatural is even more dominant and socially supported than in mainstream, white-collar America. You want more evidence that primitive man is alive and well in the twenty-first century? Pack your Imodium and venture to the third world nations of our Earth. You will return wondering what Wilson was thinking when he issued his entreaty to return to Caveman Logic.

In fact, Wilson supports our case inadvertently when he talks about our "instinctive desire to believe in unseen forces" and our need to discover "the wider significances." I agree, and so did authors James Redfield and Rhonda Byrne when they took their obscene profits from spiritual junk food like *The Celestine Prophecy* or *The Secret* to the bank. We can quibble over definitions, but to me the term *instinctive* suggests two things: this desire is species specific—that is, present in all members, even a defining characteristic of the species—and deeply ingrained or hard to change. But, having defined our need for the spirit world in this manner, it seems surprising that Colin Wilson would assume it could have been eradicated quite so simply half a millennium ago.

In any case, he clearly believes that we should work on getting it back. If I believed for one second, as Wilson does, that it were lost,

I would be out there waving flags of victory and doing all I could to see that it would stay lost. But there is just too much evidence to the contrary. We have not become those "thinking pygmies" that Wilson decried. Far from it. Our belief in unseen forces and supernatural agents is alive and well, right next to our TiVos and iPods.

Wilson also argues that "civilization cannot evolve further until the occult is taken for granted on the same level as atomic energy." Most people would find that statement absurd, but the problem lies not in Wilson's belief but in his expression of it. The "occult" has become a dirty word. It marginalizes its believer. Are "normal" undergraduate women with 3.5 grade point averages, active social lives, and loving families "occultists" because they also happen to believe in the physical presence of angels in the world as well as communication with the dead? Unless you provide a more exclusionary definition of "occult," I believe they are. And, as such, I believe they should be a source of comfort to Colin Wilson. The fact that this hypothetical undergraduate is not sacrificing chickens in her dormitory room is not the point. Indeed, that kind of expression of her belief system might get her and her 3.5 GPA expelled. It is her underlying beliefs that are in question, not how bizarre their outward manifestations are.

All this may seem unduly harsh. Is our poor, beleaguered undergraduate with her polite ghosts, angels, and "everything happens for a reason" belief any different from the rest of us who check our horoscope every day "just for fun"? Probably not, but I'm not sure this gets us, as a species, off the hook. In fact I think it may push us further on to it. It all goes back to Wilson's calling this tendency an "instinct." I'd probably opt for terms like *evolved brain architecture* or *mental module*, but we're both really saying the same thing. It is not a random pattern of activity that gets rediscovered by each new generation. This is hardwired stuff, the circuitry that is part of our evolutionary heritage. Perhaps the only comfort is that we are not talking about biological determinism. There is a small light amid all this darkness. If absolute determinism were really the case, neither Wilson nor I would have written our books. There *is* hope. There *is* choice. Of course, Wilson and I hope you will choose different things. But we both believe you have some say in the matter.

IT'S JUST NOT GOOD ENOUGH

Within certain circles, people pride themselves on being "seekers." Just what they are seeking is often left unspecified, although implicitly it is assumed to be something lofty like "the truth" or "meaning." Perhaps some of this search is triggered by a fear of death or growing signs of mortality. As novelist Julian Barnes writes in *Nothing to Be Frightened Of*,[14] "Death never lets you down." Apparently, that certainty only encourages seekers who are looking for eternal life, a quality usually reserved for one's gods. A common complaint is, "It can't be all over when I die. Please tell me that some part of me will go on living. I don't care if you call it my spirit or my soul. Just assure me that I'll go on."

Reincarnation is one way of accomplishing this by hooking one's soul or spirit up with a new body, preferably human. I've heard it said that even the species part is negotiable. Any old port in a storm. Interestingly, such seekers are not comforted by the fact that their genetic material, presently carried by their children, will be doing just what they wish. Freud put it rather poetically when he took the gene's point of view (anticipating Dawkins by nearly a hundred years) and described our present body as the "vehicle of a possibly immortal substance." But it doesn't really matter. What nature offers is not good enough for many seekers. Selfishly, they want their consciousness, belief systems, and values to stay around intact for the long haul as well.

Another concern held by many seekers is their fear of the existential void. The soundtrack for this mission might well be the Peggy Lee song "Is That All There Is?" These seekers complain, "I need *meaning* in my life. It can't just be all about finding a mate, having kids, going to work, watching TV, eating dinner, paying the mortgage, growing old, and dying. What does it all *mean*? Why am I here? What is my *purpose*?" The unfortunate thing about these questions is that they reveal a conspicuous inability to find "meaning" in what sounds like a perfectly successful existence.

Every species on Earth has been selected for its ability to survive, compete for resources, find a mate, chart out a small territory to live and reproduce, and, if you're lucky, hang around for a while afterward, perhaps nurturing your young or the young of your own offspring. What is this "greater purpose"? Why must it be about just *you* and why must it so often involve the supernatural? "What does God want of me? Why am I here?"—these are not questions about humans in general. This is all *me* stuff. Apparently, there is no comfort, peace, or fulfillment in procreating or enjoying art, literature, food, or love. Is the pleasure of exploring the real world or relationships within it not "purpose" enough? Why do most seekers need more grandiose answers to the question of purpose? They don't explicitly relegate everyone else to a supporting role, but there is an indisputable element of egotism in searching for *your* purpose. The very suggestion that one's life has been "ordinary" or without some kind of unique cosmic design seems to spread ripples of panic through a being. And so begins the uncritical and often desperate search for meaning.

As sad as I am to point this out, the classic Christmas film *It's a Wonderful Life* is a rallying cry for such thinking. Jimmy Stewart's character needs to discover that without him, people all around him, indeed the whole town, would have been a desperate and miserable lot. It is only then, after discovering how important he is, that Jimmy Stewart's character is able to carry on. He literally has to satisfy himself that his own existence has been central to the prosperity and success of everyone in his sphere of influence. Then he can get on with the business of living. Well, Jeez, Jimmy, what about the rest of us poor schmucks who may not have saved our brother's lives, as well as countless others in the bargain? Not everyone has such a salubrious butterfly effect swirling around him. Should we just jump off a bridge, as you were about to do when the movie began? Is there no point in living without being privy to that cosmic design that has singled us out to become a Hollywood success story?

JOJO, DIONNE, AND COMPANY

Although she is no longer part of the entertainment landscape, JoJo's Psychic Alliance once dominated Canada's television airwaves, competing with her US counterpart, Dionne Warwick's Psychic Friends. It was hard to get through an evening of late-night TV without running into an infomercial featuring either Dionne or JoJo. Both were the butt of endless jokes. Comedians wondered, for example, what happened to Dionne Warwick's psychic abilities when she was arrested for marijuana possession at Miami International Airport in May 2002?[15] Likewise, critics snickered when JoJo's partners robbed her blind, forcing her into bankruptcy in 1997. She claimed, "I never saw it coming."

Based in Quebec, JoJo and her big blond hairdo provided more self-parody than *Saturday Night Live* or *Second City TV* could have mustered. But while the laughter raged around her, JoJo's team of specially trained telephone psychics fielded thousands of calls a day. Only Canadian legislation that restricts the billing of each call to $50 limited JoJo's earnings. In the United States, where no such legislation is in place, Dionne Warwick's Psychic Friends went to town unfettered, resulting in an industry whose yearly earnings in 1995 were estimated at between $100 million and $500 million.

Networks like JoJo's and Dionne's employ between 1,500 to 2,000 "psychics," whose telephone work is typically billed at $5 a minute. Of this fee, the employee earns about 40 cents. They don't need telepathy to tell them there is no point in complaining about the pay scale. Their training is minimal and there are plenty of unemployed folks out there waiting to take their place on the phone lines. Psychic listeners basically allow you to tell your tale while, with a few well-placed "uh-huhs" and "mm-hmms," they manage to convince you that your mind had been read and your future foretold.

The process is quite similar to ones used by other psychic "scam artists," except both JoJo and Dionne have an obvious advantage. People call *them*. Their customers are confused, vulnerable, and needy. Those adjectives may describe the human condition in general, but callers to psychic hotlines are arguably even more unhappy than most. By and large, the number of things that confuse and upset people is surprisingly small and predictable: relationships with lovers, families and friends, health and financial woes, and dissatisfaction with work. Many callers are on the brink of a major life decision (breaking up with a boyfriend, getting married, changing jobs) but want a bit of validation for a decision they have probably already made. The callers themselves give out enough minimal cues to narrow the list down and, before you know it, their anonymous telephone companion seems like a certifiable psychic. The troubled caller might not really believe that something supernatural has happened, but they do feel sufficiently heard and understood to let the credit card charges roll along.

Although television has largely replaced the nightclub as a venue for so-called psychic performances, one of the most successful of the 1960s–1970s was a Dutch house painter named Peter Hurkos. He gained fame during the 1960s as one of the consultants attempting to help police in the celebrated Boston Strangler case. Hurkos's character even appears briefly in the 1968 film named for the case. It is of secondary importance that the Boston police were, by this time, absolutely desperate and willing to listen to anybody, and that Hurkos's advice was essentially useless.

Peter Hurkos delighted in telling the story of his psychic emergence and shared it many times on late-night TV shows. (He was a semiregular guest for Johnny Carson, Merv Griffin, Geraldo, and Phil Donahue and even appeared on Ed Sullivan's show.) The gist of Hurkos's story is, after falling off a ladder and suffering a brain injury, he lay in a coma in a hospital room. One day he suddenly awoke with "the power." Hurkos didn't know he had the power except for the fact that he immediately blurted out, "You'd better stop having sex with that doctor or his wife will kill you," which caused a nearby nurse to run screaming from the room. Hurkos was in business. Imagine that! A nurse having an affair with a doctor! Was there no limit to his psychic abilities?

Hurkos used the same time-honored bag of skills that kept most mass-market psychics in business. He would collect items such as keys and handkerchiefs from audience members and then, rubbing these items with great concentration, make pronouncements about their owners. "I'm getting something about illness," he would proclaim profoundly. The bewildered owner would reply, "Yes, my cousin is having an operation," to which Hurkos would nod enthusiastically. By tomorrow morning, the owner of the key ring would be telling friends and family that this nightclub mystic only had to rub her car keys and knew all about cousin Sadie's hysterectomy. Perhaps when you've had a few drinks and invested a $20 cover charge in some entertainment, you're a lot more open to persuasion. That, of course, was no excuse for His Holiness, Pope Pius XII, who decorated Hurkos and made kind, alliterative statements about his "God-given gift."[16]

ILLUSIONS AND DELUSIONS

Our sensory systems are beautifully designed machines that let us respond to things in the world outside our bodies. It is obviously essential to our survival and our normal functioning to know when something is out there, to interpret it correctly, and to engage in appropriate behavior toward it. The entire process is seamless: we see *something* off to our right, we interpret the image as "wife," and we greet it with recognition and affection.

The process has evolved to be automatic; it is normally not appropriate for us to stop to think of all the component parts that have gone into that smooth and rapid sequence of events. But for the moment, let's break it down and consider what is actually happening. A "thing" out there has triggered a variety of raw sensory stimuli delivered to our brains. We have taken those sights, sounds, and, perhaps, smells and *interpreted* them and responded to that interpretation. The crucial point is that, technically speaking, we have responded not directly to an item in the outside world but rather to our interpretation of a set of internal responses that it has evoked.

Most of the time there is no difference between those two things: what is actually "out there" is essentially the same as how our minds have interpreted those inner stimuli.[17] But there are two ways this system might go wrong. The more common is a glitch in our interpretation. "I'm sorry, I thought you were my wife," or "That looked like my car," or "I thought you said . . ." In each of those cases there really *was* something out there. We got that part right. It's just that the interpreter function got a bit misled, causing us to engage in inappropriate behavior. Usually, when another person is involved, a quick "Sorry, I thought you were . . ." or "I thought you *said . . .*" is enough to set things right. We've all made similar mistakes and they are normally easy to fix and forgive.

It is the second type of error—a much less common one—that is really our concern here. Just as it is possible to misinterpret what we see or hear, it is also possible to register a brain stimulus when there is no triggering event in the outside world. Keep in mind that our interpreter function will be absolutely blind to this and will set about doing its job regardless. There is nothing in its programming to validate the source of incoming messages. Once a sensory stimulus is registered, the interpreter will offer its best shot at identifying it. Everything will feel normal in such circumstances, leading us to make "I'm telling you, I *saw* my wife this morning!" statements, when the reply might be, "But sir, your wife has been dead since last Tuesday."

Under such circumstances, it is quite common for people to remain adamant about what they saw or heard. It is the interpretation they are actually adamant about. It rarely occurs to anyone that the fleeting sensory stimulus in the brain that led to the interpretation might not have come from the outside world, as it normally does. Being unaware of the chain of events that leads to perceptual experiences, most people are unprepared to second-guess that blip of activity in their brains that caused the interpreter function to spring into action. It is wrongly assumed that all perceptual reactions originate in the outside world. But they don't.

Attempting to have this discussion with a person who has already experienced such a transient spike of brain activity and interpreted it is usually a waste of time. I recently met a friend of a friend over lunch. When she became aware that I was the one writing *that book*, she lit into me with surprising energy, telling me that nobody was going to convince *her* that her dead mother hadn't visited her unexpectedly in the kitchen several years ago. That magical moment had offered further support for her "spiritual" worldview, which involved communication with ghosts of departed loved ones and also helped to ease her grief over the recent passing of her mother. I made no effort to debate with her or explain the basis of my views. These are not the conditions under which to offer a materialistic account of what can be a comforting spiritual illusion. But where do we draw the line?

Where do these spikes of internal activity—that can pass as the real thing—come from? The answer is, they are actually quite common and probably utterly random. When you think of the brain as an electrochemical system, it is not surprising that occasional and transient spikes of activity occur. Normally, there is so much signal or "real" activation triggered by events in the outside world that this background noise in the system is automatically ignored. It fails to trigger the interpreter that is already quite busy doing something else. But changes in the signal-to-noise ratio can increase the probability of an illusion. Indeed, a large number of "voices" heard by normal people—an experience that is surprisingly common—happens during quiet times. "I was alone in the kitchen and . . ." or "I was lying in bed and . . ." Such "hallucinations" became so common during sensory deprivation research of the 1960s that they became an established part of the phenomenon. Their explanation typically focused on the absence of normal background noise. Without such stimulation, internal events were likely to be registered and misinterpreted as having come from the outside world.

Thus, illusions are not great mysteries. Random activity in the brain is well documented and in no way baffling to neuroscience. Indeed, its absence would be surprising. That such blips should occasionally be interpreted as "signal" is also not surprising. The interpreter is a hair-triggered and extremely busy mechanism. Occasional false positives are part of its operating specs. It was easier, of course, to label the experiences in sensory deprivation experiments as "hallucinations" because the testing chambers were known to be empty, that is, devoid of stimuli that could trigger perception. The case is more confusing when the person is standing in a relatively quiet kitchen. Who can be sure that the spirit of a dead relative hasn't slipped in through the dining room door?

So what remains to explain? That meaningless brain signals (i.e., ones that were not triggered by anything outside the body) are interpreted in personal and emotionally charged terms? This hardly seems surprising. My friend's friend spent a good deal of time thinking about her dead parent. Interpretations are drawn from the well of experiences we each carry within us. The frequency with which these experiences are recalled, the emotional power they convey, all contribute to the raw material used by the interpreter function. In short, the attributions we make to those sights or sounds are hardly random. Don't mistake this for a conscious or willful process in which we actively seek comfort and choose our interpretations accordingly. The whole process takes place well below our threshold for awareness.

Do we simply create supernatural causal agents out of whole cloth or do we have a little neurological help in creating the ghosts and spiritual entities around us? Michael Persinger, a psychologist at Laurentian University in Ontario, Canada, strongly believes the latter and has some unusual data to back up his claim.[18] Persinger suggests that the experiences many attribute to supernatural forces have their origin in the brain's temporal lobes. Persinger is not the only one approaching spirituality in this manner. In the past twenty years, the study of religion has largely moved from the hands of anthropologists, theologians, and psychologists to neuroscientists. The field is somewhat facetiously referred to as "neurotheology." Much of this work involves the use of functional magnetic resonance imaging (fMRI). Scientists are now able to isolate precisely which brain structures are activated during various types of religious experiences and have begun to talk in terms of a "God part of the brain."

Persinger's work uses a source of low-frequency magnetic waves, which are delivered while subjects wear a specially constructed helmet that directs this energy directly to the temporal lobe region of their brains. His results are quite dramatic. Virtually everyone reports something: out-of-body experiences, visions of lights and faces, a "presence in the room," a long tunnel that draws subjects into it. Subjects describe these sensations as "pleasant" and often claim to have seen God or at least to have been in his presence. Others report the presence of extraterrestrial aliens. Persinger argues that such experiences are not confined to laboratory demonstrations. In people with temporal lobe sensitivity, naturally occurring geomagnetic activity can result in a variety of visions, ranging from the Blessed Virgin to a visitor from Venus.

STEALING GREASE IN OKLAHOMA

In the course of writing a magazine article, I had occasion to interview a man from Edmond, Oklahoma. Since I had never heard of his hometown, I took a moment to ask my source about the town and its location. Several days later, while reading *Time* magazine (May 24, 2004), I came across an offbeat story about the theft of 2.5 tons of used cooking grease. There were all the predictable jokes about the thieves making a slick getaway. The location of the crime? You guessed it: Edmond, Oklahoma.

What conclusions might I draw about these events? More to the point, what conclusions do most people draw when such things happen? I have often heard someone say, "You never heard of a place [or a new word or an actor or a musician], and once you do— you just keep coming across it [or him or her], like the universe had been saving it up." Perhaps the universe does work in mysterious ways with you as its personal target, but this doesn't seem to be one of them. Rather than seeing this mysterious process as *external* to us, it is also possible that the best account for my Edmond, Oklahoma, experience lies within me: an *internal* process.

Arguably, references to Edmond, Oklahoma, are out there, occurring at some stable but extremely low rate. Because I had no knowledge of the town, I was unlikely to pay attention or react to such occurrences and so their rate appeared—for all practical purposes—to be zero. Once I became aware of Edmond, I became sensitized to any mention of it. Actually, the term used by cognitive psychologists is *primed*. I was primed to hear or see instances of Edmond, Oklahoma. And so when the next one came down the pike several days later, it immediately caught my attention.

By transferring the account from the external world to the internal, I have stayed clear of magic or supernatural thinking and kept within the boundaries of scientific knowledge. Nothing out of the ordinary has happened in the external world; the change has been in me. And that, in turn, has shifted my attention to events around me. Can this approach to everyday life be taught? Even if we could learn to look *internally* as our first line of investigation (rather than looking for magic in the outside world), we would also have to be aware of a host of psychological processes such as "priming" that offer workable explanations of such "mysteries." Admittedly, this is a less-exciting account, offering nothing in the way of magic to brighten one's humdrum existence. But it does offer the satisfaction of understanding a somewhat baffling but widespread experience.

BEG, BARGAIN, AND BESEECH

When I was about ten or eleven years old I had a conversation about God with my mother. My own family wasn't particularly religious, although if you pushed them, both of my parents professed to believe in God. It wasn't their beliefs that confused me; it was the stuff I heard on television and from my friends.

I began with, "I always thought God was abstract, like some spirit in the sky." I'm sure I didn't use the word "abstract," but that's exactly what I meant. Somehow, I had concluded that God was just a thing, an idea, something we couldn't really grasp, and certainly not picture. You just took it on faith that he was "up there" and didn't try to draw pictures of him. It was OK to pray to him, but you didn't expect he'd become personally involved and stop a speeding bullet for you.

"How come other people talk about him like they *know* him?" I asked. "Like he's one of the guys or some old rich uncle who has a lot of power in your family. So you kind of keep on his good side and ask for favors whenever you need them. That doesn't sound very religious."

That's the confusion I brought to my mother's attention when I was a child. I needed to know how to reconcile my spiritual/abstract view of God with this "aw shucks, rich uncle watching over everything you say and do like he was in the schoolyard with you" version. Even at age ten or eleven, I knew this other view felt better, but it really seemed pretty hokey to me and I was surprised that my friends—forget about adults on TV who were usually asking for money—but my *friends*, who doubted almost everything, could buy into this. These friends were the same guys who picked up on the Santa Claus scam before I did and laughed at me until I finally came over to the adult world and acknowledged it was just my parents leaving those presents. What happened to the idea of kids as born skeptics? Why were they being so gullible?

For one thing, once we kids found out the truth about Santa Claus, all the adults in our lives admitted it. None of them tried to keep the myth going. But somehow this was different. When my friends made respectful or belief-affirming statements about God, their parents nodded piously. Teachers seemed to approve of it, as did every priest, reverend, or rabbi I ever heard about. This story seemed to have adult support, although I couldn't honestly see why.

My mother listened to this rant without interruption and said nothing at the end. So I summarized my confusion into a question: "Why do they all talk about God as if he were just another person whom we can picture and understand?"

My mother responded with eight well-chosen words that, as far as I am concerned today, contain more than a fair share of wisdom: "I guess they like him better that way."

Even then, I must have known there was something very special about that answer. What is most important is what she did *not* say. She did not tell me, "Because that is the nature of God." She never commented on that. Her reply focused exclusively on what people need God to be and the manner in which they construct him to be just what they need.

I now realize that people are not simply blank slates, constructing God as they see fit in order to bring comfort to their lives. If that were the case, there would be a lot more variability in how God was seen and described. Wherever you look, he remains essentially humanoid (often looking suspiciously like Charlton Heston), and his mind is usually quite knowable and predictable. That uniformity should tell you something. In fact, it is one of the core tools used by evolutionary psychology. When interpersonal variability shrinks to near zero, you can usually bet that the behavior (or trait) we're examining has a strong evolutionary basis.

Such is the case with God. The cognitive architecture of our species sets some very real boundaries on the way in which we will see the world, our place in it, and the things we need to do to get along. We learn early on that we are not in control of things as much as we would like to be. There are many things out there, very important things, that we can simply not control. We learn this as children. Our parents control the resources (e.g., toys and candy) and events (it's time to go to bed; it's time to come inside for supper) in our lives. They have the power. When we want more candy or want to stay up just an hour longer, we try to manipulate the one(s) with the power. We beg, bargain, and beseech to reach our goals.

These are good skills to have and we are apt, even evolutionarily prepared, subjects. The rules are simple: 1) Determine the limits of your personal power. 2) Find out who has more power. 3) Establish a working relationship with them in order to maximize the outcomes. The utility of these mental rules becomes obvious when we realize that after growing up, we still don't let go of the strategy. We still find, even as adults, that we don't have all the power over important events that we wished we did. We learn that our parents—once the source of all power—just don't cut it anymore. We can beg them all we want, but they can't control our health, success in school or at work, or interpersonal relationships. Bad stuff still happens to us. And so a little kernel of Caveman Logic gets activated. *Somebody* must have the power around here, because it sure isn't me.

It never occurs to us that maybe no power broker is out there. All we've ever known is that when we wanted something, there was someone who held the purse strings, someone we could implore and manipulate through entreaties. Why should things be any different when we become adults? And so rather than rethinking how the universe works (a sign of real maturity), we keep the same old circuitry humming and imagine some all-powerful, parentlike agent who must be running the store. And then we get ourselves into a seemingly personal relationship with him or her. We break out the three Bs: beg, bargain, and beseech. Of course, we call it prayer, but the ground rules and expectations are still the same. There is such comfort and familiarity in doing this that we have little incentive to question our actions. And even if we started to see through our own actions, there is enough consensual validity—like the person kneeling beside us in church—that we figure it must be right. This is a double whammy if there ever was one: not only does it feel "natural," but the guy next to you is also doing it. It's an official permission slip to carry on.

You combine evolutionary predispositions with nearly universal early life experience and you have a species predisposed for the beliefs and rituals of conventional religion. Even if social critics like Richard Dawkins had their way and organized religion could be swept away with the whoosh of a magic wand, there is every reason to believe that new rituals, supernatural beliefs, and group identities would emerge almost immediately to take their place. This does not bespeak the validity of religion in any theological sense. But it does tell us a lot about our species, how it is hardwired, and, to borrow my mother's logic, "how we like our gods to be."

If religion brought sunshine and light and let peace and brotherhood reign, its inevitability would be cause for celebration. But despite its lofty goals, organized religion seems to be a source of anything but peace and brotherhood. In the words of Blaise Pascal, "Men never do evil so completely and cheerfully as when they do it from religious conviction."[19] Yes, it may bring a modicum of personal comfort, but the social and organizational behavior it repeatedly leads to is cause alone to question, if not abolish, the whole enterprise. The ever-widening spread of terrorist attacks, genocide, and general ill will between groups should be a deafening alarm bell for us all. Are these problems attributable to a few extreme individuals or to one "bad" religion? That seems unlikely. The problems are nothing new. The general "My god is better than your god" and "Convert or die" mantras are a fundamental part of organized religion. As David Berreby has argued in his book *Us and Them*,[20] defining in-group/out-group membership is an essential part of human nature and will continue to fuel conflict and bloodshed between cultures and religions until humans decide to consciously transcend their Pleistocene predispositions.

DOIN' WHAT COMES NATURALLY

Many people believe that *natural* means *good*. Natural food. Natural remedies. The cognitive and perceptual mistakes we inherited from our ancestors must also be good. Why should we question our gut-level impressions? Why should we have any doubts about those faces in the clouds? Why shouldn't we view each coincidence as the universe "trying to tell us something"? As Timothy Leary told us back in the 1960s (in an acid-induced wave of insight), "Listen to your cells." That message usually finds favor when it is rediscovered in some form by each succeeding generation. Listen to your signals from *The Gift of Fear* (1999), as suggested by best-selling self-help guru Gavin de Becker.

The message is clear. The further we get from our essential nature, from being "natural," the worse we will be for it. This is also the essential teaching of the French philosopher Jean-Jacques Rousseau. Natural is good. Its enemy is progress, civilization, technology, and science. The essential message of this book is probably its enemy as well. We propose that you second-guess some important aspects of what comes naturally. What passed for wisdom or common sense in the Pleistocene era is now dangerously out of date. At worst, it can get you into serious trouble. At best, it can leave you barking up the wrong tree.

When individuals aren't too smart, species-wide predispositions will actually save a few lives. *You* don't have to be so wise as long as your ancestors' collective experience is encoded in your genes. Let's face it: most of our caveman ancestors weren't exactly Rhodes scholars. They were learning from day to day, scuffling to get by in a hostile and barely comprehensible world. Those are the times in which our cognitive shortcuts were welcome software. They got some of our not-very-sophisticated ancestors through their struggle.

Fast-forward 100,000 years and times have changed. But that "natural" circuitry remains locked firmly in place. While still not totally under our control or even our understanding, the world around us is no longer such a mystery. As recently as five hundred years ago, much Pleistocene-like ignorance was still rampant among even "civilized" nations in Europe and Asia. But that ignorance is receding. Solar eclipses, bacterial infections, thunderstorms, crop failures, and pregnancies are no longer mysteries to us. Admittedly, in some fast-disappearing corners of the world, such events remain mysterious. When that ignorance finally recedes, you can bet the superstition that came before it will not go quietly. There'll be an ugly and contentious conflict between forces of entrenched superstition and those of enlightenment.

Caveman Logic has an interesting quality. Humans are not a species that finds it easy to say, "Hmmmm. That *is* a puzzle. We really don't understand why that happens. We need to get our best scientists or thinkers on the case and try to make sense of it." Nope. That tends not to be what many humans, even the modern versions, do. Rather, we are all too likely to come up with a supernatural explanation of the event or affliction in question. Then we circle the wagons to defend that account.

If all else fails, we invent a deity whose job it is to look after whatever it is that has us puzzled. Fertility? No worries. We have just the god for you. And one thing these gods always seem to have is a willingness to listen to our entreaties. There's always someone out there to show the other members of the tribe how to appease or cajole the god who holds the reins. Beg, bargain, and beseech— the three Bs. Make sacrifices, pay homage, keep on his good side, and he will answer your prayers. Fertility will be yours. There are numerous examples of this, especially where fertility is concerned. One of the more engaging cases is Tagata Jinja, a 1,500-year-old shrine in Komaki, Japan.[21] Famous to travelers as the "penis shrine," it is the centerpiece of a yearly fertility festival that involves unwrapping an eight-foot-long wooden penis. Each year this phallus draws prayerful offerings centered on conception and safe childbirth.

Forget sending in your scientists to garner some real understanding of reproduction. Why bother with science when we can invent deities and carve wooden idols? And even if scientists do seem on the brink of unraveling whatever mystery or ailment troubles us, there are those who would withhold public support, discredit the scientists, or propose a superstitious alternative that many people will be far more comforted by. Sadly, over the course of human history, including the present day, this seems how we transact our business as a species. Superstition and supernatural lore are tenacious. They do not simply give up the ghost (literally) when higher levels of understanding are available to replace them.

The belief "What is natural is good or right" is so widespread that it has a name. Scientists call it the *naturalistic fallacy*. The view is persistent and a bit romantic since it seems to hark back to an earlier time when we weren't burdened with scientific knowledge—just our primitive, often spiritual connection with nature itself. Undergraduates who believe that natural is good are often challenged when you remind them that things like tsunamis, AIDS, pain, death, and aggression are all "natural."

So the question is, if doing what's natural is so good, why are we suggesting that you second-guess your inherited cognitive and perceptual shortcuts? The answer is simply that doing the natural thing, falling back on your default Caveman Logic, is not necessarily a good thing. Unlike your ancestors, you have alternatives available to you. Many of them are really quite spectacular, especially in contrast to those "natural" strategies.

The list of ways in which we second-guess or overcome natural tendencies is already quite impressive. We'd just like to make it a little longer. This book is largely about evaluating evidence, reaching conclusions, and formulating belief systems. Most of those processes allow you the luxury of time. Time to reconsider, ponder, take in more evidence. Arguably, if going beyond our Pleistocene default settings can be done anywhere, it is under such leisurely conditions. But consider a very different kind of example: when thrown into a crisis of life-threatening proportions, most of us fall back on hardwired strategies. There's often no time for reflection: under dire emergencies most of us trust our survival to the cognitive circuitry that kept our ancestors in the game.

Indeed, it is part of the "natural is good" argument that when it matters most, we should depend on our default settings and ask questions later. The surprising thing is, even under these circumstances, "natural" is not all that it's cracked up to be. A recent issue of *Time* magazine reports cases of mysterious scuba accidents in which people drowned needlessly, that is, when their gear was fully functional. The results of research performed at the University of Wisconsin suggest that our "natural" response to suffocation may have been the culprit. Experiencing a panic response while underwater, divers occasionally respond instinctively and tear away whatever is covering their mouths. Normally, that might remove the source of suffocation; it has quite the opposite effect when the diver is breathing through an underwater hose.

Here is more evidence that falling back on natural responses can be hazardous to your health: The US National Institute of Standards and Technology (NIST) recently interviewed nearly nine hundred survivors of 9/11 and found that even the survivors were remarkably inefficient when faced with a life-and-death crisis.[22] Few people left the burning towers immediately. The "run for safety" panic response that many assumed would prevail was barely in evidence. Some survivors took up to a half hour before leaving. Over one thousand people admitted to turning off their computers before departing the building. The NIST report also revealed that over one hundred people who had clear access to safety and time to leave the building were among the casualties. They did not sacrifice their own lives to help others. They simply did none of the things necessary to save their lives. Indeed, many who did survive the crisis were saved because they were lulled from shock or various kinds of dissociative states by others who shouted at them or literally dragged them to safety. People often refer disdainfully to horses who "go back into a burning barn" and have to be saved from their natural tendencies. Yet in this regard, we may be little better than a herd of horses.

The 9/11 results are not unique. They mirror reports of survivor behavior in another widely studied tragedy: the 1977 Tenerife airport disaster in which two planes collided while on the ground. In that accident 583 people died, although many of them died not from the crash itself but from the resultant fire. These people needed to flee to safety. Again, however, reports indicate that their natural response was to freeze, the very opposite of what they needed to do to survive. Interviews with survivors from both 9/11 and Tenerife suggest that victims either sat still or walked aimlessly, looking more like zombies or sleepwalkers than persons whose survival depended on their flight from a danger zone. Similar tales of people "standing still like statues" emerge from the sinking of the *Estonia* in the Baltic Sea in 1994. Described as one of the worst sea disasters in modern European history, only 137 of 989 passengers survived.

It is difficult to understand how such passive behavior might have benefited our ancestors, or whether our ancestors ever faced the kind of large-scale crises that occur in modern society. In any case, the message seems clear: the natural or default settings of our mental apparatus are not necessarily geared to our best interests in the modern world.

ALTRUISM: THE ELEPHANT IN THE ROOM

Altruism poses a fundamental dilemma for evolutionary biology. It is a seemingly wonderful quality of human nature, yet it just doesn't fit how natural selection is supposed to work. Altruism is, figuratively speaking, the elephant in the room.

The problem is this: Altruistic acts occur widely in nature yet, by definition, they contribute to the reproductive fitness of another organism at a net disadvantage to the altruist. How can such genes and the behavior with which they are associated pass through the filter we call natural selection?

Virtually every textbook on evolutionary biology or psychology[23] will walk the reader through this apparent paradox and suggest a twofold solution. It involves *kin selection* and *reciprocal altruism*. These are not just solutions to the problem of altruism with humans who, of course, are the primary concern of this book. These mechanisms work all over the phylogenic scale. They are *logical* solutions to how the mechanism of gene transmission, which is essentially selfish, might favor a process that occasionally prioritizes others.

Consider the fact that our relatives share some of our genetic material. The more closely they are related to us, the more of our DNA they are likely to share. Organisms are not randomly altruistic. They direct their selfless acts differentially, and the recipients are more likely to be relatives than strangers. These are not conscious volitional choices; kin selection is observed widely in species few people would assume to be great thinkers. In fact, there is no reason to believe that conscious thought or deliberation is involved for *any* species in the processes underlying altruism. It is simply a fact that altruistic acts are more often directed toward those who share genetic material with us.

This discriminative pattern leads to what is called *inclusive fitness*. From the gene's point of view, the chances of making it into the next generation are still reasonable if we save our brothers or sisters, even if we die in the act. Our reproductive fitness is thus defined not just as our own, but in a broader sense to include all of those who share our genetic material. The process is quite finely tuned. Given a choice between saving a brother and a cousin, the brother gets the nod. Given a choice between a cousin and a second cousin, the former is the more likely choice, and so on. This is known as *Hamilton's rule.*

This lesson in evolutionary biology serves a major point in Caveman Logic. Kin selection and inclusive fitness are one way that altruism makes sense within a Darwinian framework. But plainly, not all altruism is directed to kin. There are pointed exceptions to this, especially among so-called higher primate species. In such cases, the mechanism of reciprocal altruism has been invoked. This is simply a way of formalizing the "You scratch my back, I'll scratch yours" idea. Reciprocal altruism opens the door to many subsidiary issues, such as reputation, cheating, and cheater detection. These are all very big issues within the field of evolutionary psychology. Reciprocal altruism also requires that the individuals come equipped with a well-developed apparatus for individual recognition.

A hundred thousand years ago, we lived in small social groups, perhaps numbering fifty to seventy-five individuals. Most group members were related to some degree. Think about altruism, kin selection, inclusive fitness, and reciprocal altruism within that context and the mechanisms start to make pretty good sense. Even add a few more very distant cousins and it still makes perfect sense. Under living conditions like those, group cohesion is everything. Those mechanisms that reinforce group identity and loyalty will plainly be favored. The mechanism that says, "I will do for you, even at relative disadvantage to myself," is reasonable for a host of reasons, all of which make intuitive sense to the altruist, as well as theoretical sense to an evolutionary biologist.

But the process doesn't stop there. A lot of Pleistocene folks walking together through the savannah or enjoying a group hug is not the extent of the picture. Altruism has a flipside and, like it or not, it is an inevitable part of the deal. Just as there is an in-group that benefits from cooperation, trust, and good will, there will also be an out-group that does not. This is where the plot thickens very quickly and we are again faced with an aspect of our caveman heritage that does us little good in the twenty-first century.

Today, humans have replaced those small Pleistocene bands of relatives and very close friends with a variety of larger organizations that bear little similarity to what they used to be. Because the drive to affiliate remains strong, we've become rather indiscriminate in what constitutes a "group." Just as our ancestors did, we continue to use group memberships as part of our identity as individuals. This is, again, a good way to build group cohesion, but it sets the stage for some measurable nastiness. Group members enjoy the benefits of prosocial behavior. But what about outsiders to the group? How are they viewed and treated? The answer isn't always pretty; in fact, negative attitudes and behaviors directed at outsiders may be a fundamental part of group solidarity.

Plainly, group identity occurs at many levels. I am a member of my family, both immediate and extended. Under the right conditions, I will act in their support against nonfamily members. I also live in a community, and so my hometown becomes part of who I am. Perhaps that town is Dallas, Texas. I take pride in that as well. If I happen to be in the audience at a taping of the *Tonight Show* and the host mentions something about Dallas or Texas, I am going to cheer out loud for all to hear. That's *my* town. I'm proud of it. In fact, if you happen to be from Houston or, worse yet, New York, I might tease you or, if conditions should escalate, engage in a physical confrontation with you. I'm from Texas, boy, and I'll kick your ass! But if I'm from Texas, then I am also an American and you can bet that I'm willing to argue, hit, or kill in support of that as well. In his book *Us and Them*, David Berreby discusses how arbitrary and multiple these identities can be. As the humorous t-shirt says, "You mess with me, you mess with the whole trailer park."

Just stop for a moment and consider how modern group identities are an overextension of a perfectly reasonable caveman mechanism. How have things progressed from an understandable bond with our small Pleistocene group (under 100) to—using our previous example—the rabid and enthusiastic support of the population of Dallas (about 1.3 million residents), Texas (over 21 million persons), or the United States (about 300 million). And this isn't the extent of the average person's group membership. Let's not forget two other major sources of identity. Many people view their professions as part of their personal identities. I am a psychologist. I am proud of that. I feel kinship with other psychologists. We may have some internal divisions that cause occasional conflicts. Skinnerians may believe Freudians are misguided, and industrial/organizational psychologists may be focused on issues quite different from cognitive neuroscientists. But those differences are nothing compared to how most of us feel about sociologists. The bottom line is that I am a psychologist (or trucker or farmer or dentist) and I feel affinity for others in my profession, even if I've never met them and share no genetic material with them. Again, the term to describe what has happened here is *overextension*. This is a Pleistocene mechanism that has gone well beyond its original (and, arguably, appropriate) settings.

We've saved probably the most dangerous group membership for last. Aside from being a Texan, an American, and a trucker, I am also a Baptist. A Protestant. Now we're getting into some serious business because we are dealing with supernatural agents, a worldview, and metaphysical concepts like right and wrong. There is very little wiggle room here for most people. Again, the flipside of altruism, that most admirable quality of humans, is not simply the lack of altruism, but something far worse. In the earliest years of the twenty-first century, this point needs little elaboration.

In his book *In the Name of God*,[24] philosopher John Teehan discusses the paradox of how seemingly peaceful religions can generate hateful violence. His argument, rooted in evolutionary theory, is that there is no paradox at all. Teehan's point is similar to the case made by psychologist David Berreby in his book *Us and Them*. Obviously, you cannot define an in-group without reference to an out-group. And how do we view members of the out-group? While answering that question, consider that we humans, because of our natural history, seem incapable of living outside the network of group bonds and identity. Plainly, group membership brings many benefits to the individual as well as to the collective. But it holds many costs to those outside the group (who are, of course, members of *other* groups). The best that one can hope for is tolerance of other groups—be they religious or national or professional or familial. But history has shown that such tolerance is a lot to ask, especially in the realm of religious identity. There is a continuum of attitudes toward the out-group. If tolerance is the best-case scenario, it quickly moves to suspicion, xenophobia, disdain, and ultimately violence. Some would suggest the continuum is a very slippery slope.

Examine your own religious history if you have one. I was raised a Jew. I heard my share of prosocial things about the accomplishments and virtues of my own people (most of whom I had never met and was unrelated to). But I also heard occasional negative comments about outsiders. Our biggest competitors (growing up in New York) were Christians and there was no shortage of adjectives to describe "them." There was no outright violence in my experience, but the things I heard about "them" were rarely the stuff of public relations campaigns. When I became a bit older and talked at length to my Christian friends, I was surprised to learn that they had heard similarly negative things about "us." The comments were never enough to provoke a fight, and most of them had been delivered in an offhanded, even humorous way. But it was part of the identity and solidarity of both groups to criticize and distinguish themselves from the others.

Back then and there, it was Christians and Jews. The world has changed. These days it's the Muslims who bear the brunt of our fear and loathing. I've never heard a bad word about the Hindus, but then I've never lived in Pakistan. And I'm sure many Indians could teach me a thing or two about the Muslims. In any case, the stakes appear a lot higher today, but it is doubtful that the underlying issues have changed very much.

THE LANGUAGE OF US VERSUS THEM

Ask yourself, what is basic about human beings? What is it we have that other species arguably do not? That list used to be a lot longer than it is these days. Many "distinctly human" qualities (like tool use, logic, numerical skills, thinking) are now topics that students of animal cognition are actively studying. Even within this context, language has withstood virtually every challenge. We have it and they, no matter which species we're referring to, do not. Language in the sense that humans practice it effortlessly and universally remains our sole domain. It is a defining quality of our species. I mention language because David Berreby has argued quite pointedly that the tendency toward forming "insider" and "outsider" judgments in humans is every bit as hardwired and universal as language.

Think about the impact of that statement and its far-reaching implications. If "us and them" judgments are as defining a trait for humans as language, then—at the least—efforts to teach inclusiveness, tolerance, and universal brotherhood may have a lower ceiling than we might hope. Certainly, they will succeed insofar as the size of the in-group (those to whom we direct altruistic acts) can be expanded, but as for erasing the boundary between "us" and "them," the likelihood of that landmark change seems remote. If you truly wanted to erase racial or religious conflicts, for example, one way would be to create a newer and bigger "them." This is Military Science 101. Let Earth be attacked by Martians and watch how quickly Christians, Muslims, and Jews work together. All it takes is a common enemy to forge a newly expanded "us."

Try to imagine a culture that forces humans *not* to learn language. Just how might that happen? There is probably no way, short of brain alteration. The title of Steven Pinker's book *The Language Instinct* [25] says it all. The tools for language acquisition are hardwired into human brains. There is a window of opportunity in all normal humans during which inputs will be wrestled from the environment and processed in certain predetermined ways. That marvelous program will result in language comprehension and expression. That's just the way it works. Now imagine the same hardwired process for group identity and "us versus them." Keep in mind, as Berreby notes, that such a statement is value free. In other words, the mechanism for parsing the world into "us" and "them" is neither good nor bad. It is simply part of the legacy of being human. Some parts of what it means to be among the "us" group are undoubtedly positive. We experience everything from protection to a sense of "belongingness." Having an out-group to direct our conceptual (and perhaps physical) ire against also produces in-group cohesion. It is rarely good to be a member of "them," except for the fact that such membership means one is counted among their own "us" group. We are only outsiders to the people we care less about. To those we have bonded with, we are part of an "us."

Those judgments of "us" and "them" are rarely based upon anything real—like biology. Virtually any category will do: distinctions of race or "ethnicity," sexual orientation, profession. It really doesn't matter. Once the mind of an individual has seized upon an easily grasped distinction, the brain module for "us" and "them" will go to work and do its job as effectively as the language acquisition module. It is essentially uncritical about what it processes.

Does this mean the prognosis for our species is hopeless? I don't think it is. Plainly, there are circumstances under which these mechanisms are most likely to be triggered. What is inevitable is making "us" and "them" judgments. What is *not* inevitable is the malevolence or violence resulting from those judgments. But how easy is it to "just say no" to xenophobia? Can our species simply turn its back on a fundamental part of human nature? Once we decide that something about our species is unseemly, can we simply refrain from doing it?

Needless to say, there is a lot of flexibility in how we define both insiders and outsiders. Humans can be "played" by skillful manipulation of our hardwired tendencies. When political or religious leaders exploit these tendencies in us, they can turn most humans to their agenda with coordinated violence. The process can be amplified by claiming that a generally accepted deity is on "our" side. As the numbers swell, even more group members will be co-opted because of a seemingly validated threat against "us."

If we recognize the power of this module within our minds, we can be increasingly vigilant against those who attempt to trigger it.

Plainly, you do not need the language of evolutionary psychology or the tools of cognitive neuroscience to be a savvy consumer. These processes, as well as our resistance to them, operate at an intuitive commonsense level. Having the vocabulary may merely make it a bit easier to identify the process while it is occurring and hit the "pause" button. If it is any consolation, the people who rally us to their causes by triggering our "us versus them" circuitry may have little formal understanding of what they are doing. They simply *know* what works. They, too, are human. They know that if anyone comes for their sister, they will protect her to the death. The extension from sister to cousin to neighbor's sister, to someone in Texas's sister to an American's sister is a simple matter. Einstein was right when he called nationalism "an infantile disease, the measles of mankind."[26] The circuitry is not very discerning. Once it has been triggered by your guru or imam or president, your hands start reaching for a uniform and a gun.

JAMES RANDI'S OFFER

Disturbed by unsupported claims of supernatural ability and paranormal events, and frustrated by the public's uncritical acceptance of them, professional magician James Randi founded the James Randi Educational Foundation in 1996 (http://www.randi.org). In its own words, the foundation "is committed to providing reliable information about paranormal claims. It both supports and conducts original research into such claims."

The Randi Foundation has a standing offer: US$1 million to anyone who can document evidence of any supernatural, paranormal, or occult power or event. The offer began in 1968 as a "$100 challenge." Over the years, its value increased to $1,000, and then $10,000. Randi originally established the award after a radio interviewer taunted him to "put your money where your mouth is." The money is kept in a special account in the form of negotiable bonds that will be delivered to any successful claimant. The applicant is required to meet a two-stage requirement. There is a relatively simple preliminary test of each claim that, if successful, is followed by a formal test. Preliminary tests are usually conducted by associates of the Randi Foundation at the site where the applicant lives. Upon success in the preliminary test, the "applicant" becomes a "claimant" and is tested using a formal procedure, partially designed (but not administered) by members of the foundation. The design of this test also involves participation of the claimant.

This remarkably straightforward approach to the paranormal puts things in sharp perspective. On one hand we have countless millions of people actively believing in something that may not exist. On the other hand, we have someone, a foundation actually, who does not share that belief, saying, "If what you believe is true, convince us. Show us what it looks like. We will not apply an unreasonable standard of evidence. Surely, if it is out there—whether it be ghosts or telepathy or communication with the dead or clairvoyance—there must be some measurable evidence of its existence. Show it to us and we will give you $1 million for your trouble."

That seems fair (not to mention lucrative) by any standard. Yet, nobody has claimed it. In fact, no one has ever passed the preliminary stage of testing. Forget about unreasonable standards in unnatural (laboratory) settings. This has never gotten past the minimal demonstration in one's own home or haunted house. That seems a pretty strong indictment of those espousing the existence of paranormal phenomena. Not a week goes by when enormously successful supermarket tabloids don't make multiple front-page claims, any one of which would qualify for Randi's award. For those who buy the tabloids "strictly for fun," there is no contradiction. But for that indeterminate proportion of readers who *do* believe that 1) a woman gave birth to an alien baby, or 2) a corpse has come back from the dead and now heals the sick, or 3) ghosts inhabit a local house and rattle their chains every night, the time has come to put their beliefs to the test. Either this stuff is real (and someone is about to be a million dollars richer) or these beliefs are utter nonsense and it's time to renounce them.

To every horoscope-reading, "spiritual" person who lives from paycheck to paycheck, buying lottery tickets and hoping for a big payday, you're missing a golden opportunity. Find yourself a practitioner whose abilities you believe in. That shouldn't be too hard.

Then go to the Web site www.randi.org and make your claim. What's the downside to all this? Unfortunately, I think we know the answer to that question. It's "your belief in the paranormal" that might be a pretty costly thing to give up. A world without ghosts, telepathy, "everything happens for a reason," and alien abductions might be a pretty unexciting place to live. We can hear the response: "You keep the million bucks and let me keep my mysteries."

Chapter 4

SCIENCE TO THE RESCUE

COMPARED TO WHAT?

Those are three very important words when it comes to science, statistical inference, and just plain common sense. If someone tells you she has just scored 123 on a test of moral decency, you may want to utter those three words before either embracing her warmly or slipping away as quickly as possible. "Compared to what?" is embodied in the notion of control groups, baselines, and norms. Without those words it's pretty hard to make sense out of individual cases in fields ranging from medicine to athletics.

Comparisons are central to the scientific method. Indeed, they are one of the least exotic, most comprehensible aspects of all science. There is really nothing magical about the way science does its business. The most common difference between normal, everyday bright people and those who have had scientific training is not a collection of exotic facts, but rather an ability to parse the world into manageable chunks and ask and answer questions about them.

For many years I taught an entry-level research design course in the Psychology Department. I usually began by asking my students to generate an interesting question about psychology—something they thought really needed to be answered in order to further our understanding of human behavior. Virtually all of them could do this. There was almost no limit to the number of interesting questions they could generate. Next I asked them to design some research to answer the question they posed. This is where the trouble began. It wasn't just exotic statistical techniques that kept them from designing their experiments; often it was an inability to pose questions in a way that led to testable hypotheses. Many of them designed procedures that could find supportive evidence only. I pointed out that a criterion for scientific rigor is a hypothesis that can also be refuted. What would it take to reject this hypothesis? All the confirmation in the world is useless if the same hypothesis can't be rejected.

Another important theme of that course was the role of control groups in evaluating evidence. It's the "Compared to what?" question. Understanding the role of chance in this regard and being able to quantify its effects are essential, not only to statistical inference, but also to good decision making. Most people seem to know this intuitively. If I stand up in front of an audience and announce that I have a trick coin that is biased toward heads, how many flips will it take to convince them that the coin is not normal? (In this case, "normal" means a two-headed coin with the probability of heads = the probability of tails = .5.) Once we specify this, the effects of chance become easy to compute using what's called the *binomial expansion*.

If I flip it once and produce heads, can I bow and walk away? Obviously not. When you ask a nonscientific audience to explain why, they will say essentially the same thing that PhD scientists say: "Because that outcome could have happened by chance with a normal coin." When the coin comes up heads a second consecutive time, my audience remains unconvinced. A third time does little to change that. Four consecutive heads? Not yet. A fifth? A sixth? Somewhere around the sixth or seventh toss, people are beginning to wonder if maybe this is a "trick" coin. By the tenth toss, most everybody seems pretty sure. But there is a break point, say, between the sixth and tenth toss, where people begin to see that all these consecutive heads lie beyond what we'd expect to see if heads and tails were equally probable.

The nice thing about statistics is that they let you calculate the actual probability of each of these outcomes occurring by chance. It's useful to look at these values because they match up surprisingly well with our intuitions. Even if you're not a statistician, you probably knew the probability of the first toss coming up heads was .5, or one in two. When you toss the coin again, the probability of getting a second head in a row by chance was one in 2^2, or 1/4. Toss the coin again and the chance of three consecutive heads are one in 2^3, or 1/8. And so it goes, with the probability of consecutive heads having happened by chance getting progressively smaller as the number of tosses increases. The probabilities associated with a run of between one and nine consecutive heads by chance are .5, .25, .125, .062, .031, .015, .0075, .0037, and .0018, respectively. By the time you reach a string of ten consecutive heads, the probability of that event having occurred by chance is less than .001, or less than one in a thousand. In short, don't hold your breath for ten consecutive heads to occur by chance with an unbiased coin. If you see it happen, something else is probably going on. That "something else" in this case is the fact that we're using a trick coin.

It is important to note that science does not usually require such rigorous standards of proof. Plainly, scientists want to know that experimental outcomes are unlikely to have occurred by chance, but in general they do not expect the likelihood of chance to have been reduced to .001. Most experiments in the social sciences require what is called a *.05 significance level*—that is, the outcome would occur by chance no more than 1 in 20 times. That's unlikely enough so we can conclude that our results reflect something *other than* chance.

Most people may understand "chance" at an intuitive level, but they are a little fuzzy about how it translates into real outcomes. If you don't understand the sort of things that can happen by chance, you're likely to overestimate the significance of outcomes that require no explanation at all. In fact, often they lie well within the range of what can and does happen by chance.

Here are a couple of examples from two unrelated areas: sports and ESP. ESP is the more obvious case. Persons with so-called psychic abilities such as telepathy are supposed to be able to determine outcomes when no conventional sensory information is available to them. The only way we know they're doing impressive things is when the accuracy of their performance exceeds what we'd expect to happen by chance. That means we'd better have a clear understanding of the ways in which chance expresses itself. Just how probable are these "paranormal" outcomes? Many people will tell you that the "science" involved in testing ESP has to do with how well the blindfold is fastened or whether the sender and receiver are adequately isolated from each other. Granted, those things are important, but it's just as important to understand chance and probability.

In slightly different ways, understanding chance is also important to our appreciation of most sports. It doesn't come into play when we are watching a race, where individual performance is evaluated against the performance of other athletes on the field or, in some cases, the "personal best" of the runner. But, more often than not, team sports reduce themselves into a labyrinth of statistics. My own experience as a baseball fan led me to calculate batting averages for each player on my favorite team well before my tenth birthday. It was my first real experience with any form of mathematics and probably did much to immunize me against later numerical traumas associated with a university education. Baseball is a game awash in quantification. Nobody can debate the merits of their favorite player or team for very long without turning to on-base percentages, won-lost records, batting or earned run averages, and so on. Indeed, a whole new generation of baseball fans has evolved what is known as a *sabrmetric* approach to the game (a term derived from Society for American Baseball Research),[1] with reference to all kinds of numerical exotica such as secondary averages, OPS percentages, range factors, and so on. Yet, for all this statistical sophistication, we often misinterpret what we see on the field because of deeper shortcomings in how we reason statistically.

For example: any fan knows what clutch hitting is, but has anyone ever identified a clutch *hitter*? The last I looked, the search was still on for a player who reliably performed better in "clutch situations" than he did when the stakes weren't high. Players who do well in so-called clutch situations are usually players who do well in general. And so, the search continues for a player who reliably performs better under the gun. With over a century of organized baseball behind us, there is still no evidence of such differential abilities. That, however, has not stopped managers, coaches, sportscasters, and fans from describing someone as a "clutch hitter" with little trace of uncertainty in their voices. Why does this happen? Obviously, if we observe a player hit a game-winning home run in the bottom of the ninth with two outs, we are likely to remember that event. Often, it's transformed into a hypothesis about that player that gets further supported by future positive outcomes. But can this hypothesis be as easily disconfirmed by future (or past) negative performance? The answer is probably no. Again, it is the salience of positive cases and our inability to disconfirm that renders this conclusion illogical. We simply don't keep track of baselines adequately, and we tend to emphasize occasional "hits" disproportionately.

In most sports there is a pervasive idea of a "hot hand" or a streak. Players are described as being "in the zone." During these elusive periods, their performance, we are told, reaches nearly Herculean proportions and they can do little wrong. They score more goals, sink more baskets, catch more passes, hit more home runs, or strike out more hitters than anyone expects. We've all witnessed such "streaks" although we can't quite explain what causes them. In fact, the streak often becomes an explanation of itself. He's hitting this way because he's on a streak. "He's a streaky hitter," we are told by the announcer. "You don't want to face him when he's hot like this." Hardly anyone, from players and managers and coaches to sports commentators and journalists, seems to doubt the existence of the streak.

Psychologist Thomas Gilovich and his colleagues published a detailed investigation of sports streaks and concluded that, at least in the realm they studied, streaks were illusory.[2] Gilovich and his colleagues examined NBA performance and reported that while basketball players occasionally run up impressive strings of "hits" (e.g., four or five baskets in a row), these clusters do not exceed what one might expect by chance alone. Gilovich et al. used each player's own performance as a baseline. For example, if a player sank 60 percent of his free throws that season, how often might he be expected to sink five in a row? What is the probability associated with this outcome happening by chance over the course of a season? Whatever the answer, you'd better have that information available before you start talking about the psychological, perceptual, or motivational reasons for a "hot hand." If the performance in question doesn't lie outside the boundaries of chance, what's the point of trying to explain it?

The underlying problem is that most of us don't really know what chance looks like. Worse yet, we *think* we do. Most undergraduates will tell you that the purest example of chance in a $p = .5$ binary situation like a coin toss is an outcome that looks like H–T–H–T–H–T–H–T. Back and forth and back and forth: 50–50 on the nose. We expect some deviation from pure alternation but the question is, how much? It is here that many observers run into trouble; they underestimate the amount of streaklike clusters that are likely to occur under a truly random distribution. Any but the mildest deviations from regularity is likely to trigger our suspicion. We are very quick to see biased coins or streaks or hot hands, when in fact we are looking at nothing more than chance. As Gilovich points out, there is a 25 percent chance of seeing five consecutive heads if a normal coin is tossed twenty times. Most observers have great difficulty reconciling five consecutive anythings with the idea of chance. And so we are quick to reject chance in favor of more exotic alternatives.

Taking this back to the basketball court, it is easy to see how a cluster of five baskets in a row might send us running for the record books. Our impoverished sense of the many faces of chance leads us on a pointless quest for explanation. Call in the color commentators to ramble on about the player being "locked in" or "in the zone." My colleague Scott Parker has devised a humorous tale to illustrate this point in reverse, namely, a case in which ignorance of chance leads us to *minimize* a truly exceptional feat. A man billed as the "World's Greatest Coin Tosser" steps before an audience and produces five hundred consecutive heads. He then takes the same coin and produces five hundred consecutive tails. The audience sits in silence until someone stands and says, "Big deal. Fifty–fifty— anyone can do that!"

Our problems with chance would be far less troublesome if they were confined to the basketball court. Obviously, they aren't. Whether talking about sports or gambling or the stock market, the stage is set whenever a binary set of outcomes (e.g., heads/tails, win/lose) lies outside our control. Our explanatory skills, needlessly dragged into play, do not often reflect what is brightest and best about our species. Whether invoking cycles of the moon, karma, or curses, we attempt to explain what needs no explaining. This is not to deny that *something* caused that head or tail on the coin toss. Of course, it did. But the issue here is not to account for the physical and psychological forces that cause every event on Earth. Our concern is with the *sequence* of events and whether *it* lies beyond the random fluctuations we can expect as the universe unfolds. More often than not, it does not.

SCIENCE'S GREATEST HITS

Just how much knowledge of science is out there? It's not an easy thing to measure. In the last year or so, I've run an informal survey using what is often termed an "opportunistic" or "convenience sample." In short, I've asked just about everyone with whom I came into contact. That might have been a disastrous approach if I were a more typical academic or shy about talking to strangers. Fortunately, I am neither. And so I asked this question of literally hundreds of people: "What do you think science is?" These six words usually produce a pause, which I immediately fill with the easier question, "What do you think of when you think of science?" That question intimidates fewer people since there is plainly no wrong answer. If someone says, "The *Mona Lisa*" or "Elvis Presley," then so be it.

But nobody has. Their answers are all far more relevant, and surprisingly consistent. I've talked to undergraduate students; gas station attendants; baseball fans; grad students; colleagues; folk, jazz, and rock musicians; food and hardware store sales people; financial advisors; servers in restaurants and pubs; ex-girlfriends; and my housekeeper. The list is actually quite a bit longer and more varied, and many people in my sample are difficult to classify since they fit multiple categories. Their education ranges from some high school through PhD degrees.

With the exception of most of my colleagues and a few grad students, this informal census has yielded a surprisingly consistent pattern. Because what I report isn't about being right or wrong, it doesn't shed light on the issue of scientific literacy. But it does address the public perception of science. Most people think about the *results* of science, rather than its *methods*. More than 95 percent of the people I spoke with mentioned things like "space travel," "medical cures," and "wonder drugs." Some people said "$E=MC^2$" or mentioned Einstein. People talked about computers, and a few included plasma screen TVs and iPods. Cloning was a popular response and a few referred to stem cell research. And that was basically it. This is what most people I spoke with think about when they think of science.

As much as anything, this is essentially a "Science's Greatest Hits" list, as reflected by media coverage. Conspicuous by its absence is any reference to the *methods* of science. The idea of gathering evidence, formulating or testing hypotheses, and building theories appeared in a very small percentage of responses, almost all of them coming from my colleagues or graduate students, all of whom are in the business of *being* scientists. This should surprise no one, but it is a sobering thought. For most people, the methods of science consist of hardware rather than logic. Perform your own survey and you will find that most people think that scientists go about their business using exotic instruments like particle accelerators or electron microscopes, and then they share their discoveries with the rest of us, who either accept them (if we can understand them) or stay clear of them. But if we accept them, it is on faith or through appeal to authority. ("Scientists report that . . .")

The scary part of this is that the fundamental methods of science, which lie well within the grasp of the average person, are not widely taught or appreciated. It is this lack of critical thinking, not the failure to do gene splicing or run an MRI unit, that dooms the average person to vulnerability at the hands of charlatans and purveyors of quackery and mysticism.

DOUBT IS EVERYTHING

Most people believe that training in the scientific method confers some kind of immunity to the sorts of mental errors we are concerned with in this book. People with no scientific training, indeed people with little formal education, often misunderstand why this is so. They assume that scientists are less likely to hold irrational beliefs because scientists have learned *things* that contradict such widely held nonsense.

It rarely occurs to less-educated persons that what gets learned during scientific training is not an exotic body of facts, but rather a set of logical and critical thinking skills. This is why scientists, in the main, are skeptics, whereas less-educated people are not. Authority, as a reason for belief, holds almost no allure to most scientists, whereas it is distressingly persuasive to people with less education. Higher education, especially in the sciences, leaves one with mantras such as "To live is to question" or "Doubt is everything." As comedian Bill Maher says, "Keep asking questions or it becomes a religion." These viewpoints do not translate well across cultural lines. Indeed, questioning or doubting may well be seen as a sign of disrespect in less-educated subcultures. Certainly, we know that most organized religions do not nurture such tendencies among their members.

Scientific education makes several specific contributions to a healthy intellectual life. First, like most higher education, it leaves us with a high regard for just how much we do *not* know. The more education one has, the more he or she is likely to profess ignorance. It is that simple.

Second, even those things that are known have a somewhat tentative quality. Most scientific knowledge comes with an expiry date on the label. Things appear correct within the present context. But as our knowledge grows, we often have to question and reevaluate our present collection of "facts." Some students find the tentative nature of knowledge to be infuriating, even intolerable. Such persons have an easy time of it; there are many alternative belief systems out there that offer absolute facts. Just accept and there is no need to question or doubt. A black and white universe is there for the taking, and you'll have the company of like-minded persons in the bargain. About the only thing you sacrifice is accuracy. But when was accuracy ever a competitor to comfort and reassurance?

So far the legacy of a scientific education seems to be a knowledge that we actually know very little. Added to that, it is *difficult* to know things and what we *do* know is subject to change as our knowledge grows. You can see why science education is not a product with particularly wide appeal, given the competition. This is probably the time to admit that not all scientific training is created equal. Gilovich has made an important distinction between what he terms the "deterministic" versus the "probabilistic" sciences. When I went to graduate school in psychology, several friends used to tease me that I ought to get into a "real" science. Even my first-year professors admitted that psychologists were often self-conscious about their lack of scientific precision. We were given a sense that, as sciences went, psychology was a second-class citizen. "Real" sciences, like chemistry and physics and astronomy, typically made statements about relationships in the physical universe. Gravity wasn't something that worked nineteen out of twenty times. You stick potassium permanganate and glycerine together in a test tube and there wasn't a .95 chance the compounds would react violently. They simply did. Truth is truth. Determinism, we were told, was the basis of real science.

In turn, we in psychology were offered a probabilistic view of the universe. This is the way things are most of the time, we were told. But the truth is, we're dealing with a very complex, multivariate universe and since we don't really have a handle on all those other factors, the best we can do is state with some statistical probability that we understand the relationship we're studying. You want precision, we were told somewhat defensively, go study geology or chemistry. In time, we all got used to it. About the only downside was that we had to learn all about inferential statistics and fancy multivariate procedures in order to wrestle meaning out of the jumble of results our experiments produced. But the truth is, the universe is a messy place. It's not so much that God is playing dice with it, as Einstein famously observed, but that even the simplest situation was awash in factors that could be functionally related to what you were studying. You control as many of them as you can and hope for the best. Even a lone rat in an impoverished-looking Skinner box can be an explanatory nightmare. You give it your best shot and if your results can be replicated nineteen out of twenty times, you get to hold your head up with the big boys. It may be far from physics or chemistry, but it's how most of us do business in psychology.

Now, all these years later, it turns out there may actually have been an advantage to being a psychologist. Gilovich argues that traditional hard sciences such as physics and chemistry deal largely with a straightforward determinist universe and, as such, offer little in the way of useful scientific method when one is confronted by unusual or speculative belief systems. In contrast, psychology offers a more appropriate logical framework from which to evaluate such claims. Things are not so black and white within the psychological universe. Patience, skepticism, and even-handedness are useful skills to have when faced with what Gilovich calls the "messy probabilistic phenomena that are often encountered in everyday life." Causes are usually multiple; even when we find one, it may be necessary, but it is rarely sufficient to account for the event in question. Psychologists are often challenged by tough cases. Behavior and perception may reveal as much about the mind of the individual as they do about the world outside.

Evolutionary psychology and cognitive neuroscience have helped us to see that we are not simply blank slates, responding to the external environment. The evolved structure of our minds brings a lot to the party. Without taking such things into account, simple linear causality, as practiced in the "hard" sciences, is not likely to be helpful. A basic course in research design taught by a psychology department will hammer home ideas such as regression to the mean, the importance of control groups, random sampling, statistical confidence intervals, and the role of chance. These concerns may reflect the untidy nature of psychological science, but they also offer the student precisely what she needs when facing contentious claims.

Learning these techniques is no guarantee they will be applied appropriately. Many years ago I had a student who performed extremely well in my research methods course. She was consistently at the top of her class. When the course was over, she came to see me in my office, thanked me for an interesting class, and informed me that she was a fundamentalist Christian. She basically told me, "I learned everything you said to do when faced with unsupported conclusions, illogical arguments, and supernatural accounts for natural phenomena. I simply applied what you taught us on all the classroom examples and examinations. I gave you everything you wanted to hear. Now that the course is over, I'm going back to who I am and what I believe." She smiled broadly and shook my hand and left with her A average and honors degree in psychology. I told her then that I appreciated her honesty, and I still do today. Likewise, any of our A-level students can finish their reading assignments on logical reasoning, go back to their dormitory and listen uncritically, even supportively, as one of their roommates goes on about a psychic experience she's just had. In short, a rigorous education grounded in scientific method does not provide foolproof immunity against uncritical listening and irrational beliefs. But, all things considered, I wish more people had such an education.

IT'S ONLY A THEORY

The term *theory* has gotten an increasingly bad name in the popular press. What should be a grand compliment has become a damning indictment. The creationists now point out with glee that evolution is *only* a theory. In Cobb Country, Georgia, the board of education insists on placing stickers in biology textbooks reminding students and teachers alike that evolution is not a fact; it is *only* a theory. To them, that means, "You don't really know for sure. And if you don't really know, you should be teaching alternatives (such as intelligent design) side by side. The two should have equal footing since they are both merely possibilities." Actually, as Richard Dawkins pointed out in the May 21, 2005, *London Times*, creationists are saying even more than that. They argue that whenever any ignorance or gap in the fossil record can be revealed, the winner by default is intelligent design.

To discredit something as merely being a theory misunderstands what science is all about. Calling something a "theory" is, in fact, quite a compliment. It means the possibility has been stated in such a way that it can be tested. Two things can happen when you test a theory: The evidence we gather may support the theory. On the other hand, the evidence we gather may refute it. Theories stand or fall on the available evidence. You cannot cling to them for sentimental reasons or by faith alone. Evolution by natural selection is stated in such a way that evidence can disconfirm it. This is no small thing. It is like doing a high-wire act without a net. If fossilized remains of rabbits are found in a pre-Cambrian stratum, then evolution is wrong. It must be consistent with the fossil record. That is what being a theory is all about.

Creationism, aka intelligent design, is not a theory. It is a belief. The bumper sticker says it all: "The Bible says it; I believe it; That settles it." There is a name for this approach to knowledge. It is called *fideism*. It is an aggressive irrationality, a refusal to discuss or justify statements of belief. Many children go through a stage in which they use the word *because* as if it were a reason. "Why?" "Because." Needless to say, most children successfully grow past this irrational early stage of cognitive development. Obviously, not all of them do.

The next time you witness or participate in a debate with a creationist, ask him what kind of evidence it would take to refute intelligent design. The truth is, there is none. It cannot (and will not) be refuted in the mind of a creationist. That alone tells you why intelligent design is not a theory. Creationists may see that as a strength, but it is just the opposite. In any case, it is precisely the reason that intelligent design has no place, no matter what your local board of education says, in the curriculum of a science class.

I teach a fourth-year class in my university that is termed a "capping course," that is, an attempt to summarize or integrate much of what has gone on for the past eight semesters. If the process has gone well, my department would like to have instilled more than a collection of facts. I use a take-home exam in this course rather than the usual fact-based, multiple-choice format. I find it amusing that the same students who decry multiple-choice exams often do much better on them than they do on open-ended essay exams. At least the ones I give.

In this case, I wrote a special question that I will probably have reused several times by the time you read this. I thought it might be a particularly good question when I created it, but I had no idea how well it would discriminate between good and bad students. That, of course, is the ultimate criterion for the success of any exam question.

The question asked them to imagine a patient with a puzzling phobia. Her family doctor calls in two consultants. The first, an evolutionary psychologist, suggests that her phobia reflects what is called a "prepared association": an evolutionary predisposition for certain types of Pavlovian conditioning that would manifest itself as a phobic reaction. That our ancestors' adaptations would affect our present-day thoughts and actions is the essential tenet of evolutionary psychology. The second consultant in my hypothetical scenario is the ringer. He examines the patient and reports that she experienced, in a previous life, some trauma at the hands of her father and had carried forward this trauma to her present life. If there is any doubt in the reader's mind, past lives may be all the rage in some parts of popular culture, but they have absolutely no standing in scientific psychology. You may not know that if you watch reruns of *The X-Files* or *Medium*, but after four years of university education and a major in psychology, you should recognize this kind of nonsense when you see it.

A shockingly large portion of students did not. Far too many of them treated this supernatural account as if it were any other theoretical viewpoint within psychology and gave it serious consideration. Curiously, a number of students described the reference to "past lives" as a Freudian account, which it assuredly is not. But most troubling was the position expressed in about 20 percent of the papers: that the two accounts, Darwin and past lives, had equal standing. As one student put it, "Past lives is just a theory, like Darwin."

In grading her paper, I underlined that sentence in red and, might it not potentially cause her embarrassment, I would have posted the sentence on my office door. It goes to the heart of what is wrong with science education and certainly, in this case, underscores one of the failures of a four-year education in my department. I wrote the offending student a memo but could barely do justice to the magnitude of her error. No, I explained to her, so-called past lives is not "just a theory" at all, and the idea is in no way comparable to the theory of evolution by natural selection.

The biggest problem, again, is the word *theory*. Suffice it to say that to the average person with no scientific training (which this student was not), *theory* is synonymous with *hunch*. But there is a big difference between everyday or folk use of the term and what it means within science. For something to have been elevated to the status of theory, it has undergone extensive critical attention and formal testing. It reflects a trail of intellectual activity of the highest order. In fact, it is the very opposite of a hunch. So, yes, Darwin's view of evolution by natural selection *is* a theory. And one of the most successful ones in all of science. In fact, it is the very cornerstone of biology. What *isn't* a theory is the belief in past lives. To dignify it with the status of theory would be to suggest that it has been stated in a manner that leads to hypothesis testing, much less that there has been one shred of empirical evidence to lend it support.

WHAT A COINCIDENCE!

People seem inordinately impressed with experiences that are in no way exceptional. Such circumstances can be explained away with relative ease, yet the experience itself feels overwhelmingly powerful. Walking through a gallery in a foreign city, I bump into my high school art teacher. For days I can't stop talking about the coincidence. Can you believe that? My *art* teacher. In a *gallery*! In a foreign city, no less. I mean, what were the odds!?

Don't try to tell me while I am in the throes of the coincidence, but the answer is that the odds were actually quite good. Not for *that* particularly gallery or that particular person, but the odds of experiencing this kind of coincidence are surprisingly large. There are two reasons for this: One is that by leading active lives we are constantly sampling a tremendous number of experiences—persons, places, circumstances—any one of which can enter into a coincidence. Second is what we have earlier termed *multiple endpoints*. Our definition of coincidence is tremendously flexible. A lot of different possibilities qualify for the award of "Amazing!" Viewed from this point of view, what is truly surprising is that this sort of thing doesn't happen even more frequently.

As rational as this may sound, it is no match for the emotional impact of living through the experience. You know you have an anecdote on your hands almost from the moment it occurs and, like all good anecdotes, it becomes embellished to the point where it sounds like those events were truly unique and only those events would have qualified for the "meaningful coincidence" label. This makes the result seem even further from "chance" and closer to the *Twilight Zone* than it actually was. Consider a parallel situation that is probably known to every teacher of statistics in the world. If you are in a class with about thirty students, you can amaze them by telling them that there is a very high probability that two of them have the same birthday. Students who have never heard about this demonstration will find it counterintuitive and argue with you. Yet it works, time after time. In fact, if the number of students lies between thirty-five and forty, it is a virtual certainly. Even thirty students offer a very good chance your demonstration will succeed. There is no magic involved, no slight-of-hand. It is only impressive because—as in the art gallery example—people fail to consider just how many cases are actually being sampled. Of course, as that number grows, so does the likelihood of a "hit." Most students falsely conceptualize the birthday example as if you were asking a room of thirty people whether they had one particular birthday. But you are not. In fact you are asking each of thirty-plus students whether they were born on any of thirty-plus different days. That creates a lot of opportunities for success, just as walking through life or European art galleries offers numerous opportunities for the "exceptional" to occur.

The final piece of the puzzle is suggested by Thomas Gilovich, who notes that all of this repeated sampling of events is not even obvious to the person. As far as she is concerned, she is simply living. Yet, for all intents and purposes, she is repeatedly flipping a coin or playing the roulette wheel. We fail to see the repeated sampling as such, however, because unlike roulette or tossing coins, we are constantly sampling different kinds of events as our lives unfold. There is almost nothing to remind us that we *are* repeatedly sampling until we experience a "hit." At that moment, we understandably feel as if a very unlikely thing has happened. "I wasn't even playing the roulette wheel and I won!" If we could be made aware that we had been doing almost nothing *but* playing the roulette wheel from dawn to dusk each day, would the occasional payoff seem like an episode worthy of the *Twilight Zone*?

NONSCIENCE, PART I: ESP

Let me begin by making a simple claim: If our ability to gather and evaluate evidence were not so deeply flawed, there would be no need for continued discussion of ESP. Certainly, there would be *talk* of it, the same way there is occasional talk of x-ray vision or walking through walls or reincarnation. But the clear absence of reliable evidence for any of ESP's most common forms, such as telepathy, precognition, clairvoyance, or psychokinesis, would remove it from the realm of serious consideration or rational debate.

As we know, this is far from the case. Belief in ESP is widespread and it is by no means confined to those with marginal intellectual gifts. There is even evidence that belief in ESP may correlate positively with education. How can this be?

Rather than debating whether ESP exists in any of its well-publicized forms, it is probably more instructive to examine 1) the kind of evidence we would need to confirm the existence of ESP, and 2) the kind of evidence we actually have. Needless to say, to believers, there is an adequate match between 1) and 2). To nonbe-lievers, there is not.

Debating ESP should not be like debating the existence of God; that is, its acceptance should not be based on faith. ESP is a phe-nomenon that rightly or wrongly has been dragged into the realm of the natural world. Confirming its existence should depend on well-established empirical and logical techniques. Science offers us a value-free body of skills for collecting data and evaluating evi-dence. These should pertain as readily to ESP as they do to astronomy, sociology, or molecular biology. Why, then, does the debate continue?

The answer is that we can't seem to agree on the rules. For some, the tests *have* been run and the evidence overwhelmingly dis-confirms the existence of ESP. But for others, the so-called negative evidence isn't particularly relevant and might even be construed as positive. Thus, the search continues and the belief remains strong.

These discussions do not take place behind closed doors. In his book *How We Know What Isn't So*,[3] Thomas Gilovich surveys evi-dence and cites the report of a blue-ribbon panel constituted in 1988 by the National Research Council. Offering an even-handed overview of 130 years of research, the panel concluded there was no evidence to support belief in ESP. A reasoned exchange between believers and skeptics appeared in 1987 in *Behavioral and Brain Sciences*,[4] one of the most respected journals in the area of cogni-tive science. More than one hundred pages of journal space was devoted to the debate, which ultimately centered on the issue of *replicability*. The ability to repeat a result is a cornerstone of sci-entific credibility. The very idea that a finding occurs only once, and only in one place, is anathema to science. Yet it is what character-izes much of the evidence for ESP.

Because believers can anticipate that skeptics will point to the fleeting nature of their findings in any debate, they, themselves, have begun to raise the issue. A good offense is the best defense. By attacking the criterion of replicability before it can be used against them, believers have stalled serious discussion. This should not be confused with the case of old enemies who finally agree to sit down to work out their differences, only to be sidetracked by arguments about the size of the table or the color of the walls. In this case, the disagreement could not be more fundamental.

Replicability is the hallmark of the scientific method, and ESP supporters want immunity from it. There are two very good reasons not to allow this to happen. First, the history of ESP research is replete with examples of faulty methodology and outright fraud. Indeed, there may be no other area of psychological research where these problems are more glaring. If anything, history shows we need to tighten the strictures of the scientific method, not loosen them.

Second, ESP is a tremendously important possibility. If its existence could be proven, it would change the very way in which we see ourselves and the universe around us. This is no small matter, and, if anything, we want to be extremely sure of ESP's existence before we embrace it. This hardly seems to be the place to lower the standard of evidence.

NONSCIENCE, PART II: ALTERNATIVE MEDICINE

Just about everyone, including practitioners of conventional medicine, agrees that conventional/Western/AMA medicine doesn't have all the answers. This is a good start: agreement from all parties. The problem is, where do we go from here? Does it follow that if A doesn't have the answer, then B must? Logic certainly does not suggest that, yet people flock to alternative forms of healing. In some cases, they meet earnest practitioners who might hold some promise. In too many other cases, they meet quackery. Some of that quackery (like so-called psychic surgeons) is outright fraud, designed to prey on the desperate and gullible. Other brands of alternative medicine are not so cynical. The worst you can say about them is that they waste your time and money. That's not the end of the world—people waste their time and money on bad books, movies, and relationships all the time. It's theirs to waste.

Our concern here is not to distinguish between good and bad forms of medicine. Rather, we are concerned with the mental errors that lead to *beliefs* about alternative medicine. Why do we really think various therapies work when, demonstrably, they do not?

How can we be so clueless in the face of clear evidence? Presumably, people do not want to hold erroneous beliefs about medicine, yet many of us do.

Just how widespread is the use of alternative approaches to medicine? Depending on how the question is phrased and which practices are included, the US National Institutes of Health report that about two-thirds of the population employs "complementary alternative medicine" (CAM). There is a lot of variation in what people turn to in addition to their family physician. For some it may be glucosamine plus chondroitin tablets for their arthritis or St. John's Wort for their nerves. For others, it's prayer or prayer groups or faith healing. For some, it may be iridology or applied kinesiology. Other patients visit a naturopath or chiropractor or homeopath. Roughly a fifth of the population purchases and uses "natural" remedies from health food stores or specialized sections of pharmacies.

How many of these approaches have been objectively tested and documented to actually help? The answer is, virtually none. Certainly, there have been studies that provide suggestive evidence—exactly the kind of thing that should prompt larger-scale, more rigorous testing. But such tests require sizable investments of time and money, neither of which seems to be in great supply. It is far easier to go on speculative or anecdotal evidence. How much does a package of echinacea lozenges cost anyway? Even if it doesn't work, it isn't going to kill you.

There is a fundamental flaw that runs through virtually all reasoning about alternative medicine. It is simply this: the body is likely to heal itself in time, regardless of what you do. This means, whatever you are doing at the time of this natural healing will receive undue credit for the improvement. Adding various chemicals and practices to the mix will simply complicate things when it comes time to understand your health and how to keep it. By analogy, think of one of those old-fashioned radios, televisions, or amplifiers that worked on vacuum tubes. You turned on the TV and had to wait for it to warm up. It *would* come on, but not immediately. Now imagine someone desperate to hear or see his favorite program. He turns the "on" switch and . . . nothing. He becomes anxious, rotating other dials needlessly. Still nothing. He paces, maybe turning circles in the room. Still nothing. Finally, he smacks the set on the side and immediately on comes the screen. From the wisdom of our vantage point we might understand that the smack to the side had no part in attaining the desired outcome. But at the time, frustrated by a lingering silence, desiring an outcome that seemed overdue, the connection seems reasonable. If the timescale were a little slower and the outcome were not *I Love Lucy* but your return to health, might you not be a little intrigued by that new herbal remedy you took just last night before you woke up feeling better?

In terms of scientific method, this is another case of the missing control group. You can't just listen to someone raving about how quickly her cold was cured when she took gobs of vitamin C or tablets of zinc and goldenseal. You've got to compare that cure with a patient who took nothing, or was given a placebo or prayed to Sneezo, the god of colds. Anecdotal reports, even from good friends or family members, can suggest possibilities, but they don't constitute evidence.

In his book *How We Know What Isn't So*, Gilovich makes the intriguing point that were it not for this erroneous tendency to associate cures with preceding treatments, conventional medicine, itself, might never have survived the eighteenth and nineteenth centuries when its offerings were pretty marginal by today's standards. The bottom line is that virtually all forms of healing benefit from the same mental mistakes. Whether it's conventional antibiotics or holistic medicine or faith healing, once we are invested in the process we are likely to attribute any improvement to it while discounting its failures as somehow irrelevant. In this regard, faith healers are perhaps the most resistant to criticism. Their approach is Teflon-coated as far as negative results go. If you're a good person and God wants you healed, then the treatment will work. If my touch does not work, don't blame me. I'm only God's instrument. He's the one who's made the judgment not to heal you and in all likelihood that reflects something unsavory about you. Thus, not only does the unhealed patient have to cope with continuing illness, but she also has to bear the stigma of God's judgment. A double whammy.

Some time ago my partner and I visited a very successful local naturopath. He checked us both, and told my partner she had intestinal parasites. I was spared the shame of parasites, but was told I had serious dietary allergies that contributed to my general sense of weakness, a state I didn't recall having until it was both identified and explained in one visit. I asked him if there was anything that could ever go wrong with me that couldn't be understood in terms of his methods. He looked a little cagey but replied, "No." I then asked if he could imagine anything, any kind of outcome that would suggest to him that his approach had failed. He again shook his head, explaining that negative outcomes most often reflected deficiencies in the patient or his or her compliance with the therapeutic program. It's been over twenty years and, to the best of my knowledge, the man still has a thriving alternative medical practice.

NONSCIENCE, PART III: HANDWRITING ANALYSIS

It's a time-honored gimmick to use in Introductory Psychology classes. Before your students—most of them new to university—get the message that you're going to be critical of pseudoscience, you announce that you're going to offer a demonstration of handwriting analysis. You tell them there's a visiting expert in the department who has offered to help.

You ask each student to write a meaningless sentence like "The purple cow jumped over the moon," and then you instruct them to place the papers carefully in unsealed envelopes, write their names and ID numbers on the outside of the envelopes and pass them forward. Inform them that this will take some time but you will return the results of the handwriting analysis in about a week. The delay is not necessary, although it builds suspense. The only time you'll have to spend is inserting a formally typed piece of paper into each envelope.

On the big day, you return the now-sealed envelopes, which contain their handwritten sentences along with an analysis of their personality based on their handwriting. On your signal, everyone opens his or her envelope and reads the analysis, which consists of a single sentence. There is usually quiet in the room, punctuated by a few nervous giggles. After a moment, you ask them whether their analysis seems accurate. Many will shake their heads up and down quietly, trying not to draw attention to themselves. You can rephrase the question, such as "Does it seem like he knows what he's doing?" and you'll get an even more enthusiastic response.

Finally, ask them if anyone would be willing to read his or her analysis to the class. At first there will be no volunteers. Finally, someone will raise her hand and barely audibly will read out loud what is written on her paper. That sentence might be, "Although you are outgoing, happy, and extroverted sometimes, you are quiet, reserved, and introverted at other times." Or it might say, "You have found it unwise to reveal yourself too quickly in social situations." Or perhaps, "At times your sexual experiences have involved difficult adjustments for you." At this point there is stunned silence as people look to the left and right of themselves in growing recognition of the obvious. They've been had—they've all received the same analysis. There is usually an interesting mix of emotions. Some are rolling their eyes or groaning. They wondered from the first whether it was phony. Others look genuinely disappointed; they were really into this and they wanted it to be real. Now they're starting to wonder why you did it to them.

You can turn this into your next question. Why does it work? What have we learned? Why is it part of an Introductory Psychology course? This might be the most important moment in the course so far, because they realize that many of their preconceptions about themselves and the field of psychology might be wrong. If they're willing to pay attention, this course might shake up their world more than they anticipated.

So why *does* it work? Apart from the obvious stuff about trusting authority figures, there are some insights here into how their minds work. The important message isn't about handwriting analysis and whether or not it works. What matters is that they were prepared to accept some pretty flimsy evidence as proof that it did. Why were they so gullible? What was it about the analysis they all received from the "expert"? To begin with, they have gotten what sounds like a highly specific message and yet, as they now see, it is quite general. Those embarrassing personal insights turn out to be glib generalities that fit just about everyone in the room. Just how far could we have pushed their credibility before it broke?

Were they predisposed to believe in things like handwriting analysis because they have heard about them all their lives without ever hearing a criticism or disproof? If I told them I had an ancient and blind Hindu prophet in my office who would run his hands over their aura and produce an analysis of their character, would that have worked as well? What about a German shepherd who could sniff them and press one of a dozen pedals with his paw, thereby printing out the analysis they received? If the dog still sounds credible to them, how about a trained rat with various levers in his cage that could trigger the printouts? There are plainly limits to our gullibility, but they are rarely absolute. To most undergraduate students, a handwriting analysis by an "expert psychologist" is well on the positive side of credible.

NONSCIENCE, PART IV: MEN ARE SUCH JERKS

Not for a second would I dispute the occasional accuracy of this section's title. How *general* the indictment may be is another matter. What's relevant to our discussion is how evidence of this delicate issue was collected and analyzed. In 1976, an author with few professional credentials named Shere Hite put together a book called *The Hite Report*.[5] Subtitled *A Nationwide Study of Female Sexuality*, the book was a runaway hit, ultimately selling more than 35 million copies worldwide. Not surprisingly, this initial book spawned a franchise resulting in four *Hite Reports* and two later works as well. In her initial *Report*, which Hite often claimed to be "scientific," the author presented a relentlessly negative and depressing view of heterosexual relationships that failed, almost uniformly, because of the attitudes and behavior of men. Report after report came from angry and sexually unsatisfied women detailing the abuse they had suffered at the hands of the men in their lives. Hite made some attempt to classify these reports by category, added two covers and a title page, and then watched her work climb the best seller lists.

Part of the book's appeal lay in the undeniable sense of validation it provided to unhappy and abused women. Given the extent of some of the cases, the book probably also offered a perverse comfort in knowing that someone out there was even worse off than the reader. In this regard, no one can blame the readers, the author, or her informants. The problem lies in assuming that there is anything *scientific* about any of this. Yet, that is just what many journalists believed (the book was listed by the *London Times* as one of the Hundred Key Books of the Twentieth Century). The case is worth examining quite apart from the personal pain or feminist politics at its core.

First, large sample sizes do not render findings "scientific." The case is analogous to asking all those who have been abducted by aliens to send me a one-thousand-word summary of their experience, then stapling them together and publishing them as scientific proof of alien abductions. The problem isn't with the number of stories or even their accuracy, which are both issues raised by reviewers who argued for the legitimacy of the *Hite Report*. In fact, I am willing to concede as truth every word of those harrowing tales of abuse. I am equally impressed by the sheer number of women who wrote to Ms. Hite. And none of that has anything whatsoever to do with science.

To make important statements about what jerks men are, we need to know how general the indictment is. Otherwise, your tale is nothing more than your litany of woe, even if your neighbor agrees with it. To explore generality, we cannot simply ask wounded women to tell their stories. The issue isn't whether there are some men who are sexually insensitive, abusive jerks who have mistreated their partners. That much is undeniable. The issue is, again, generality. To that end, we need a random sample of women talking about their relationships with men. Only then can we begin to understand how widespread the problem is. To her credit, Ms. Hite attempted to achieve this. She sent out questionnaires to hundreds of organizations, potentially sampling over 100,000 women. The problem stems from the fact that very few of them (fewer than 3,000) replied and, of those, most were very hurt and very angry. Those are the reports that were cobbled together, so to speak, and sold to the public. Presumably, women who were reasonably satisfied in relationships with their partners did not feel the need to tell Ms. Hite about it. Indeed, a collection of such reports would probably not have made very interesting reading or garnered much in the way of financial reward for Ms. Hite and her publisher.

The bottom line, once again, is that it is not sufficient to form an interesting hypothesis and test it by gathering as much confirming evidence as you can. Yet, as we are learning through the efforts of cognitive science, that is precisely how our minds work when faced with the mass of information in our lives. Form a belief and then look for evidence to confirm it. That's many things— including Caveman Logic—but it isn't science. And, even as non-scientists, it is not a good way to run our personal lives. Important hypotheses or belief systems should be *tested* before we invest our egos or lives in them. Once again, this requires stating the belief in a way that allows for either confirmation or disproof. Then gather as much evidence as you can from as large and unbiased a sample as you can find. And then see what kind of conclusion the evidence supports. Perhaps men *are* sexually unfulfilling jerks, but we'll never really know it from reading *The Hite Report*.

Chapter 5

A DEEPER LOOK AT WHAT'S WRONG

THE LOYAL OPPOSITION

Sometimes it's helpful to put a face on the resistance you're going to encounter. It can be a bit sobering to get a sense of what keeps people from embracing your ideas. What do they oppose or fear about what you're offering?

My partner and I found ourselves sitting next to four high school teachers at dinner during a recent vacation in Florida. Our neighbors were bright, friendly, and outgoing, so we began to chat as we made our way through several bottles of wine. The woman sitting closest to me was a biology teacher named Joanne (not her real name). The others taught chemistry and social studies. After the usual small talk about escaping the northern cold, I asked Joanne whether she faced any problems teaching Darwin in her biology class.

"Not really," she replied.

"So you're able to teach evolution without having to apologize for it?" I asked.

"Well, I like to be fair so I teach them both sides of the issue."

"So you teach creationism in your biology class?" I inquired.

"Yes," she replied, aware that our conversation was beginning to move beyond casual vacation chatter. "I want to be respectful of the Christian kids too. The Bible *does* have something to say about all of this, you know."

"And you think science class is the place to teach it?" I inquired.

"Sure. Why not?" she asked. "Where else would you teach it?"

"How about your friend's social studies class?" I asked.

"I suppose so," she conceded, "but I just like to give a balanced picture of the issue. It seems fair."

It struck me that a lot of important questions had already been raised:

1. Shouldn't a science class be reserved for the teaching of science? Have we missed a precious opportunity to educate these children about the methods and findings of science?

2. Does every opposing idea, regardless of its empirical or logical status, deserve equal time in a curriculum whose time is already drastically limited?

3. Doesn't including a faith-based belief system as an equal contender within a science education disrespect *all* the students? Why confine notions of "respect" and sensitivity to the Christian kids? Aren't atheists, Jews, Muslims—to name but three obvious groups—also being disrespected by teaching Christian theology?

4. Joanne's wording suggests that Darwin is respectful only to atheists and non-Christians. Like many people, she believes that science is an affront to Christians. Is the only way to show them respect to teach the Bible?

I have little doubt that Joanne does a fine job teaching her students about photosynthesis or the difference between vertebrates and invertebrates. But arguably she is not doing as good a job when it comes time to explain one of the most fundamental principles about life on Earth (the subject matter of biology). These students are likely to go away thinking that Darwin is "just another theory" and the Bible presents an equivalent alternative hypothesis about life on Earth.

When I inquired whether she would also teach her students that Earth was five thousand years old, she replied, "Of course not."

"Why?" I wondered. "If this is about respecting Christian kids, aren't there many who also believe that age thing?"

Her reply was essentially a "Yes, but . . ." I was left with the impression that *fundamentalist* Christian beliefs exceeded her own and were thus beyond her threshold for fair treatment. Because Joanne didn't believe Earth was five thousand years old, she was not prepared to include it in her syllabus. Nor was she prepared to offer equal time to the Flat Earth Society or other such "foolishness" (her word). Darwin, however, was another matter. On this issue, Joanne stood shoulder to shoulder with former president George W. Bush in believing that "the verdict is still out."

After another glass of wine, Joanne confronted me. "Let me ask you something. Can you look at us and see a random process?" Without waiting for an answer, she added, "Every time I see a flower or a beautiful bird I find myself siding with the intelligent design kids. Do you really believe there is no thought, no purpose behind such beauty? If this were a random world, would anything be so beautiful?"

This final point was presented with a "Take that!" demeanor, which led me to believe the conversation was over. It wasn't. But what I had just heard reminded me that there is a widespread assumption out there that beauty can only happen by design. "Randomness" or "chance" are seen as alternatives to "design." They are both godless and can only result in chaos or ugliness. Beauty, the idea goes, doesn't just *happen*. It must result from conscious, purposeful design. Of course, once you admit "design" into your system, it's a fairly short step to a "designer." There is only one candidate for that job.

The connection between beauty and God seems very intuitive to many people and has wide social support among those to whom the sight of a flower confirms theology. For such people, the nature of beauty itself goes unexamined. *Why* do some things strike us as beautiful and others not? Is beauty simply a *thing* that resides in some items but not others? Perhaps we might wonder why we perceive certain things as beautiful and others as ugly. Or is it enough to simply let beauty accumulate in an unexamined way until we are convinced that beauty → design → designer → God?

Joanne viewed these questions as a big waste of time. She asked, "Why do you think you're sitting here, at this table, next to us? Do you believe *that's* a coincidence too? Do you not see that *everything* in the universe has meaning and purpose?"

This moment underscored the enormity of the challenge facing this book. Almost every error of fact, logic, and perception discussed in *Caveman Logic* seemed to be present in Joanne's thinking and the arguments she made with considerable force. These attitudes and beliefs were present in a normal, intelligent woman whose job it was to educate hundreds of children each year. These are children whose minds are already predisposed to the same mistakes that Joanne wore on her sleeve. These are children who would already be hearing similar thinking from their families and friends, as well as from people they respected in all walks of life. And now their educators were piling it on as well, perhaps winning teaching awards in the process.

A controversial subject matter and a teacher who professes ambivalence about it are not a recipe for good education.

"Do you think you understand natural selection?" I asked Joanne.

"Probably not as well as I ought to," she admitted.

This, too, underscores the dilemma: Should a teacher who does not understand an important subject very well be entrusted with teaching it to the next generation, as well as making decisions about the extent to which it should be taught at all?

Joanne was very clear. *Chance* is a cold, ugly process that can only result in empty sterility. It can never produce beauty. Beauty can only result from conscious design. Joanne's viewpoint is actually more enlightened than some. It is a dual system that relegates ugly-looking weeds or warthogs to natural selection (score one for

Darwin!), but ascribes things like roses and bunny rabbits to God. Nowhere inside these beliefs is there any reflection on the possibility that beauty might reside in the mind of the beholder and not in the rose. And if it does, that sense of beauty might result from an evolutionary process whose existence Joanne doubts.

Creationists sometimes use the analogy of a tornado blowing through a junkyard. When the wind subsides, you find a perfectly assembled jet engine. Now how likely is that? they ask with glee. To many, evolution goes beyond silliness and if a bunch of godless academics want to put it in some fancy book, that's their business. Joanne, like any team player, will dutifully present evolution in class (with no great enthusiasm), but she'll damn well remind the kids that it's "only a theory."

The second scenario has both common sense and comfort on its side, not to mention the fact that it doesn't stir up protest from the parents. Common sense and comfort without conflict: an unbeatable combination. This scenario simply says that someone very wise and very powerful spent time in that junkyard and *designed* that jet engine and left it for us. If anyone asks why, you can suggest that he loves us. Plainly, this is the scenario many teachers favor for both personal and pedagogical reasons. You've just got to hope that your class doesn't include some smartass atheist kid who points out that it doesn't take much to insert that heavenly jet engine into a plane and fly it into a building.

REJECTING MONKEY SEX

"They're no fools, those believers. You may think of them as weak-minded sheep, but there are some pretty smart people out there who believe in God."

I've heard this from more than one colleague who knew about this book and wanted to help. I agree with them. We already looked at the smart/dumb, atheist/theist correlation table in chapter 2 and found it less than helpful. There are better predictors of religious belief than intelligence. Certainly, cleverness is not in short supply among the religious. How else to account for the billboard on display in the Nashville, Tennessee, area bearing the words, "Exposure to the Son prevents burning"? Atheists could use a few good slogan writers to work for them.

So what do we make of the almost intractable resistance one finds to logical Darwinian arguments? If you listen carefully to what opponents tell you at unguarded moments, a recurrent theme emerges. What we often learn is that concerns about morality are absolutely central to rejecting Darwin. You can argue the fossil record until you're blue in the face. You may win some unenthusiastic concessions, but only up to a point. That point was well expressed recently in the Arkansas State House of Representatives. In essence, "If we teach children they're descended from monkeys, they'll act like monkeys."

That fear of "monkey sex" is so basic to creationist resistance that no amount of scientific evidence can budge it. "Throw out God and you'll throw out morality." That's what you'll hear, along with fears about fornicating in the streets. "Within a single generation we'll lose every bit of decency, self-restraint, and morality we've worked hard to instill in them." *Them*, of course, are the children who are viewed as moral blank slates upon which religion's mighty pen had better start writing. Seen from the conservative Christian/creationist point of view, this debate is a battle for civilization itself, not some academic difference over paleontology. To understand or engage it in those terms is to embrace failure.

Darwinians and scientists in general might be better advised to focus on this rarely stated core of resistance and not worry as much about the academic-style arguments they were trained to make to convince their students and colleagues. There are relevant papers out there like Frans de Waal's "Primates: A Natural Heritage of Conflict Resolution," and books like Matt Ridley's *The Origins of Virtue* and Marc Hauser's *Moral Minds*.[1] But they are neither written for, nor widely read by, creationists. This is an entirely different adversary. They are frightened—not about the particulars of natural selection, but about its implications for everyday life. A colleague of mine who occasionally debates creationists makes a point of bringing his wife and two young sons with him to the events. As he observes, "Seeing me surrounded by a normal-looking family may do more to give them second thoughts about Darwin or atheism than all of my best logical arguments put together."

So, if we can't persuade them using our usual arsenal, can we at least immunize ourselves (or perhaps some of them) against such wrongheaded beliefs? We've already noted that creationist/anti-Darwinian beliefs have a considerable advantage in the market-place of ideas. When you pair that natural advantage with modern teaching aids like Kenneth Miller's article in the April 2007 *Parents* magazine, "Giving Kids the Gift of Faith" (available at www. beliefnet.com), it's a wonder atheism is still around to protest.

Fortunately, technology has been put to use on both sides of the spiritual divide. There is a full library of children's books and videos on subjects such as secular humanism, critical thinking, skepticism, and atheism. A series of offerings by Dan Barker such as *Just Pretend: A Freethought Book for Children*[2] encourages them to question and doubt the religiosity they will find everywhere. The publicity surrounding these products seldom uses the word "immunize," choosing instead to say things like, "In a world flooded with religious literature, there is a need for material that nonreligious families can present to their children that validates their decision not to believe in gods or myths." Longitudinal studies examining the effects of such early experience on later beliefs would be useful to determine whether early "immunization" can overcome later religious indoctrination.

It might also be useful for these longitudinal studies to document the fact that nonindoctrinated individuals do not routinely become drooling, amoral sexual predators or mass murderers. There are those to whom that simple fact might be somewhat surprising. It won't put the debate to rest, but it's a step in the right direction.

CONFIRMATION BIAS

The confirmation bias is one of the most insidious and pervasive bits of software in your head. It is as much a part of being human as having two eyes, one nose, and two feet. To avoid evaluating the

world through the confirmation bias, you have got to take conscious steps against it. Even then there is no guarantee you'll succeed. If you allow your mental software to operate on its Pleistocene default settings, you will bring this bias into play.

Worse yet, you won't even be aware of it. In all likelihood, if you
are confronted with what you are doing, you will probably deny it.
You might even bring some righteous indignation to the denial.
When its rules and properties are spelled out, the confirmation bias
is actually quite unappealing to most people. They agree that it is *not*
very reasonable or fair. It is not the kind of mental style they want to
associate with themselves. People prefer to see themselves as open-
minded, rational, and fair. Those are admirable qualities, indeed, and
it is good that we value them so highly. It's just that those qualities
are almost the opposite of how we function in the real world.

So just what is this dreaded confirmation bias? It refers to the
fact that we form opinions, social perceptions, and judgments very
quickly—and often by rules that we would not want to bring before
the Oxford Debating Society. Once these opinions, perceptions, and
judgments are in place, we do not hold them up to critical scrutiny.
Instead, we look for confirming evidence and seize upon it as
quickly as it appears. We spend virtually no time seeking negative
evidence about our beliefs and, even when such information forces
itself into our awareness, we find ways of discounting or dismissing
it altogether. In short, we don't play fair. We are emotionally invested
in supporting our beliefs and worldviews. We have an almost inexhaustible supply of "Yes, buts" when some of that threatening negative evidence peers around the corners of our belief system.

This is nothing new. It is entirely reasonable to suppose that the
confirmation bias has been a fundamental part of human mental
functioning since we were certifiably human. It is nothing new in
another sense also. Describing and diagnosing the confirmation bias
is not just the domain of modern cognitive or social psychology. Evidence of this fundamental "unfairness" in human mental life has
been known for centuries. It is hardly a well-kept secret. Francis
Bacon wrote about it in his *Novum Organum* in 1620. Bacon's language may appear quaint to us today, but there is no doubt that he
was talking about this same glitch in human mental life. He spoke of

our "drawing all things to support and agree with" our opinions, and "neglecting or despising" negative evidence even though "there be a greater number and weight of instances to be found on the other side." Bacon spoke of our need to keep our "former conclusions" as "inviolate" and described the mental tricks we used to do so as *"great and pernicious"* (italics mine).

Evidence of the confirmation bias has advanced from earlier questionnaire studies by social psychologists to more modern neuroimaging techniques of cognitive neuroscientists. A 2006 study by Drew Westen and his colleagues[3] used functional magnetic resonance imaging (fMRI) of a group of "strong" Republicans and Democrats as they responded to George W. Bush and John Kerry contradicting themselves during the 2004 presidential elections. True to form, the Democrats found a way to let their candidate off the hook for his verbal transgressions while remaining strongly critical of the Republican candidate's gaffes. Republicans responded to Kerry in the same manner. The study's primary contribution was to report that areas of the brain normally associated with logical reasoning—the dorsolateral prefrontal cortex—was all but missing in action during this processing. Instead, the most active regions of the brain were those associated with the processing of emotions and conflict resolution. Once subjects had reached a decision to support either Kerry or Bush, the "pleasure centers" of their brains were highly activated.

In a press release accompanying his findings, Westen noted, "We did not see any increased activation of the parts of the brain normally engaged during reasoning. What we saw instead was a network of emotion circuits lighting up, including circuits hypothesized to be involved in regulating emotion and resolving conflicts." Westen describes the overall process in terms that resonate with Bacon's prose from nearly four centuries earlier. "Essentially it appears as if partisans twirl the cognitive kaleidoscope until they get the conclusions they want, and then they get massively reinforced for it, with the elimination of negative emotional states."

Commenting on these findings, *Skeptic* editor Michael Shermer notes that such irrational information processing is hardly confined to the political arena. Because it is a fundamental part of human nature, the confirmation bias emerges everywhere humans are forced to reach and maintain conclusions as evidence continues to accumulate. All of our personal beliefs fall under this heading. Is this a just world? Am I lucky (or unlucky)? Is the president a great leader? Have we had previous lives? Does God love me? Do we have a divine purpose that will be revealed to us through signs in our lives? These are areas where we're likely to find evidence of the confirmation bias in action. The conclusions were long ago reached; now we are in the business of weeding through the evidence in a way that keeps us feeling good about how "right" our viewpoints are. Most of these opinions are highly personal and may ultimately have little impact on the lives of others. However, Michael Shermer looks at examples whose implications may be greater, such as a juror assessing the innocence or guilt of a defendant or a high financier making decisions about the actions of his own company or a competitor.

Shermer also examines how the confirmation bias might affect the beliefs and behavior of a scientist. This example is particularly important for two reasons. First, science is a great example of where you might find the confirmation bias at work. The fate of scientific theories depends upon how information is gathered and interpreted. If science in general or a theory in particular depended upon the information-processing skills of one individual—perhaps one with a vested interest in the outcome—then we might be in for some serious trouble. After all, there is no reason to believe that scientists in general are any better equipped to keep the confirmation bias at bay than nonscientists. Scientists are first and foremost human beings, and they are as likely as most to seize on positive data and discount disconfirming evidence. But science does not advance because scientists have evolved to a higher mental standard than other people. The virtue of science is built into its collective process. As Shermer notes, "Extraordinary claims require extraordinary evidence." Hypotheses, by definition, are stated in terms that lend themselves to empirical testing. Such testing is performed widely, by individuals without emotional ties to the hypothesis. The essential self-correcting mechanisms of science are an antidote to the flaws of the confirmation bias. It is as if the rules of science, with its endless need for replication and reexamination, were constructed by individuals with a deep understanding of the flaws of human reasoning. The individual practitioners can be flawed, as long as the rules they are forced to follow are not.

Shermer laments the dangerous impact of this bias on fields like law, business, and politics. He goes so far as to suggest that political debate should, for example, require opponents to argue each other's positions. Shermer concludes that skepticism is the antidote to the confirmation bias. That may be true, but it is not particularly helpful to say so. As we have argued, the confirmation bias is a natural state of affairs for us. Even bringing it to the level of awareness does not necessarily preclude it. The forces that underlie the confirmation bias are powerful, emotional, and supported by a network of evolved mental circuitry. That is a formidable adversary. Skepticism, on the other hand, is—at present, anyway—an unnatural state practiced by a small minority of the population and prized by very few. We are more likely to name our daughters "Faith" than "Doubt" or "Skeptic."

ANTHROPOMORPHISM: SEEING OURSELVES IN EVERYTHING

"The attribution of human qualities to nonhuman things"—that's the simple definition of *anthropomorphism*. We all do it, mostly unconsciously, and far more frequently than we realize. Anthropomorphism is not some aberrant cognitive trait confined to the stupid or uncritical among us. It is a normal quality of the human mind, affecting both thought and perception. It is doubtful that anyone ever went broke selling anthropomorphism and some (e.g., Walt Disney) have gotten very rich. Is anthropomorphism just a quirky little human trait that never hurt anyone? Not according to Yann Martel's best-selling novel *Life of Pi* (2006). The title character, the son of a zookeeper, learns in no uncertain terms that the most dangerous species on Earth is what he calls "*Animalus anthropomorphicus.*"

Although there are many positive things one might say about anthropomorphism (it has added sentimentality and compassion to our treatment of animals), it also leads us to misunderstand many of those same animals. The mental modules that underlie anthropomorphism must have provided a selective advantage for our ancestors and, even if the trait has become selectively neutral today, there is little selection pressure to abandon it. Indeed, the only culture/subculture I can think of that specifically discourages it is scientific training, especially those areas where contact with nonhumans is an important part of the experience. No self-respecting (or, for that matter, respected) comparative psychologist, learning theorist, or ethologist could remain actively anthropomorphic while functioning at a professional level. Even animal welfare activists, along with some more moderate animal rights advocates, have taken pains to remind us that those pets we adore are not human surrogates that thrive when we treat them like furry little humans with tails (or feathers). They are members of another species with needs, abilities, and agendas that are often far removed from our own.

Like other forms of mental shortcomings discussed in this book, anthropomorphism stems not from a broken or nonfunctioning mental ability but from one that is functioning quite well. It is being triggered far too frequently, and in contexts where it just doesn't belong. When dealing with other humans, it is appropriate for my "intuitive psychology" or "theory of mind" module to be triggered. The benefits of understanding and anticipating another's thoughts and motives are obvious. However, the application of this intuitive psychology to various classes of nonhumans is another matter.

The following is a list of creatures or things in whose presence you are likely to find yourself one day. Just how anthropomorphic are you likely to be in each case? The list is not arbitrary. I have known people to make anthropomorphic attributions about each of them. Were they right to do so in all cases? Are some more appropriate than others?

1. A chimpanzee
2. A dog
3. A rat
4. A lizard

5. A fly
6. A vegetable
7. A rock
8. A toaster
9. A car
10. A computer

This is not a trick question. The strictest answer is that none is correct. Human characteristics should be applied to humans. To do any more is to distort understanding (and prediction of behavior). But isn't that unnecessarily tough? Doesn't that chimp share nearly 99 percent of its genetic material with you? Yes, and you can dwell on that side of the equation while you look into those big soulful eyes, or you can focus on the enormity of that 1 percent difference. That chimp might tear you apart limb from limb and have you for dinner while staying within the norms of its species' culture. It also may fail to comprehend some of the most basic abstract relations between events that even your slow-witted brother-in-law grasps unthinkingly. As Steven Pinker observed in *How the Mind Works* (1997), while our species reaches for the stars and ponders issues such as the ones in this book, chimpanzees remain an endangered species, clinging tenaciously to a shrinking habitat in a corner of Africa. So much for mixing sentiment and science.

Like the chimp, the dog was on the list to sucker some of you into saying yes. They may be man's best friend, but they are an entirely different species, whose natural history intersected with ours hundreds of thousands of years ago, but whose mental and physical lives are immensely different from ours. We share enough, through phylogenetic development and domestication, for us to get along famously—probably better than any two unrelated species have a right to. But come the crunch, dogs are still dogs. They are neurologically closer to wolves than to the humans who love them. Their needs may occasionally overlap with our own, but more often than not they diverge in ways that we can barely understand.

Like dogs, rats are highly intelligent and adaptive mammals and make excellent pets. I can assure you from personal experience that, under the right conditions, they seek contact with you and even come when you call them. But they, too, are a different species from us and attributions about their motives or emotional states may be misleading, at best.

Few people I know would get anthropomorphic about a lizard (they're simply too reptilian looking), and no one I've ever met attributes much in the way of human mental states to a fly. Anthropomorphism typically leads to more humane treatment and, in the case of a housefly, most people draw the line at not swatting them. Adoption and nurturance seem out of the question.

Many people I've met fuss over their plants and talk about their "needs" in ways that suggest more than strict botany. I actually had one friend tell me she felt more of a connection with her philodendron than with her cactus. Somehow, because it came from the desert, she did not feel as "attuned" to it.

Each of these cases involves a living organism, which might seem a minimum requirement for anthropomorphism. Humans certainly have the capacity to distinguish between animate and inanimate objects, and for good reason. Animate objects move under their own steam and have agendas. Inanimate ones do not. Items 7–10 on the list above can be grouped together as inanimate. The houseplant is a bit of a judgment call for many people. I've heard people argue that hacking one's way through the underbrush with a machete is akin to a killing spree. But let us set that issue aside for now and simply say that nonliving entities such as rocks, toasters, cars, and computers are less likely to trigger attributions of human qualities in most of us. Certainly, it is true that many humans grow up playing with, and becoming extremely attached to, dolls. But those dolls are modeled on human anatomy and might be expected to trigger mental attributions, especially in the very young. However, a variety of inanimate objects, which bear no similarity to human form, continue to trigger attributions of human qualities, and not just by children. During the 1960s, people (admittedly some unusual people) kept pet rocks, on some of which human faces had been crudely painted.

I included a vegetable on the list of contenders to reflect an exchange I had with a seven-year-old boy. We were bringing his dinner to the table and a French-fried potato fell off the plate. He jumped off his chair to rescue it from the floor before I could throw it out. As he popped it in his mouth, I asked why he felt so strongly about this particular piece of potato. "I didn't want it to feel left out," he explained. "It came all the way from the factory with its friends, and I didn't want it to end up in the garbage after all it had been through." I have seen people treat their pets with less compassion.

What's good enough for a potato is certainly good enough for a household appliance or a car. I was amused to learn that Caribbean patois often included statements like "The pot wants cleaning" or "The car wants washing." Beyond treating these metal devices with compassion, people often describe mechanical failures in anthropomorphic ways. Breakdowns by toasters, computers, and cars are not uncommonly described in terms suggesting an internal agenda on the part of the failed appliance. "My computer is out to get me. I swear, of all the nights it could have broken down, it picks *tonight* with the paper due tomorrow." Similar statements are frequently made about automobiles, which apparently never break down at opportune times. This, in turn, suggests a malevolent or malicious spirit lurking just behind the Ford sticker. Forget that it's a hunk of metal. Anything with timing like that must have a mind. "It's still pissed off at me for not getting the oil changed on time."

The instructive thing is that we have the capacity to laugh at the folly of the above examples while knowing full well that we are not immune to such perceptions or statements. This is the power of anthropomorphism. We come hardwired for it. We engage in it unconsciously as well as on occasions when we are fully aware of what we are saying and how outrageous it is. It's *fun* to be anthropomorphic. Animals the world over are the beneficiaries of much kindness that might otherwise not come their way. None of this is problematic. Can our anthropomorphism module be brought under control? People understandably hold funerals for their deceased pets. (Although here, again, species seems to be a large determinant of the degree of ritual. Often dogs are buried but goldfish are flushed.) But do we and should we memorialize and mourn our cars, computers, and toasters?

Not all scientists working with animals are militant in their opposition to anthropomorphism. My colleague Gordon Gallup has argued for what he calls "critical anthropomorphism." It is best seen as a middle ground between the relentless and uncritical approach taken by most persons without scientific training, and the reflexive "it can bring no good" attitude held by many scientists. Acknowledging that anthropomorphism is deeply ingrained in all of us, Gallup suggests that at the least, anthropomorphism may benefit our observations and fuel hypotheses for later testing. Just as anecdotes cannot substitute for rigorously controlled observation, they—like anthropomorphism—can have their role in science as sources of ideas that can eventually be tested under controlled conditions.

In his book *Faces in the Clouds* (1993), Stewart Guthrie states, "Anthropomorphism is universal in human perception." Guthrie's book is subtitled *A New Theory of Religion*. Not surprisingly, his thesis is that the widespread and unfettered use of anthropomorphism is at the core of religious belief and behavior.

What are the advantages of anthropomorphism, or at least of the cognitive predispositions that give rise to it? Whether anthropomorphism is an adaptation, per se, or what Steven Jay Gould calls an *exaptation* (a feature that was not produced via natural selection for its current function) is an open question, but there is every reason to believe that it continues to serve some function. Here is the proverbial baby and bathwater problem. Expunge anthropomorphism and you may be losing an essential and highly adaptive part of human nature. True, our entertainment would no longer consist of talking mice and ducks, our religions might take a giant step in the direction of abstract deities with inscrutable goals and no interest in our prayers, our pets might be treated more like members of their own species, but are these improvements our species wants to make?

SPECIESISM: FIRST COUSIN TO ANTHROPOMORPHISM

Given a choice, most people would rather welcome a golden retriever into their home than a scorpion. This normal attitude has a name: speciesism. It's rare to find an "ism" that is politically correct. Racism. Sexism. Ageism. None of those things are valued by enlightened people and most of us have learned to suppress racist, sexist, and ageist impulses in order to behave in a more socially acceptable manner. Sixty years ago there was plenty of social support for acting in a racist, sexist, or ageist way. Comedy routines on the radio and in motion pictures—both a good reflection of prevailing attitudes—supported behavior that makes us cringe today.

While certain forms of discrimination may come easily to us, they are not necessarily good things and, with a little work and social support, they can be eradicated. Two points are worth making: speciesism is still alive, well, and quite prevalent among us, and that may not be an entirely good thing; in addition, speciesism is probably one more instance of Caveman Logic. It certainly appears to be the default setting for our minds. If we are motivated, we can get beyond it. But it will take work as well as social support. Without both, we will simply default to our Pleistocene settings.

This is not a polemic against speciesism. But I think we can use speciesist attitudes as a way to understand Pleistocene thinking in general. To do that, it is useful to share a speciesist moment. We can experience what an evolutionary predisposition feels like in terms of emotions and cognitions. First, we should replace those fancy academic words with plainer terms. Instead of "cognitions and emotions," let's talk about "thoughts and feelings." Instead of "evolutionary predispositions," think in terms of what comes naturally to you. In fact, think about what comes so naturally that you cannot imagine it being any other way. This is certainly what happens in other forms of Caveman Logic: alternative thoughts or beliefs do not even seem to be options until they are explicitly called to our attention.

In a shopping mall not far from my home, I found a store called something like "Nature's Ways." It was a welcome respite from the endless array of clothing stores geared to teenagers. And so I went in.

I found a wall full of third world products like wooden masks, animal carvings, and primitive-looking pottery. Most were imported en masse for distribution and sales in North American outlets to people like me. Among the animal art, I found pieces of plastic in which actual insects had been encased. They were called "Bug Art." Most of them contained small specimens, including many varieties of beetles. But some did not. The plastic cases contained scorpions and spiders and were as large as 6 by 6 inches. What does it mean to find a tarantula encased in a 6-by-6-inch piece of plastic? I observed shoppers as they encountered these items. Many reacted in revulsion to the sight. Some (usually young males) picked up the display item—carefully, I might add—and teased their companions (usually young females), who reacted with varying degrees of horror and glee. I discussed the items with the sales staff and was told that they made "unusual and challenging gifts." None was purchased in the time I observed, but from the quantity on hand, I would assume they are a successful item.

Arachnophobia is widespread in the population. It may actually be the most common phobia and is generally held to be a vestige of our evolutionary heritage. As with any trait in the human genome, you will find a normal distribution of expression. Some people are utterly blasé about the creepy crawly things that terrorized our ancestors; others are absolutely phobic with a response that borders on panic. Certainly, I could induce a healthy demonstration of arachnophobia by projecting an image of one of those encased tarantulas onto the large screen in the lecture hall where I teach Introductory Psychology to six hundred undergraduates. But I don't want to buy the item. The truth is, I don't want to support the cottage industry in trapping these creatures that has sprung up in the third world.

Like many or most persons, I react with some revulsion to the sight of a large and hairy spider, even when it is encased in plastic. I don't enjoy finding the occasional wolf spider loose in my home in the woods. When swimming or boating in the lakes of northern Ontario, I don't enjoy sudden meetings with what we call "dock spiders." But—and this is an important "but"—I have worked very hard to get past my first line of response to these creatures, which is to shudder or squish them. I have to consciously take a deep breath, count to ten, and force myself to stay in their vicinity. When I find spiders, large or small, I make a point of capturing them alive (a large-mouthed glass placed over them quickly and a sheet of cardboard slipped under them will usually work) and transporting them back to the great outdoors.

It takes work, but I have overcome my "natural" emotional

response with one that is more reasoned. I believe this is a good thing for any number of reasons, but this is not about morality. The most important point here is simply that it is possible to transcend Pleistocene default settings, even on something as emotional as encountering an unexpected and large creature in one's home. The revulsion toward a large spider or scorpion is not unlike many of the other examples of Pleistocene logic we have discussed in this book. If you give into those Pleistocene default settings, you will find all kinds of social support for your beliefs and actions.

Let's return to the concept of speciesism. Imagine, for a moment, that the store in question also sold small mammals encased in plastic. Imagine looking down at a 6-by-6-inch piece of plastic and finding a mouse or a baby squirrel looking out at you. What might your reaction be? Note that the store does sell rodent art, but it consists of ceramic replicas or wood carvings. Why is it not OK to encase a squirrel in plastic and sell it? The answer lies in speciesism, which, in turn, stems from deep inside our evolutionary predispositions. Once you avoid the revulsion, the whole business (literally) of encasing animals in plastic raises new questions. For example, how were these spiders killed? Just how were they transferred into that solid block of plastic? Are they gassed and encased while still alive? That seems a hell of a way to die. Why is it OK for tarantulas but not squirrels or chipmunks?

Despite my occasional save-the-spider missions, I am still a speciesist. I may live-trap mice and (less frequently) bats, but I also swat mosquitoes and black flies with impunity. My rationale is simple: mosquitoes and black flies are actually trying to dine on my blood. Moreover, these bites bring discomfort and the potential for disease. Tarantulas (which are not native to southern Ontario) and wolf spiders (which are) are not actively pursuing me as a food source. So, armed with this rationale, I save some and swat others. By definition, then, I am still a speciesist, although my boundaries may be different from yours. The important thing is that I have taken control of the process and moved those boundaries in a direction that suits my own value system. The impulse to flee or squish may have served my ancestors well, but, like much of what served them, it is something I do not need in my life.

SUCCESSFUL SCIENCE FICTION

Because our minds evolved here on Earth, they reflect all the physical and psychological realities of human life on this planet. Both your perceptions and your behavior are earthbound. If and when we have to make accommodations to understand or interact with extraterrestrials, it will require both knowledge and effort.

None of that stops us from creating fantasies about extraterrestrials. Of course, they are extraterrestrials who have been invented by human minds. With all the science fiction that has been created in the past century, why has none of it dealt with truly alien creatures with nonhuman consciousness? The answer is quite simple: It would bore the socks off us. Science fiction as we know it is written for local consumption. Sir Arthur Eddington, an early twentieth-century physicist, wrote, "Not only is the universe stranger than we imagine, it is stranger than we *can* imagine."[4] The essential elements of successful science fiction must be recognizably human, even if the events occur on alien worlds and the protagonists have green skin and two heads. Think of this as the *Star Trek* syndrome. Gene Roddenberry, who created the iconic science fiction series, often professed to be writing westerns set in outer space. The behavior of aliens encountered by Captain Kirk or Captain Picard is rooted in what we know about life on Earth. It is doubtful that a science fiction writer could think outside the assumptions of the human mind to write truly alien stories. Adventures about Martians had better be written by earthlings if they are to succeed on this planet.

When I was a counselor in summer camp, my ten-year-old campers used to ask me to tell them a story before they went to sleep. What they really wanted was for me to make something up. If I had pulled out a collection of works by Charles Dickens or Mark Twain, it just wouldn't have been the same. On most nights I could create some kind of tale, often continued from night to night, about a detective or baseball player or space traveler, and they would listen with droopy-eyed pleasure until we hit the "To Be Continued" point. It turns out, I was pretty good at it. I never knew where the material was coming from, but there seemed to be an ample supply of it. The stories made sense. There were heroes and bad guys.

There was justice and unfairness. There were conflicts and resolutions. When the story took a turn for the boring or incoherent, I knew it as quickly as they did. Putting the events into evolutionary terms, there was selection pressure on what I did. Because I shared some very important cognitive architecture with these ten-year-old kids, it was natural for me to keep the stories on target without laboring to do so.

If Camp Ferosdel had employed an actual Martian counselor, it's a safe bet that his or her (or its) stories about Mars would have left something to be desired. Assuming hypothetical Martians are very different creatures from us, their stories would probably not have entertained the campers; much of it might have been imponderable to a human consciousness. For example, humans do their everyday counting in what is called "base 10." (We use ten digits between 0 and 9.) We also happen to have ten fingers, which is probably more than a coincidence. If Martians turn out to have two arms, each containing three fingers, their counting system may be built on base 6. That's the least of the differences we might find, and it alone might pose some interesting communication problems. If you want to hear stories about life on Mars, it's a much better plan to get someone on Earth to make them up. They may not be accurate, but they sure will be satisfying.

Think about these things when you examine the deities who populate the world's religions.

ABNER DOUBLEDAY, ELVIS, AND CREATION MYTHS

There is no shortage of creation myths. Virtually every culture and religion has one. They approach a common question (Where do we come from?) and, as any anthropologist will tell you, they provide a dazzling array of answers. If one of these myths is correct, which I doubt, then all the rest (which provide conflicting details) must be wrong.

But even if creation myths provide social cohesion and the illusion of understanding one of life's mysteries, it is quite telling that they all get it wrong. You'd think some portion of human groups would stumble on an accurate answer, but they do not. Almost every human mind on the planet has, individually or collectively, addressed a common question and come up with the wrong answer. That is quite an indictment of this piece of evolved software with which we process information. There is so much that our minds do well, yet in certain domains we find it difficult to rise above our Pleistocene default settings. This is not to say that questions about origins or starting points can never be answered. Of course, they can. We can ask, "Who was the first president of the United States?" and expect an uncontroversial answer.

But when the topic shifts from the first president to the first human, or at least to the origin of humans, the results become controversial. Is it simply because opposing belief systems—in this case, religion versus science—are involved? Would the "first president" question be equally controversial if religion and American history each had a strong stake in the issue? This seems unlikely. Instead, the problem seems to lie in the *kinds* of accounts offered by science, in this case, versus religion and how well those accounts fit within our minds.

Consider what science has to offer: evolution, the fossil record, and anthropology. The simple truth is that none of these offers a particularly good story. Compared to the average creation myth, they're downright unmemorable. Even if one culture or generation were to get it right, these are not the sort of stories that transfer well between listeners. Pascal Boyer, Daniel Sperber, and Susan Blackmore have convincingly shown that certain types of stories contain elements that are well remembered and transmitted between individuals and generations.[5] Our minds are not unbiased receivers and transmitters of information. They are highly selective in what they are likely to understand and repeat. All variations—or, to use Richard Dawkins's term, all *memes*—are not created equal. They do not stand an equal chance of retention and transmission. The parallels between memetic and genetic evolution are striking. Just as some phenotypes will thrive and spread throughout the species, so too will certain ideas, stories, or myths be highly successful in the telling and remembering.

All the creation myths out there today are already evolutionary winners. Like a child's game of "telephone," they have all been shaped into a form that is most likely to be transmitted and retained. Although evolution is difficult to imagine because we can rarely see the losers, there were many alternate myths that did not have what it took to move from person to person and pass through succeeding generations with a minimum of change. Like unsuccessful physical mutations, most of them are no longer available for examination. They were "selected out."

Creation myths have a decided advantage over genetic mutations. The latter are simply copying errors in an organism's DNA and there is no guarantee that they will confer any selective advantage on the individual. In fact, most of them will not. However, myths are quite another story, so to speak. They are not drawn from a random array of possibilities. On the contrary, they hold a very strong advantage. Myths and stories were all created by human minds. That guarantees that some filtering has already taken place. Just as the human mind is only capable of grasping and transmitting certain kinds of information, so too is it limited in what it can invent. There is a strong likelihood that this creativity will lie squarely within the range of what the mind can comprehend.

In a 1989 article in the magazine *Natural History*, Steven Jay Gould offers some fascinating insights into our search for creation myths.[6] Gould draws a thoughtful analogy between our need to identify the starting point of our own species as well as that of baseball. This strikes me as important. It shows that ultimately the problem has nothing to do with religion, per se. We are hungry, even to the point of being blindly uncritical, for stories about where, when, and by whom things began. To be successful, these stories should offer precise dates, places, and protagonists (whether natural or supernatural). Gould is clear that if we make such demands in areas as mundane as baseball, we are certainly going to do it when the origin of our own species is concerned.

Gould's point is that the quest for such information, even when it conflicts with reasonable evidence and common sense, is a driving force in our need to *know* or to bring order to the world around us. We are here; that much is certain. So is baseball. Surely, there must have been a time when neither we nor baseball were here. Somewhere between then and now, things changed. We need to know when, where, and how that happened. Preference will be given to accounts that provide a location, a causal agent, and a date. Whenever possible, this information should be specified in frames of reference or timescales we can readily understand. In this regard, the idea of a 5,000-year-old Earth is a lot easier to grasp than one that is 5 billion years old.

I will add a third example of our quest for origins that follows the same pattern. Because of my involvement in popular music, I often hear the question, "Where did rock 'n' roll come from?" or "What was the first rock 'n' roll record?" This question allows us to identify the artist (causal agent) and date. The premise is that rock 'n' roll *started* with a particular record, whose details can be specified. Although the essential information about rock music's origins is, like baseball's, quite trivial when compared to the origin of our species, the mentality behind all three questions appears to be the same. They are drawn by our *need* to know as well as limitations in our *ability* to know. They all presume a discrete starting point as opposed to a gradual evolution. The latter, while often true, is simply harder to grasp and less satisfying.

If I, as a pop culture historian, am interviewed and asked for the name of the first rock 'n' roll record, I can be a real crowd pleaser and answer, "Oh, that's easy. It was Elvis Presley. His record of *That's All Right* was released on Sun 209 in July 1954."[7] In fact, if I really want to show off, I might instead select Jackie Brenston's record *Rocket 88*, released on the Chess label and recorded in Memphis in 1951. My interviewer might reply, "That's three years before Elvis," to which I would respond, "Yes, but this record was made in the same location at Sun Records, 706 Union Avenue in Memphis." This may all seem rather silly, but there are numerous books and articles in respectable magazines and journals that dwell on such matters in precisely this way. It is far easier to get one's mind around an intuitively obvious time like the 1950s and a cultural hotbed of musical hybrids like Memphis. You may not have heard of Jackie Brenston, but at least you now have a name to put on the plaque that will no doubt commemorate the event and draw tourists and music fans to the spot. We've got the who, the when, and the where in terms that make closet creationists happy.

Consider the alternative: When asked to name the first rock 'n' roll record, I might reply, "That's really a very difficult question. In fact, there may not *be* any answer. Rock 'n' roll evolved from many musical forms. It took decades to bring all the ingredients together into something that is recognizable as rock music. It was a slow, painstaking process that occurred over time in fits and spurts. There were many innovations. Some were dead ends; others were incorporated into what would eventually become 'rock 'n' roll.' As such, there was no 'first record,' which means there is no single causal agent (singer/musician), no place, and no date. As we get closer to the rock 'n' roll revolution that occurred around 1955, more and more records sounded similar to what we now recognize as rock 'n' roll. It's not always easy to see how the earlier versions are connected to the present form, but there are identifiable things about those early records that reveal the gradual evolution of the music. So, much as it makes life simpler to think of a clear starting point (name/date/place), it is more meaningful to think of musical styles as things that evolve slowly with no clear beginning point or end. No magic date, no street corner studio, and no first artist."

Can you imagine the impact of such an answer? If pressed for specifics, I could mention a slew of 1940s titles in a related genre called "country boogie" that fed right into the 12-bar format that early rock 'n' roll incorporated. I could even go back to the 1920s and 1930s and point to recordings by Jimmie Rodgers or Robert Johnson that influenced rock artists more than half a century later. And what about the emotional vocal styles of pre-rockers like Frankie Laine, Dean Martin, or Johnny Ray, whose performances influenced Elvis and, through him, a multitude of early rockers? Sam Cooke[8] came from the black gospel tradition, another genre that was co-opted by early rock 'n' roll. Indeed, Cooke's earliest records appeared on the Specialty label, which gave voice to Little Richard, an iconic figure in rock history. The lines weave, crosspollinate, and end in a hopeless tangle from which no clear starting point emerges. Just like any evolutionary account, this offers little comfort or satisfaction to those questing for clear origins. By now, the person interviewing me wishes he had never asked the question. His eyes have glazed over and the audience has probably changed the station.

Having drawn the analogy to music, let me briefly deliver Gould's case against creation myths in baseball. Because baseball fans are also closet creationists operating with an imperfect human mind, they also want to know the who, when, and where of baseball's origin. Although actual historical records clearly paint a very different picture, the plaque at the Baseball Hall of Fame offers exactly what fans are looking for. Abner Doubleday invented baseball in Cooperstown, New York, in 1839. What could be tidier? The comfort of a creation myth speaks to our species far more convincingly than history, evolution, or paleontology. The idea that baseball *evolved* slowly from related bat and ball games played for centuries on different continents is more difficult to grasp and far less satisfying. As Stephen Jay Gould has argued, "Too few people are comfortable with evolutionary modes of explanation in any form." Once more, the creationist *Poof!* is more compelling to our minds than the cumulative effects of slow change.

SMART VIRUSES

The June 18, 2007, issue of *Time* magazine featured an article by medical columnist Alice Park about what she called drug-resistant "bugs."[9] The article outlines the usual litany of concerns about our excessive use of antibiotics and how this, in turn, ups the ante in our arms race with bacteria and viruses. The article concluded that our present practices might yield a new generation of microorganisms that are more resistant to our present arsenal of drugs. The article is peppered with Darwinian concepts like "selection," "mutation," and "extinction." The casualness with which these ideas are introduced reminds us how intuitively appealing basic Darwinian concepts are. Few people seem threatened when they are applied to microorganisms, rather than to beings like ourselves. That in itself seems odd. Aren't the fundamental principles of natural selection the same, regardless of whether they are acting on a porcupine, a paramecium, or a person? Are the laws of gravity different for your cousin or your cat?

In any case, what is particularly relevant to our concerns is that in order to communicate what's happening out there at a molecular level, the entire natural selection process has been translated into language that makes it even easier to grasp. Unfortunately, that translation may distort what is really going on.

Park (or *Time* magazine's editorial department) refers to the new generation of microorganisms ("bugs," if you prefer) as being "smart." This may be a dangerous choice of words. To many persons—myself included—*smart* suggests things like *mentally alert* or synonyms like *clever, bright,* or *witty.* Smart individuals can analyze the situations they encounter, sort through their existing options, and select or synthesize their best response in order to maximize success.

This gives a lot of credit to a single-celled organism. In fact, no such credit is due. While it is true that natural selection has resulted in the survival of mindless "bugs" that stand a better chance of making it through the defenses we throw at them, it has nothing whatsoever to do with their being smart in the sense that humans normally understand that term.

But it sure does make the biological arms race easy to understand. These bugs must be smart because they have beaten us at our own game, right? We can agree that in order for us to come up with the antibiotics, we had to be smart. We had to think, extrapolate, speculate, and do all those things that smart humans, especially scientists, do. But our opponents did not. They had merely to experience a differential survival rate in the face of what we threw at them. In other words, some survived and some did not. We don't think of the viruses that died as "stupid." Well, neither should we describe the ones that survived and reproduced as smart. The real process is a lot simpler than that. Some heritable differences made it through the filter we created. The survivors got to reproduce, thus creating more offspring that share the tiny genetic advantage that conferred immunity to our arsenal.

Maybe this is nitpicking. Perhaps most people who read that article in *Time* magazine will understand that "smart" is just a metaphor. But do those readers understand that, in place of glib metaphors like "smart," there is a straightforward biological mechanism called natural selection that accounts for what happened?

That this mechanism works all around them, to produce morphological changes and, eventually, new species? Perhaps some people do understand this, but in a nation where more than half the citizens (and their elected political leaders) claim not to "believe in evolution" or argue that it's "just a theory," it is not altogether clear that *Time*'s looseness of language is such a good idea. Authors like Steven Pinker and Richard Dawkins (in books like *How the Mind Works* and *The Selfish Gene*) show that explanations can remain simple without sacrificing accuracy. It is one thing to suggest, for example, that bacteria act *as if* they have their own conscious agendas. It is quite another thing to suggest to an uncritical audience that bacteria *do* have agendas. In this sense, the *Time* article by Alice Park has squandered a golden opportunity to educate.

DISTORTING PROBABILITY

We are generally not a clever species when it comes to understanding probability. Nassim Nicholas Taleb has written a widely acclaimed best seller about the massive impact of what he calls *Black Swans*, highly improbable and unpredictable events. Taleb believes that "you can't be a modern intellectual and not think probabilistically." Yet he argues that when it comes to probabilities, so-called experts rarely are and, as consumers, most of us are "beyond suckers." Steven Jay Gould concurs, noting that if we humans understood probabilities better, Las Vegas would still be a truck stop in the desert.

The problem seems to be that when confronted with partial or probabilistic information, we are hit by a cognitive one-two punch: Not only do our mental calculators fail to work accurately, but we have a battery of hair-trigger coincidence detectors waiting to jump in and wring fanciful conclusions about what lies before us. We saw ample evidence of this in chapter 3 in our discussion of Jung and synchronicity.

Here's another example of a probability distortion. Let's assume you and I decide to play a game that requires thirteen cards. I carefully shuffle the deck and deal us each a hand: thirteen randomly drawn cards from a normal deck of fifty-two. So far, so good. Open your hand slowly and examine it. Nothing special there—an assortment of high and low numbers, a few picture cards, maybe examples of all four suits. Pretty unremarkable. No magical/mystical event modules in your mind have been triggered yet. But wait—the probability of that hand, the very one you are holding, occurring by chance alone was somewhere in the neighborhood of 1 in 635,013,559,600. Why aren't you jumping up and down?

In fact, why aren't we jumping up and down every time a hand is dealt? We've just been handed a singular event that occurs by chance about once in every 635 *billion* shuffles of the cosmic deck. You don't believe it? Shuffle the deck and deal thirteen cards again. Did you get the same hand? Nope. How about next time? No again. In fact, if you did nothing for the rest of your life but receive shuffled hands of thirteen cards once a minute, twenty-four hours a day, seven days a week, fifty-two weeks a year for seventy-five years, it is virtually certain that you'd never see that hand again. That's how improbable it was. You can even pass the franchise along to your heirs and let them continue to receive shuffled hands of thirteen cards at the rate of one per minute for the next ten thousand generations and they'd be unlikely to see that particular hand you just drew. That's how many possible thirteen-card hands are in the deck and how rare your original hand actually was. But somehow, none of this impresses you very much. That hand sure didn't look so special when it was dealt to you.

Imagine that I had dealt you all thirteen hearts in the deck. *Now* we have something to talk about! "Incredible!" you'll say. "I bet the odds of that happening are low as hell." And you're absolutely right. They are in fact, 1 in 635,013,559,600. Does that number look familiar? The average person has to work hard to get his mind around that. How can those two probabilities be the same? One of those hands was totally *ordinary* and the other was unique! In fact, that hand full of hearts would probably get your Jungian synchronicity detector working. Maybe this is a good day to go out and buy a lottery ticket. You might be on a roll! The universe is sending you a message. Say yes to that Internet stock offer. Go ask that special person to marry you. Strike while the iron is hot!

Here, once again, you can see that one-two punch: a faulty

information processor (it evolved before probabilities were a major part of our information universe) and an overactive agency/pattern detector. So why does a hand of thirteen hearts seem so exceptional while that other hand seems so ordinary? Mundane things must have a higher probability of occurrence, right? Wrong. The simple fact is that the "random" unexceptional hand you were dealt a moment ago is just as unlikely as any *particular* hand in the deck. There are, in fact, over 635 billion of them just waiting for you. The confusion comes from the fact that you have mentally lumped all "undistinguished" hands together into a single category. There is even a name for this mental mistake. Psychologists call it the *representativeness bias*. It's one of the easiest ways to distort calculations of probability.

There may only be a couple of dozen hands that would strike you as exceptional: for example, all hearts, spades, clubs, or diamonds, or perhaps six of one suit and seven of another. You might also find clusters of four jacks, queens, and kings an equally noteworthy hand, regardless of the thirteenth card. You have some intuitive sense of a "special hand" and you also know (from previous card-playing experience) that its probability is low. The trouble is, Caveman Logic has lumped all unexceptional hands together *as a group* that they don't really belong to. Collectively, they do have a much greater likelihood of occurrence. But taken as individual events, which is what they are, they are every bit as exceptional as a straight flush from ace to king. They, too, are cause for celebration from a statistical point of view, even though they won't win you anything in a card game.

This example offers an easy way to see—some people would say to *feel*—just how poorly our minds are designed to understand probabilities. The basic principle becomes easier to grasp if we reduce the numbers drastically and move from playing cards to a drawer full of socks. If you own a dozen pairs, only one of which is orange, what is the probability of reaching blindly into the full drawer and pulling out the orange pair? Most people understand the answer to be 1 in 12, or .0833333. Does that mean reaching in there twelve times will guarantee you success? Of course not. By continuing to sample from that drawer of twelve pairs, there's a good chance you will repeat some of the earlier choices before you finally grab the orange pair. It may take fifteen or twenty tries, or you may hit the orange pair the very first time. That's precisely what might happen with our deck of cards. And remember that "non-orange" is not a single category. It consists of eleven different outcomes (e.g., blue, red, black, brown), every one of which has the same probability as orange. Chances are, you'll receive some of those "losing" hands or socks a second time before you finally get to the one you were looking for.

ROLL THEM BONES

Gambling is a wonderful place to look for distortions in human perception and cognition. Although life and death are rarely at stake, the experience is usually symbolically strong enough to trigger some pretty fundamental circuitry. Researchers interested in perceptual distortions, cognitive biases, and errors in judgment and decision making have invested major effort studying those who gamble.

Just to be clear, we are not talking about *pathological* gambling. The kinds of errors and distortions that are studied are by no means the work of diseased or abnormal minds. That's just the point. These mental deficiencies are likely to occur in normal people whenever a hand of cards is dealt or a pair of dice are rolled. There is an entire literature of such cognitive research including journals dedicated solely to studies of gambling behavior (*Journal of Gambling Studies, International Gambling Studies*) as well as those with overlapping interests (*Journal of Behavioral Decision Making*). The results have revealed a fairly consistent and not altogether glowing report about how our minds work when information is fragmentary and probabilities are involved.

Gambling situations differ in how much control the gambler actually has (e.g., betting on the lottery versus playing poker), but even in situations in which the gambler has no control over the outcome, most gamblers do a passable job of convincing themselves that some kind of control exists. It is a rare person who buys tickets at a local convenience store for some kind of state-supported numbers game and doesn't try to bring a measure of personal power (e.g., betting a child's birthdate) into a situation that is demonstrably out of his or her control.

People will tell you that they really *know* such strategies don't work, but such knowledge doesn't mesh with the results of studies in which gamblers provide ongoing verbal narratives during games of chance. Whether or not people truly understand what randomness or independence are, they certainly act as if these were alien concepts. For example, we are not only bad at recognizing randomness, but we cannot even do a passable job of creating it. Back in the precomputer days when psychology experiments needed a random number sequence, it was common knowledge that the worst strategy was to allow the experimenter or his assistant to make one up. They were almost invariably nonrandom in easily demonstrable ways. Embarrassingly, some research from my own lab[10] demonstrated that even rats could see right through our pathetic human attempts at randomness.

In 2003, Sevigny and Ladouceur[11] monitored the thoughts of gamblers before, during, and after playing a slot machine. Prior to the experience, 98 percent of subjects believed that the outcome of such games was primarily determined by chance. That number dropped slightly to 91 percent following the experience, but remained a sizable majority. However, during the game, in the heat of battle, as it were, the majority of subjects' thoughts were classified as erroneous and irrational. The authors suggested that two sets of beliefs exist and most subjects "double switch" effortlessly between them. Arguably, subjects know what is sane and reasonable and readily say it when interviewed by a psychologist. However, once thrust into the heat of the game, some other "self," whose perceptions are distorted and whose judgments are irrational, takes control of the body.

There does not appear to be a single study of gambling that doesn't underscore how irrationally humans behave. The extent of our mental malfunctioning is truly staggering. The research is not far-fetched; our mental deficiencies are simply that apparent.

The best known of these cognitive distortions is called the *gam-*

bler's fallacy. Imagine you are in a casino observing a roulette wheel being played. Incredibly, it has landed on red ten consecutive times. You may not have the binomial distribution with you, but you know that outcome seems pretty extreme. In fact, the odds of getting ten consecutive reds (in an unbiased red-black binary system) by chance alone are 1 in 1,024. Suddenly, someone hands you a thousand-dollar bill and tells you to bet it. What do you choose? This is where the gambler's fallacy kicks in. Most people will choose to bet on black. Why, you ask them? They will tell you "because black is overdue." In the great cosmic ledger book in the sky, in which black and red have equal probabilities of occurring, we're going to have to play some serious catch-up to get black back up to that 50 percent total. This trial is as good a place as any to start compensating.

Interestingly, those who do not bet on black tell you they have to choose red. Why, you ask? Because, they explain, there's obviously something amiss with this roulette wheel and it's clear that whatever mechanical or ethical quirk is at fault here, it's going to keep on happening.

The truth is, it's hard to fault either account and harder yet to see why they represent some kind of breakdown in mental functioning. But they do. The reason is simply that in both cases the bettor has failed to realize that each spin of the wheel is an independent event, neither influenced by nor influencing any adjacent trial. In short, the real probability of rolling an eleventh red after ten consecutive reds is not 1 in 2,048, but 1 in 2. Most people will simply tell you that account feels wrong. And so we have a handful of psychologists telling the rest of the human race that they shouldn't listen to mental circuitry that has taken hundreds of thousands of years to evolve.

This impasse is tied to the fact that gambling casinos are every bit as unnatural environments as psychology labs. In the real world events are *not* typically independent of each other. You can, indeed you *should*, use past cases as predictors of present ones. In that sense, gambling casinos, like psychology labs, are dangerous and misleading places where unnatural things can happen. Casinos are not registered charities. They are there to take your money and they depend on your making foolish choices. Your mental modules can get you into trouble, but that is not because they are faulty. It is because the environments in which they evolved are very different from where they are being tested. If you can anticipate that and take a moment to second-guess the messages delivered by those modules, you'll be in much better shape.

The usually unstated corollary is that such mental errors are not confined to gambling. Gambling is simply a value-neutral way to trigger irrationality. There is no other domain in which we dare hold the human mind up to such ridicule. We *know* what is correct in a gambling experiment. If a person believes that a previous outcome on a roulette wheel influenced the present one, we can say, "No, it didn't. Your perception is faulty. We are right and you are wrong." We do not have to worry about being politically incorrect or offending a powerful group who can affect our advertising revenue or our national security. Who cares if we tell some nitwit at a roulette wheel that he is seriously deluded? Hardly anyone will come to his defense. But can you imagine telling someone that winning the lottery was not proof of the power of prayer? In social or political terms, not all Caveman Logic is created equal. The underlying mechanisms may be the same, but the manner in which these distortions are expressed runs the gamut from silly to sacrosanct.

And so, using gambling as a venue to study mental distortions is socially acceptable. In fact, it is even highly valued. It's not that humans are in a hurry to discover the inadequacies of their minds. Rather, the major impetus for studying these cognitive distortions—at least as far as the public is concerned—is the alleviation of problem gambling. Problem gambling is bad, and we want to "cure" it like we do any other addiction. Such research is thus on the side of the angels; it will reduce human suffering. Of course, try to take our findings from gambling research and apply them to everyday, socially supported situations and one will find a quick end to government funding for this line of research.

THE VIRTUE OF A DESIGN FLAW

Just ask any of my colleagues who happen to be in their forties, fifties, or sixties and they will be only so glad to tell you what is wrong with their memories. This litany of complaints runs the gamut from petty annoyances ("I've lost my car keys again," "I can't remember that student's name") to more serious concerns about incipient Alzheimer's disease. Few people I know are happy with how their memories are working.

Part of the problem is that we are keenly aware of the occasional frustrating or embarrassing flaws and almost oblivious to the majority of cases when our memories serve us well. This alone makes us highly suspect as data analysts, since we are prone to what we have previously labeled as the confirmation bias ("I have a rotten memory and now I'm going to collect evidence to prove it.") Worse yet, we are unlikely to view those occasional lapses as evidence of something good. However, rather than signaling that we are going straight to cognitive hell, such infuriating glitches might actually suggest that everything is working according to factory specifications. In *The Seven Sins of Memory*,[12] Daniel Schacter concludes that memory's most common failings are "by-products of otherwise adaptive features of memory, a price we pay for processes and functions that serve us well in many respects."

The problem is simply that the architecture of our memories has been designed by evolution to serve us well in the *majority* of cases. And it does. But, by definition, there will be exceptions in which the same strategies fall flat, leaving us to wonder how human memory, especially our own, can be so flawed. Experimental psychologists and cognitive neuroscientists love to design situations to short-circuit normal memory. Such research is not necessarily geared to discrediting the facets of cognition that have served us and our ancestors well. Rather, it allows us to understand the mechanisms of memory more clearly by revealing its boundary conditions.

Here are some examples: We cannot possibly recall all the information to which we have been exposed. It is reasonable, even desirable, to set aside information (like unused phone numbers) that we no longer actively require. On those occasions when we are required to retrieve such dormant information, we are likely to come up empty. Is this really a design flaw? Perhaps it feels that way during the palpable struggle for retrieval. But consider the alternative: everything is slavishly encoded and stored. Nothing is lost. The trade-off seems obvious. Yes, that dormant phone number (or old license plate) can be retrieved, but the entire system is slowed down by the sheer weight of storing and retrieval of all-but-useless information.

Schacter goes on to detail a variety of cases in which forgetting is a virtue and how the inhibition of irrelevancies keeps us functional in a constantly demanding world. But there are downsides to occasional problems with human memory as well. The effects of suggestibility can have devastating effects on courtroom testimony. Confusion about the source of a memory (even when the content itself is intact) can lead to misattribution or unintentional plagiarism. There are numerous instances of this in the music business, for example, when a composer mistakenly believes that he has written a melody, which in fact stems from an earlier listening experience whose source has been forgotten. Examples of this include well-known composers and compositions: George Harrison's "My Sweet Lord" turned out to be an unconsciously plagiarized version of "He's So Fine" by the Chiffons. Not even jazz musicians are immune to the process. The jazz anthem "Misty" came to Erroll Garner during a dream, he often reported. He may have been sleeping, but the song he was dreaming of was called "Ebb Tide," which was a major pop hit at the very time Garner spontaneously wrote "Misty."

These are obviously not life-threatening events, but, along with errors in eyewitness testimony and false memories, they do underscore the fact that our cognitive architecture, designed to solve certain types of problems faced by our ancestors, is far from perfect in the modern world. In their 2008 paper, "Adaptive Memory: Remembering with a Stone-Age Brain,"[13] James Nairne and Josefa Pandeirada approach memory as if it were a treasure trove of evidence for Darwinian natural selection. Memory is a package. Its faults are, in Schacter's words, "an integral part of the mind's heritage because they are so closely connected to features of memory which make it work well." Sue Halpern concurs in her 2008 book, *Can't Remember What I Forgot*. Never mind that detailed information about deterioration of the hippocampus or the prefrontal cortex. The bottom line is that it is normal to forget, and such forgetting is not inevitably linked to pathology such as the dreaded Alzheimer's disease.

Memory lapses are not a major cause of Caveman Logic. But similar consequences of how our minds work, such as superstition or religion, are. They follow the same paradigm we have just discussed with regard to memory. They are based on cognitive malfunctions that turn out, under closer scrutiny, to be evidence not of design flaws but rather of the misapplication of otherwise useful circuits. Superstition and religion are the "I've lost my keys" of information processing. But unlike memory lapses—which are generally disdained—superstition and religion are valued and enshrined in a society of key-losers, who somehow view such glitches as a higher form of functioning.

EXPLOITING MENTAL DEFICIENCIES

More and more authors today are trying to raise your consciousness about our mental shortcomings, alert you to the kinds of mistaken beliefs you may be drawn to, and give you tools to immunize you against these mistakes or to correct them.

Not everyone wants to see such growth. Certainly, many religious leaders do not want you to transcend your Pleistocene mind for reasons we have explored. Likewise, the purveyors of much alternative medicine and New Age spirituality do not want you to get smart. They make money on your Caveman Logic and, like everyone else, they have mortgages to pay and food to buy for their children.

There is another group that trades on your mental inadequacies. This group will require little defending to the average person. They are lawyers. Lawyer jokes ("What does a lawyer use for birth control? Answer: His personality") are more frequent than blonde jokes on the Internet. Like all opportunistic foragers among us, lawyers find and exploit mental weaknesses in those around them.

Attorneys routinely screen potential jurors, seeking to exclude those who may be unsympathetic to their goals. But such pre-screening is never 100 percent effective. When all is said and done, attorneys face twelve men and women who may have been screened for race, ethnicity, age, religion, or other biasing factors. But they are still human. Unless they are very special, they will still be vulnerable to the mental deficiencies we are discussing in this book. The courtroom is no place to remedy it; it is a place to exploit it. Juries can be played, manipulated, and taken advantage of. The interesting thing is that in order to exploit Caveman Logic, you have to know that it exists. How did lawyers get so smart?

Obviously, as a group, they are no smarter than anyone else. So they hire consultants. Consultants, like lawyers, range from very savvy to a total waste of time and money. The savvy among them are likely to have consulted the specialized corners of the psychological literature. Maybe they've read the very books or articles we've been referring to. Maybe they've read *this* book. In any case, they are likely to learn things like "people are generally very bad at reasoning with probabilities." Most people are also confused about the difference between "possible" and "probable." You can watch this confusion spelled out nearly weekly on some version of the TV series *Law & Order*. Imagine some outrageously improbable alternative scenario: Instead of some ex–football star murdering his wife in a fit of jealous rage, perhaps aliens from Jupiter landed in his backyard and roughed her up, before taking off again unseen. Now imagine the defense attorney grilling the forensic expert, who is there to deny the plausibility of this account. "But is it *possible* that it happened this way?" he finally asks. "Possible? (Exasperated pause) I suppose so, technically speaking but . . ." "Thank you," the defense lawyer says, walking away quickly and cutting off the witness. Possible means "not impossible" and to many people that is equivalent to "reasonable doubt. " Amazingly, some jurors are ready to acquit on such testimony.

The defense attorney was smart: plainly smarter than the people he was dealing with. They should have known that virtually anything is possible. That in itself is a meaningless piece of information. Possibility is a binary variable and most events in the universe probably lie on the positive side of it. What jurors really want to know is whether it was *probable*, and if so, *how* probable. That answer is not binary (yes/no); it can be located along a continuum. And so, a good prosecutor might have said, "Redirect, your honor? Doctor, you appeared to have something else to say before my colleague stopped your response. Would you share that information with us now?" To which, the expert might reply, "Thank you. Yes, I wanted to add that while a murder by men from Jupiter is technically possible, it is such a low-probability event that it can realistically be excluded as an account of this crime. The probability of it happening, given everything we know about life here on Earth and in our universe, is conservatively more than a trillion to one. In other words, "possible," sure. But likely? About as likely as the sky turning purple and raining dollar bills over Newark tomorrow morning. In fact, your honor, the purple sky and dollar shower seem far more likely to me than the hit men from Jupiter." Now *that* is the kind of testimony a jury can get its teeth into.

Remember, juries are drawn from the human race. You can count on some species-wide human deficiencies being present in the courtroom. Those expert witnesses can drone on and on about the probability of this or that happening being very high or very low, but the jurors are likely to glaze over when the reasoning gets statistical. Their ancestors didn't understand probabilities back in the Pleistocene Age, and most of their descendants haven't done a whole lot to remedy that flaw. Prosecuting attorneys know exactly how to phrase their presentations or cross-examinations or, worse yet, how to openly distort perfectly good information that has been presented by experts.

"If people are going to continue to behave stupidly," an anonymous attorney friend of mine said recently, "then I'm going to continue to take advantage of it." He was talking about juries and their gullibility. He used the term *blind spot* to describe some of the themes in this book. Had he known the phrase *Caveman Logic*, he might have used it. Blind spots are gaps or loopholes in our ability to think logically. As long as we do not see them as gaps, blind spots, or loopholes, and as long as they are socially supported, there is little hope they will be remedied. It goes way beyond selling some more snake oil or scamming the results of a jury trial. We're talking about allowing humanity to descend further into ignorance and superstition when a world of wonder stands ready for us to discover.

GOD HATES TELEVISION

Bad things happen all the time. Even to good people. Sometimes they are the result of an agent who means you no good. Reasons like a grudge or vendetta lie well within the realm of the natural world. Sometimes bad things happen for no "reason" in the sense we usually use the term. You slip on the ice and fall, breaking your leg. You get into a car accident. Your dog dies. Surely, there are "causes" for all of these events—for example, your dog had leukemia—but they are not at the level of understanding most people seek. Caveman Logic demands a different kind of account. *Who* did that to me? *Why* did he do it to me? *How* can I make him stop doing this? Whether a disciple of voodoo, a believer in New Age spirituality with an aversion to coincidence, or an average God-fearing American with a guilty conscience—all are predisposed to look for a powerful agent who watches and punishes.

Few people are inclined to humor when examining unpleasant events in their own lives and what they might "mean." But sometimes when we step outside our own experience, the results of such Caveman Logic can seem mighty funny. I've recently finished reading Michael Ritchie's fascinating book on the history of early television called *Please Stand By*.[14] Ritchie describes enough technical disasters to convince anyone with a healthy dollop of Pleistocene reasoning that some deity was personally invested in the failure of early television. For example, the BBC, after screening hundreds of applicants, hired two young women for their new television news program in 1935 (the British were well ahead of Americans in the development of mass-market TV). On the day of the show's premiere in 1936, one woman was confined to home with a throat infection and the second—her emergency replacement—was hospitalized with an emergency appendectomy. What were the odds of two no-shows after all the months of preparation and screening? It appears that God, dead set against British television, was flexing his powerful muscles.

Similarly, the day full-scale telecasting was scheduled to begin in Los Angeles, the region was hit by a major earthquake. Compared to the Brits, this event seemed absolutely biblical in scope. You can bet that when it came time to "make sense" out of what had transpired, the notion of "punishment" or a powerful agent with an agenda was raised.

Both of these "coincidences" are instructive. They contain the kind of cognitive distortions that keep tabloids in business and tabloid readers confined to the Pleistocene era in terms of their understanding of the world around them. Admittedly, the probability of those particular women being indisposed on the same day, especially the premiere of a show they had just been hired to host, is quite low. However, the distortion lies in the way this evidence has been evaluated. The focus was never really on *these* two women, but rather on any event that could have been interpreted as "bad luck" surrounding early television. If we truly believed that God did not want early television to succeed, then there were numerous events (*multiple endpoints*, to use the term we've discussed earlier) that could have supported our view and that manage to seem like low-probability outcomes.

There is something else to be learned here. The earthquake that occurred in Southern California in the 1930s was presumably a random occurrence in the geological course of events. If you studied the tectonic plates in question, you might have predicted that such a quake was more likely than not in the next fifty years, but its occurrence hardly astonished geologists or required supernatural explanations. However, consider the countless millions of human events taking place on the day of the earthquake. How might some of those coincidences looked to the persons involved? Mothers gave birth on the day of the quake. Persons died. Would the occurrence of the quake on that particular day have prompted some—arguably unwarranted—assumptions about how God felt about the passages in their lives? Should the families of those who were born or died the day *before* the earthquake have felt cheated (unloved by God) or reprieved (spared from this negative omen)?

Consider a young woman on her way to an illicit sexual liaison, or a young man who had just screamed at or hit a loved one? Might they view the earthquake as something provoked by their wrongdoing? A message from God? "I screamed 'Goddamn you' to my wife (or husband or child) and immediately the earth moved and buildings fell." Can we blame such a person for making the connection, even if we know that none really exists? The fact that there were tens, maybe hundreds of millions of things going on that day begs the question: Which of them provoked the earthquake? They couldn't all have done so. The fact that some "innocent" people may have died in that quake makes it a costly thing for a vengeful deity to have used to signal some woman to stop having an affair. Admittedly, *she* may have read the event as a message, but was it really so? If we can see the error in her cognitive system that led her there, does that help to immunize us against making similar mistakes?

DOWNGRADING THE DEITY

Having designed a memorable and awe-inspiring deity, you might expect that humans would interact with him, her, or it in a dignified manner. You'd think that when faced with such an entity one would remain awestruck and silent, realizing that the scope and design of his plan was well beyond our comprehension, much less our control. But it turns out that the same evolutionary circuitry that drove us to construct this deity in mundane terms also dictates how we approach and negotiate with him. Because the underlying modules were originally designed for social exchange with other humans, the deity receives exactly what we have to offer, and no more. From an evolutionary point of view, there *is* no more to offer.

Short of a mutation in cognitive architecture, the best we might offer to whatever supernatural power hovers wordlessly around us is an honest professing of our lack of understanding. Such humility might be a good start, but it is unlikely to happen. Remember, humans did not invent supernatural agents with whom they could bargain so that these agents would remain aloof. It is our need to control things that drove us. And if that need produces some undignified and disrespectful groveling in the process, so be it.

The trouble is, when it's not the village chief we're dealing with but a grand, all-knowing, all-powerful supernatural entity, you'd think we'd upgrade our approach just a little bit. That we don't tells us something not only about the bargainer (and the limited mental software he's using), but also about the bargainer's view of the deity whose power is up for grabs. It's not a very respectful picture.

The limited scope of the deities we create and embrace is very similar to the limited imagination of 1950s science fiction movies. To today's audience, it seems laughable and rather quaint that all their fantasies and projections about the future reflect the limited technology and knowledge of the 1950s. "What else could they base them on?" you might ask. Philosophers even have a term to describe this limitation. It is called *epistemic constraint*. Fair enough, but then the same criticism can be leveled at the deities who populate the world's religions. How can we go beyond our own limited imaginations? Very few depict God as an infinite, abstract spirit, unknowable and unimaginable to creatures such as ourselves. Rather, they fill in the blanks with what they can imagine— just like the 1950s science fiction movies. The difference is, a half a century later we all know those movies were nonsense.

To the best of our knowledge, there is no published empirical survey of the content of prayer. Our experience and informal surveys suggest that beyond pure unqualified thanksgiving, the most common category found in human dialogue with a deity falls in the realm of "If you let my child live/give me this promotion at work/let my team prevail in the World Series, I will quit my drinking/stop having this affair." Clearly, the tendency for social exchange runs deep in the human mind. What is surprising is how indiscriminate it is.

It is a rare human who, believing in God, says, "I can't possibly understand you or your plan. The best I can offer is a humble 'Thank you.' Other than that, I'll sit back and let events unfold as you will them to. I will not disrespect you or shame myself by offering anything in trade for my wants, even though I accept that they are under your control. How could I be petty or presumptuous enough to believe that the rate at which I consume alcoholic beverages or mistresses will be a bargaining chip with you or affect your cosmic plan?"

Chapter 6

ASSIGNING THE BLAME
Television, Religion, Politics, and the Movies

A PERSON OF FAITH

Last week I spent some time talking to a friend I hadn't seen in a while. For some reason, the conversation got a bit more serious than it had before. I was conscious of trying to keep the exchange as lighthearted as possible, but I obviously failed.

"Don't you have faith?" she asked me, with genuine surprise in her voice.

For a moment I was absolutely stumped. I did a quick inventory of what I believed about my friends (including her), my job, my politics, my family, my favorite baseball team, and concluded that I was indeed a person of great faith. And I said so.

As you might imagine, this did not satisfy her. In fact, it provoked her. She thought I was being sarcastic. Perhaps even knowingly offensive.

"You know what I mean," she said. "Don't you believe in God? In Jesus Christ?"

"No to both," I replied. "Is that what you mean by faith?"

She gave me her best "talking to an idiot" face and the conversation soon came to an end.

When did the word *faith* become co-opted by the forces of religion? Is there no such thing anymore as faith in secular matters? Obviously, I had failed to read the October 27, 2006, *Harvard Crimson*, in which Steven Pinker pointed out that the word *faith* had officially become a euphemism for *religion*. Pinker noted that "an egregious example is the current [Bush] administration's 'faith-based initiatives,' so named because it is more palatable (and perhaps more legal) than religion-based initiatives."

Faith, at least the religious variety, has a number of curious properties. As far as I know, no form of secular faith follows any of these rules. The process is described in detail by Richard Dawkins in his book *A Devil's Chaplain*.[1] According to Dawkins, the more outrageous the belief, the "better" the faith. To have faith that the sun will rise tomorrow hardly raises eyebrows or marks one as a noteworthy person in the faith department. But to believe in a God who walks on water or comes back from the dead (or flies through the clouds or passes through walls, for that matter) is the kind of faith that will turn a few heads. In short, less evidence makes for better faith. Outrageous is good. Less is more in the faith business. Dawkins wonders whether "some religious doctrines are favored not *in spite of* being ridiculous but precisely *because* they are ridiculous."

My friend certainly took pride in her faith. She didn't just experience it quietly. Compared to me, she embraced all kinds of supernatural possibilities, and she was damn proud of them. She was also a bit surprised (and measurably disappointed) that I did not share her unsupported belief system. She and I will continue to talk about food, wine, and mutual friends, but "bigger issues" will probably now be on the taboo list. I am not a person of faith.

IS RELIGION THE PROBLEM?

The past five chapters have argued that, cognitively speaking, our species is a mess. Part of the problem lies in our mental apparatus itself. It's hard to fault our species for this. That would be like criticizing someone for being short or having brown eyes. There's no sense picking on the phenotype. For better or worse—and there is surely a case to be made for both—this is the hand our species was dealt.

But it's another matter to blame those individuals or institutions who exploit faulty perceptions or beliefs for power or profit. There is a huge opportunity to cash in on fear, pain, loneliness, and grief, and there is no shortage of practitioners in this department. How can we look at the history of our species over the past two thousand years and not conclude that religion is to blame for what is worst about us? From the Crusades to the atrocities of 9/11, religion always seems to be at the core of our greatest violence.

Yet we may be missing the bigger picture when we blame religion. Religion is not an external institution that has been imposed upon us to our detriment. It is misguided to claim, "If only this destructive thing could be expunged from our culture, we would be free to pursue higher, more peaceful callings." The truth is, if religion were not here today, we would be busy inventing it by tomorrow. The problem lies within the structure of our minds, not within the institutions they create. It may seem at times that these institutions are external to us, acting independently to subvert our progressive or peaceful instincts. But this view misses the underlying issue. Just as rap music or violent TV shows are not a root cause of societal ills, neither is religion. They are all products of the human mind and—especially in the case of religion—their occurrence is all but inevitable.

Granted, a particular pope or imam or TV evangelist may do some particularly nasty work, but the basic potential for violence and destruction of outsiders/nonbelievers is the deeper issue, and it predates any of history's villains. In some cases, removal of a particular leader may cause a movement to misfire, but its essential nature remains unchanged. There is an endless supply of replacement figures who are capable of energizing true believers toward destructive and violent ends. Undoubtedly, some of these leaders will be more charismatic than others, but it is unlikely that the basic process can be altered. In fact, this is doubly dangerous when martyrdom is a backbone of such belief systems. Killing a dangerous leader can ultimately strengthen his position.

The problem becomes worse year after year because of the growth of technology. There is absolutely no reason to believe that the fanaticism of present Islamic fundamentalism is any greater than that of thirteenth-century Christianity. What differs is the technology available to these two groups with which they can punish unbelievers. It is simply easier today to bring death and destruction on a mass scale. That they would do so without a second thought is fundamental to their religious fanaticism. There is no reason to believe that anything fundamental to human nature has changed. The fervor with which a neighboring village will be wiped out is driven by the same mental circuitry that leads one nation (or religion) to unleash its wrath on another. If the Crusaders had had mass media, airplanes, and dirty bombs available to them, rest assured they would have used them with gleeful abandon. And know also that they would have believed they were doing God's work and done so with that singularity of purpose that only religious conviction can provide.

So, in short, don't blame religion. Blame the cognitive architecture that gives rise, over and over again, to religion. We can deal with it each year or each decade, but it will continue to surface until there are some basic changes in our species, or in how reflexively we respond to those hardwired impulses. *That* is the agenda of this book. If I tell you that the leader of a theocratic state who was threatening to rain down nuclear destruction on all infidels has finally been assassinated and you reply, "Thank God," what have we gained?

RELIGION'S SPECIAL STATUS

Obviously it is not permissible in North American society to be openly critical of someone's religious views. This is true both in casual conversation as well as in the mass media.

To some extent, this is understandable. For one thing, America was founded upon an ideal of religious tolerance and we seem particularly touchy about anything that might call our views into question, even 230-plus years after the American Revolution was fought. But the problem seems to run a lot deeper than national history. What remains verboten is not simply restricting what someone can believe or which church he or she can join. Rather, it seems as if the very topic of religious belief has become taboo. Shortly after taking over the *CBS Evening News*, Katie Couric instituted a segment titled "Free Speech." The idea was to have prominent speakers briefly address some aspect of the topic in order to inspire discussion or, perhaps, trigger pride in how we as Americans carried on our business. In any case, one of the celebrities approached for the assignment was outspoken social critic Bill Maher, host of a weekly show on HBO called *Real Time with Bill Maher*.

As he reported on the September 16, 2006, episode of his show, Maher's experience was not quite what he had hoped. "I had them on a pedestal," Maher said of CBS News, invoking images of Edward R. Murrow and Walter Cronkite. However, it was a "deal breaker right from the start" when Maher told Couric's producers that the topic he would like to discuss was "religion." He was then given a list of "acceptable topics" about which he could practice free speech on her show. Maher's audience, a decidedly liberal crowd, howled with derisive laughter when this was reported. But the story really does not end there.

Free speech is a marvelous ideal, but it is rarely unrestricted as a matter of law. Here in Canada, where I have written much of this book, there are restrictions on what can be said in different venues. Ernst Zundel, a latter-day Nazi working as a high school teacher in Alberta, was fired from his job for repeatedly teaching his students that there was no Holocaust in World War II. Zundel's right to "free speech" stopped well short of distorting history and knowingly teaching it to his students as fact. Likewise, my colleagues and I do not have unlimited license to make sexist, racist, or other derisive remarks targeted at individuals or specific groups when we do our teaching. Nor would my university knowingly allow public speakers who appear on our campus to offer rants targeted at gender, sexual orientation, ethnic, or religious identity. This offense would be considered even more egregious if the speech were seen to instigate violence. Indeed, a "Let's go kill the Jews (or Catholics or Muslims)" speech would be viewed as a "hate crime" in Canada and treated as far more than a misdemeanor. I am happy to live in a nation that restricts "free speech" in this manner. Plainly it is a trade-off, but ultimately I believe it enhances the quality of life my fellow citizens and I are likely to enjoy.

A second addendum to my Bill Maher story concerns what happened next on his broadcast. Maher got lots of support from his studio audience for lampooning the "acceptable topics for free speech" edict by CBS. That lay within the liberal bias of the audience. But what he did next did not. Maher then proceeded to do a rant about the inconsistencies of religious belief—presumably as he would have done had he been given carte blanche on the *CBS Evening News*. The routine was not well received. Some laughed or tittered, but the response stopped short of the kind of enthusiastic rapture that often greets his tirades. It was simply not OK to laugh at the idiocy of religious beliefs and the people who hold them. "The nature of God" was not an acceptable topic for satire.

On the opening episode of *Studio 60*, producer Aaron Sorkin offered a behind-the-scenes look at a *Saturday Night Live*–type television show, on which the (fictional) producer is fired after the network cuts a four-minute sketch called "Crazy Christians."

"You can't have free speech without offending some people," he argues to no avail. The unanswered question is whether, on television anyway, such decisions are about money or cherished beliefs. Are network executives fearful that conservative religious groups will boycott a sponsor's products, causing them to withdraw financial support? Or, like many of us, do they simply hold that religious beliefs are off-limits to criticism or disdain? If so, such restriction should be seen in context. It is not off-limits to make fun of ethnicity, sexual preference, physical appearance, or intelligence (too much or too little). Just don't think of poking fun at someone's commitment to the supernatural.

I applaud Bill Maher for having the courage of his convictions and using his own television show as a platform for atheism.

Indeed, the points made by Maher struck me as a reasonable critique of one aspect of Caveman Logic. But the bigger issue here is that in the act of lampooning the CBS network for shying away from criticizing religiosity, Maher revealed the very reason they had done so. Most people, including liberals on social and political issues, are not atheists. Maher's audience, which seems to venerate him, is solidly behind his liberality. Atheism is another matter. The audience was not ready to detach themselves from the cognitive distortions that fuel supernatural thinking. Worse yet, people can get really testy when you hold their beliefs, indefensible as they may be, up to ridicule. They may not stop watching your show or boycott your sponsor's products, but they sure as hell won't laugh along with your comments.

Richard Dawkins has repeatedly argued that ideas are ideas. They all compete in the marketplace—as do physical traits (phenotypes). Only the best survive. That is, in fact, how you define success in evolutionary terms. Not the prettiest, not the brightest, but those that enjoy greatest reproductive success: those that successfully make it through into the next generation and ultimately spread in the population. Ideas are like phenotypes. They are subject to immense competition—selection pressure, if you will. As Dawkins has put it, ideas need to be "attacked." Maybe a more socially acceptable term is *challenged*. In any case, they have to encounter some turbulence or we'll never know how viable they are. If an idea withstands the challenge, it continues to live another day, to be transmitted from person to person for yet another day. If the idea cannot withstand the challenge, then down it goes. The junk pile of ideas is large. It is far larger than the number of ideas we presently hold. Phrenology didn't make it through. Neither did the belief that Earth lies at the center of the universe. A lot of ideas have fallen under the weight of new evidence, as they should. This weeding out is crucial for the expanding knowledge base of our species. Debate and challenge are fair game, even essential to the process.

Why, then, is religion immune to this process? The answer is rooted in social rules. It is simply not polite to challenge religious beliefs. It is perfectly OK to risk offending spoon benders or psychics, but if you question the doctrine of papal infallibility or, for that matter, the existence of God as a guiding, controlling force in our everyday lives, you are violating the rules of polite social discourse.

As a university professor, I am rather careful when I tread on to the path of religion. There are powerful forces out there (very much of the natural world) that would challenge my right to academic freedom were I to dwell on someone's religious beliefs or seriously call them into question. Flat Earthers are fair game; Christians, Muslims, Jews, or Hindus are not. If I were to repeat Christopher Hitchens's case against Mother Teresa[2] or utter his description of her as "the ghastly bitch from Hell," I would no doubt find myself in a meeting with my department chairman, dean, or university president. If I were to describe Darwin (or Lysenko) as an idiot, I would probably find I had carte blanche to do so. By not offering challenges to religious belief systems, we allow them to stagnate. In evolutionary terms, we are probably even weakening them.

SEPARATING GOD FROM MORALITY

Putting aside "taxation without representation" for the moment, wasn't America founded on the basis of religious freedom? Isn't the right to worship the supernatural entities of your choice a fundamental right, enshrined in the American Constitution? Doesn't American money boldly proclaim, "In God We Trust"? Aren't American political leaders evaluated on the basis of comparative piety? How can there be anything wrong with religion? A few Catholic priests, maybe, but those were just sick individuals, right? Surely, it's not an indictment of the church itself, or of God or religion. Aren't we going just a bit overboard here? What is it about this period in history that seems to be generating so much discussion of atheism? So much God-bashing! What's a decent person to do?

The answer, at least the one suggested by this book, is to hold fast to that decency. God is not and has never been a prerequisite for human morality. The Founding Fathers seemed to understand that message quite well, although the principle has gotten lost over the years.[3] Nowhere is the distinction between morality and religion clearer than in the so-called Jefferson Bible. The third US president created this manuscript to retain the moral principles of Jesus, while excluding the supernatural "nonsense" (Jefferson's word). Jefferson described the contrast between these essential moral teachings and the unnecessary supernatural ballast as being "as easily distinguished as diamonds in a dunghill."[4]

Morality runs deep in human nature. Indeed, as author Matt Ridley has argued, a moral sense is coded in our genes and with good reason. "Moral," "decent," and "fair" social interactions were essential conduct in the small social groups in which our ancestors lived. These positive traits would have been selected for, just as strength, agility, or language would have been. Likewise, Marc Hauser's book *Moral Minds* makes clear the transformation in how scientists understand the development of morality. Fifty years ago, the emphasis was on social learning and cognitive development. From that viewpoint, one might have concluded that, without religious indoctrination, humans might remain boundaryless brutes, capable of all manner of moral atrocities.

This is far from how moral development is now viewed, although conservative religion is in no hurry to let you know about the change. The cornerstone to understanding moral development today is evolutionary psychology. Marc Hauser's book goes so far as to argue the parallel between an evolved language instinct and an evolved moral instinct. Hauser is talking about hardwired neural circuitry whose job it is to produce moral decisions and behavior. There is nothing about acting in a moral way that requires supernatural belief or intervention. It is true that many religions encode rules of moral conduct in their teaching, but it is naive to view those codes as the *basis* for morality. In *God Is Not Great*, Christopher Hitchens has put the issue even more bluntly. Is it reasonable to believe, Hitchens asks, that before Moses delivered the Ten Commandments containing the rule "Thou Shalt Not Kill," his followers believed that it was perfectly all right to do so?

The separation of religion and morality is an extremely difficult idea for many people to grasp. Some of my students are appalled to hear me suggest that morality does not come directly from God or, at least, from religion. In his novel *Arthur & George*,[5] Julian Barnes recounts a conversation between Arthur Conan Doyle and his love interest, Jean. They are discussing religion and morality, and Jean observes, "If people, ordinary people, do not have the church to tell them how to behave, then they will relapse into brutish squalor and self-interest." When Arthur disputes her view, Jean announces that she feels a headache coming on and ends their conversation.

The link between morality and religion is embodied in everyday language. The Colorado Rockies, a very successful baseball franchise in 2007, noted publicly that the management of their organization was guided by "Christian values." Not surprisingly, this message was offensive to many non-Christians, including Jews, Muslims, Hindus, and atheists. There was a lot of Internet discussion of Colorado's position, and much of it underscores the point we make here about the separation of religion and morality. When asked to itemize some of those values, management listed such things as "decency," "honesty," and "charity."

"Oh, you mean *Jewish* values," one fan noted.

"No, *Buddhist* values," another replied.

"Hindu values," yet another said.

"You're all wrong," commented a fourth discussant. "These are *human* values. I'm an atheist and these are core values of the secular humanist organization I belong to."

How quickly a Christian organization had laid claim to these cornerstones of decency and morality. They didn't merely espouse the values that most people admire. They took *ownership* of them, suggesting in no uncertain terms that personnel decisions, like other parts of organizational policy, had reflected these attitudes. Although no such statement was made, it seems a short distance between this view and posting a "Non-Christians Need Not Apply" sign on the door.

A friend of mine who works thousands of miles away from Denver experienced a similar bias while working for a public (as opposed to a Catholic or "separate" school) board of education in Ontario, Canada. She had worked to implement a "community service" requirement into the curriculum of a civics course, only to receive an angry letter from an anonymous source. It contained a passage from the June 2006 issue of *Catholic Insight* magazine. It was essentially an attack on the public schools for meddling in "character education." The article said in part that virtuous acts such as community service had to be rooted in "an understanding of the overall meaning of human life." The article goes on to argue that only a Catholic teacher could instill a "virtuous character." For non-Catholics, the teaching of such acts would be empty gestures with "only a semblance of moral respectability." The basis for such a charade was obvious (to the writer): "Public schools don't have the luxury of quoting the scriptures or speaking about God." In summary, it is an "illusion that character education can bridge the gap between religious and non-religious schools." Leave the good works to God's people (better yet, to Catholics). Works alone are meaningless without character, and character can come only from accepting God. Our God.

In the October 9, 2006, issue of *Time* magazine, Andrew Sullivan argued cogently that embracing doubt in the area of religious belief was a core requirement for individual rationality and perhaps even world peace. Sullivan's ire was directed at religious fundamentalists of all stripes and the rising tide of fundamentalism in world politics. Qualities like being utterly certain and uncompromising in judgments while preaching "absolute adherence to inerrant Scripture" are reserved for Sullivan's sharpest criticism. Yet, for many, they are among the most attractive features of religious affiliation. Being infantilized by absolute notions of right and wrong continues to resonate with many people. For them, the separation between religion and morality is unthinkable.

Andrew Sullivan does not share the antireligious stance of the present book. In his book *The Conservative Soul*,[6] Sullivan argues that the problem lies not with religion, per se, but with its fundamentalist, assertively nonrational believers. It is certainly true that a holy war between two opponents who are utterly convinced that they are doing God's work by smiting nonbelievers is scary business. And there is much to fear. American involvement in the Middle East cannot stand apart from a geopolitical system that is deeply rooted in religious history and perceived mandates from conflicting deities.

Although we are not making a case for mild-mannered, moderate religion, it is certainly to be favored over absolute, fundamentalist belief. The former may be wrong; the latter may be lethal. Sullivan has actually put the case quite strongly. Citing sixteenth-century writer Michel de Montaigne, Sullivan concludes that "complete religious certainty is, in fact, the real blasphemy." He goes on to argue that "true belief is not about blind submission." Sullivan, interestingly, proposes a faith built on doubt. This may be a viable cornerstone for a personal belief system, but it seems an unlikely mantra for any organized religion. Certainly, it seems a poor match for what we know of the world's major religions and their usual practitioners.

RELIGION AND TYLENOL

Religion appears to be one of the defining characteristics, if not of our species, then certainly of the cultures we create. Why is this so? What makes religion so widespread? Philosophers, theologians, and psychologists have grappled with this question quite unsuccessfully for thousands of years. It seems surprising that anything so widespread would be so resistant to analysis. In the opening chapter of his recent book,[7] Stewart Guthrie addresses the lack of a satisfactory theory of religion, citing a small sample of previous attempts, and uses 167 notes to document his conclusion.

It is only recently that advances in cognitive neuroscience, coupled with an interest in evolutionary psychology, has begun to cut a meaningful path through this mass of theorizing. Arguably, previous accounts have been misguided. By focusing on religion itself as an adaptation, one may be led to ask the wrong questions about how it came to be and why it persists. Because this is not a book on religion, per se, these debates lie beyond our immediate concern. A brief summary, however, will help to draw the issue of religion into the framework of Caveman Logic.

Previous approaches by believers and skeptic/scholars alike have often confronted the "why" of religion by asking, "What benefits does religion confer on the believer?" This functional analysis confuses *benefits* with *causes*. It assumes that once identified, the benefits of religion will explain why it was chosen or persists.

Thinkers like Freud or Marx—to name the most famous of this viewpoint—concluded that the intolerable anxieties of everyday life, whether spiritual, economic, or social, lead humans to search for something to dull the pain. Freud argued that religion was "born from man's need to make his helplessness tolerable." Marx's famous phrase "the opiate of the masses," patronizing as it may be, embodies this same viewpoint.

Although many have accepted this approach to the "why" question, there are at least three problems with it. First, as many writers have noted, much religious doctrine invokes as much anxiety as it relieves. Indeed, religious devotees often bask in florid depictions, both artistic and lyrical, of the sort of torture that lies ahead of them in the afterlife. As sources as diverse as painter Hieronymus Bosch's grotesque *The Descent of the Damned into Hell* or musician Chuck Berry's "The Downbound Train"[8] confirm, religion has the potential to agitate as many people as it soothes.

The second problem with the functional or "utility" analysis of religion lies in its assumption that people are simply acting as unconstrained free agents selecting what makes them feel good. It is as if most people in our culture find themselves with a headache and turn to each other, saying "Hey, my head is really throbbing. Any idea what I can do for it?" And the answer comes back from anyone you ask, "Take Tylenol. It's great for headaches." And before you know it, more and more people are taking Tylenol and recommending it to others. One day you look around and realize that virtually the whole human race is taking Tylenol—or whatever the local equivalent may be in areas where Johnson & Johnson has no distribution. The headache really hasn't gone away, and Tylenol-crazed people are flying airplanes into buildings or attacking other people who use Bufferin, but the Tylenol use grows daily.

When an investigative reporter asks, "Why do so many people take Tylenol?" she is told, "Because it cures headaches." Yes, but so do lots of other things. Why Tylenol? And so she wonders, Were we really all neurochemical blank slates suffering from headaches? Can it really be that, independently, almost every person on Earth has arrived at the same strategy for curing his or her headache? This seems improbable at best. Something must be going on besides analgesia. Might it not be possible that we come equipped with some sort of neurochemical predisposition that Tylenol grabs on to like a pair of vice-grips?

It's not like the folks who make Tylenol did it on purpose, but they sure managed to exploit a chemical predisposition in their consumers. No one in her right mind would argue that taking Tylenol is an adaptation. But when those predispositions started to assert themselves, Tylenol use was going to spread like crazy once the human race got a taste of it. A lot of people would wonder where Tylenol came from and why it was so popular. On which receptors was Tylenol piggybacking its success? But don't be duped into asking the wrong questions about Tylenol. Its success just rides the coat tails of some other qualities of human existence that were in place well before Johnson & Johnson came on the scene.

One more thing to remember: this story is not about a few chemically unbalanced individuals; rather, it is *Homo sapiens* in general who display this collection of biochemical quirks and predispositions. And given what we are beginning to learn about human neurochemistry, it appears that our descent into Tylenol use was inevitable.

And so, questions like, "What selective advantage does belief in God confer?" are off-target. It is more productive to ask, "How could belief in God have occurred so easily and frequently in humans given what we know about the human mind?" What are the (already existing) features that lend themselves so well to the creation and maintenance of religious belief? This question has been answered differently by various authors, although it seems a step in the right direction to combine overactive pattern and causal agency detectors with a tendency toward anthropomorphism.

The latter is a vital component of religion. A simple exercise will underscore its importance. Remember that religions, like all cultural things, face strong competition. The ones that are most successful are able to mesh with evolved characteristics of the human mind. If you doubt that, ask yourself whether the following religion would catch on:

1. God has no humanlike qualities, either mental or physical. You cannot picture him. There is no art and there are no artifacts in this religion.

2. God is "infinite" and we are told that his mind is beyond our comprehension. He does not listen to prayer. He is not interested in your praise through word or song. He is benevolent and he is in charge, but he is not interested in bargaining with you.

3. In short, God is there, although you can't imagine him. His plan may be fair but it is beyond your comprehension. He is not interested in hearing from you. Just let him do his job.

Do you think this is a religion that is likely to be devised by humans? If it were, do you think it would catch on and spread? What does this tell us about the role of the human mind in determining the content and success of religion or any supernatural belief system?

A PIOUS PARASITE

Whether or not religion, per se, is a good thing is not the issue. Surely, there are those who believe that organized religion is at the core of what ails our species. Oxford biologist Richard Dawkins argues persuasively and passionately that the world would be a safer, more intelligent and compassionate place were it not for our species' descent into religion. I dwell on religion or the various ways that gods are constructed by human societies simply because religious belief and religious membership are two of the chief beneficiaries of what is wrong with our minds.

How would you complete this sentence: If there were no _____, there would be no religion (or no God). Various philosophers and authors have offered their answers, which are surprisingly different. One approach, perhaps argued most persuasively by Pascal Boyer in his book *Religion Explained*,[9] is that death, or more specifically dead bodies, are the primary impetus for religion.

Matthew Alper[10] makes a somewhat similar case, arguing that there is a specific "God Part of the Brain," to quote the title of his book. Alper sees religion as an evolutionary adaptation, prompted by primitive man's early realization of death and ultimate need to establish some sense of immortality. Dean Hamer also argues for a hardwired spirituality in his book *The God Gene*.[11] On the other hand, some theologians might simply argue that the question, itself, is meaningless. Their case might be: there will always be religion because there will always be a God, and it is just a matter of time until humankind finds the way to him.

My own view is that religion and man's quest for supernatural agents are not in and of themselves adaptations. Others share this view. Neither author Scott Atran nor Ara Norenzayan believe that religion, per se, is an evolutionary adaptation. One way or another, each makes the case that religion itself is not an adaptation, but rather the beneficiary of many cognitive and emotional traits that *are* adaptations. Perhaps a stronger way to put this is that religion is, in a sense, a parasite. It takes full advantage of how our minds perform. In this sense, religion is not unique. Traits may be selected for because of the reproductive advantage they confer, but once the phenotype is in place, there is no restriction on the secondary uses to which its components can be put. In some cases, traits can combine in ways that were not part of the original selection process. As Atran and Norenzayan put it, the qualities of our minds that form the backbone of religion were, themselves, probably "evolved for mundane adaptive tasks."

It is thus possible that religious thinking and behavior are mediated by mental mechanisms that are, in their own right, absolutely ordinary. It is their unique combination that has given rise—probably quite unexpectedly—to something central to our species. Putting the case even more strongly: *Religion is the inevitable by-product of how our minds* misperform. It is the result of mental misfiring, so to speak. Of course, once such belief systems are socially transmitted and well established, there is a rapidly decreasing likelihood that they can be dislodged. Breaking free from both beliefs and group cohesion become a very costly process.

Seeing religion in this way is not a mainstream point of view. It is far more common to note the universality of religion, assume it is adaptive, and ask how it has contributed to our reproductive fitness. Whether that might be "alleviating anxiety," "providing comfort," or a host of other glib attributions, the conclusion is usually that religion is an independent adaptation. I disagree, and argue that religion serves no evolutionary function whatsoever. It is certainly possible that a man and woman might meet at a Wednesday night Bible study group and embark on a rich reproductive life together. Happy endings aside, that story falls well short of meeting the criteria for a species-wide increase in reproductive fitness.

Once one views religion as an inevitable outgrowth of our inherited mental defects, it becomes clear that religion is really just a symptom of the problem. The problem is in that defective underlying software. Being religious is simply an easy, one might even say lazy, use of our minds, which are capable of so much more in the way of processing ability. In this regard, religion is a sign of intellectual laziness. It is far easier to believe in God than to question or deny his existence.

THE FUTILITY OF PRAYER

There is probably no life experience that illustrates better than prayer just how inadequately we collect and evaluate evidence. One-third of Americans surveyed by the 2008 Pew Trust poll[12] reported that they "receive answers to their prayer requests at least once a month." Needless to say, people aren't running experiments when they pray. But those who report how their prayers have been answered and those who argue for the efficacy of prayer in general are making strong statements that require a reasonable standard of evidence. These are important issues. Should we not have our wits about us when we address them?

It is probably safe to say that billions of prayers go unanswered every day. The case is dramatically illustrated during prolonged natural disasters that cause suffering and death. Presumably, many of those affected spend considerable time praying. Most of those prayers, by any reasonable standard, are not answered. As Carl Sagan has argued, "Their failure constitutes data." As most of us realize, data of this nature is unlikely to be acknowledged, much less elevated to the level of hypothesis or theory. Yet occasional, often shaky, evidence of success will be shared between individuals or touted by the news media.

There is a loophole that can silence these concerns, although it is rarely invoked. This position states simply that prayer "works" because it makes the person feel better. Just uttering the prayer, regardless of its outcome, is helpful. The mechanisms don't even have to be specified. Perhaps it is the release of endorphins, endogenous opiates designed for just this purpose. At a less reductionist level, perhaps it is the illusion of control in a sea of huge, largely uncontrollable events that provides the comfort. From this point of view, prayer is a useful strategy and would remain so whether or not God existed. In fact, by setting the standard so low, prayer can be said to work 100 percent of the time.

But this is not what people mean by "the efficacy of prayer." When they tout the benefit of prayer, it is usually about prayers being answered—about outcomes that match the content of requests. It is rare to hear someone say, "I prayed to the Lord to make the flood go away and to spare my house and cherished possessions. I prayed for him to roll back the waters as I know only he can. But it didn't work. I lost everything. My house, my stuff, it's all gone. Washed out to sea. But I sure felt good there for a while praying to the Big Guy."

If more arguments sounded like that, people like myself would spend less time questioning the efficacy of prayer. Again, it is when specific claims are made for tangible consequences that were unlikely to have occurred otherwise, that scientists become curious or are drawn into the fray. Sometimes they put that curiosity into action. The March 31, 2006, issue of the *New York Times* published a story headlined, "Long Awaited Medical Study Questions the Power of Prayer." The widely publicized study (later to appear in the *American Heart Journal*) was the most detailed and thorough investigation of the topic, taking almost ten years to complete and involving over 1,800 subjects. Nevertheless, the research became the stuff of comedy routines almost immediately and prompted a wave of criticism by advocates of prayer who were unhappy with the results.

Not surprisingly, this was not the first attempt to scientifically test whether prayer works. The *Times* article points out that at least ten studies on the effects of prayer have been published in the past six years. The present work, led by cardiologist Herbert Benson, was designed to remedy design flaws present in earlier work. In effect, the study tested whether prayers offered by strangers had any effect on the recovery of patients who underwent heart surgery. They did not. Worse yet, patients who knew they were being prayed for actually had a higher rate of postoperative complications. The researchers speculated that these complications, such as abnormal heart rhythms, may have resulted from additional pressure to "do well" felt by the patients who knew they were being prayed for. Subjects were divided into three groups prior to receiving coronary bypass surgery: two of them received prayer and one did not. Half the subjects who were prayed for had knowledge of that prayer; the others did not. Unfortunately, the study did not include a group that received no prayer but were told that they had. The study, which cost $2.4 million to perform, employed three teams of persons who were instructed to "pray in their own way" but to use a standardized phrase "for a successful surgery with a quick, healthy recovery and no complications."

Prayer givers were asked to identify the patient to God using only the patient's first name and the first letter of his or her last name. Presumably, this was sufficient information for God's purposes, although Carl Sagan's comment about why God would need to be prompted about who needs help seems relevant here. There was concern expressed by some that the study was confounded by having no control over the occurrence of prayers by family members and friends. Presumably God would listen to such entreaties also, even if they had not been sanctioned by Dr. Benson and his team. Obviously, design of the study could have been improved, but there would have been ethical concerns had Benson et al. forbidden prayers by the loved ones of patients in his no-prayer group. Indeed, some critics worried about general prayers that are routinely offered for all the sick and afflicted everywhere. How highly does God weigh those messages? Are they worth as much as a specific prayer from a wife or a customized prayer from a stranger using only first name and last initial of the patient? Also left unanswered are questions about whether God would fail to heal a patient (or, worse yet, throw impediments in his way) simply because no adequate "prayer quotient" had been received on his behalf. Such a deity could be said to victimize atheists and their families. Obviously, these are complicated metaphysical questions and without their resolution it will be hard to design a definitive study.

Even if this long-term project had done a better job, can you imagine a scientist stating prior to data collection, "We'll go ahead and test this hypothesis, but even if the data disconfirm it, I'm not going to give it up. I just know in my heart it's right, so the results don't matter." How long would science last if that were the prevailing approach? But that very attitude seems to do no damage to religion. Bob Barth, the director of Silent Unity, the Missouri-based ministry used as a source of prayers in the study, made it clear that the results of this study would not affect the beliefs or actions of his ministry. "We've been praying a long time and we know prayers work."

Then why do the study? Had the results shown unequivocally that prayer asking for divine intercession into the fortunes of surgical patients actually increased their chances for recovery, there would be no shortage of religious leaders quoting the data. Suddenly science would become the friend of religion, which would tout its virtues in finally answering a great spiritual question. But when the data offer no such support, the religious community lets fly with everything from methodological critiques to denying the possibility that science might ever address questions about the power of prayer. Once again, the game has been rigged so that only positive evidence is relevant.

THE NAMES AND FACES OF GOD

Churches may be a major component of culture, but they also depend upon cultural things to sustain themselves. The American

South is a case in point. Churches compete for attention every bit as much as car dealerships and long-distance telephone companies. Like these businesses, churches resort to billboard advertising that ranges from professional to extremely amateurish. Sometimes they border on mean-spirited. A sign posted outside the Cleveland Avenue Church of Christ in Long Beach, Mississippi, placed there by the Reverend Dan Huggins, read, "There is one God and His name is not Allah."[13] The sign was displayed on September 11, 2002. According to Rev. Huggins, this was not a barb aimed at his Muslim neighbors on the one-year anniversary of the terrorist attacks. "I do these signs to provoke thought. This was never meant to be antagonistic." Nevertheless, the sign was changed within four days, "but not because of the negative publicity it generated," claimed the minister.

Focusing on the sign's theology rather than its politics, Sabree Rashid, a spokesman for the Biloxi Islamic Center noted, "If you look up 'Allah' in the dictionary you'll see that 'Al' translates as 'The' and 'Ilah' means 'God.' A clear translation means 'The God.' The prophet Mohammed comes from the same line as Abraham. Our scripture tells us our God is one and the same. Christians who speak an Arabic language call God 'Allah.' The French call him 'Dieu.' Is [Reverend Huggins] going to say his is a different God because the language is different? To say they are not the same God is crass ignorance."

If the name of God divides people, you can imagine the results of putting a face to the deity. Andrew Sullivan's book *The Conservative Soul* stresses the fact that we cannot know the face or the mind of God. Yet, for many believers, this would be a deal-breaker. A God who is not personalized and understandable in human terms is no God at all.

Humans evolved to understand and deal successfully with other humans. It remains the sine qua non of social life. Not surprisingly, our gods conform to what we see in and expect from other humans. Thus, gods the world over get "angry," are "pleased," grant favors, demand something in return, and so on. They are essentially powerful humans in supernatural suits. It is what we can understand and—more cynically—what we are likely to invent.

The belief that "God created man in His own image" is exactly backward. Voltaire put it even more bluntly when he wrote, "If God made us in his own image, we have more than reciprocated." There is more to this than clever wordplay. Along with well-documented sex differences in the perception of God, there is no clearer evidence of just how many versions of God seem to be out there than Stephen Prothero's book *American Jesus: How the Son of God Became a National Icon.*[14] Turning to popular culture, Prothero examined the many faces Jesus wears to his believers. It turns out that rather than embracing a common deity, followers of Christ seem to invent or define their God in terms that reflect their values, priorities, and cultural preferences.

Putting the case mildly, Jesus is many things to many people. He is variously conceived not only as the Son of God, but also as a Hindu avatar, a Muslim prophet, a Jewish rabbi, a warrior, a pacifist, and a black Moses. In the words of journalist Tricia Brick, Jesus is variously viewed as "an enlightened sage, in the fashion of Thomas Jefferson, a macho wielder of Teddy Roosevelt's Big Stick, . . . a brother, a confidant, a soldier, a CEO, a yogi and a feminist." And let's not forget Jesus Christ, Superstar. In short, he is all things to all people. He is, in the language of psychoanalysis, a projective test. What do you need him to be? Whatever your answer, that's what he will be to you.

As Brick notes, Americans have a long and colorful history of making Jesus over in their own image. This flexibility would seem to tell us more about the mind of the believer than the properties of the deity. The "many faces" approach puts believers in the odd position of sharing a God in name only. American Christians may call Jesus by the same name but make few of the same assumptions about who he is, what he wants, how he operates, and, not trivially, how he looks. This latter point is particularly telling. Prothero's book is replete with illustrations that reveal just how differently Jesus is perceived. In some, Jesus is white; in others, he is black. In still others, he is Asian. His demeanor ranges from beatific to corporate. In Stephen Sawyer's painting *Undefeated* (www.ART4 GOD.com), Jesus is a muscular, long-haired prize fighter.

As we have repeatedly seen, the human mind brings its own agenda, even to seemingly neutral situations. The perception of Jesus reflects much about the mind of our species, but it also reflects individual cultural differences as well. Jesus is, again, a deified projective test, waiting for us to complete the painting with a canvas that best meets our needs and expectations. As Prothero's book points out, this flexibility in how we perceive Jesus is particularly telling since, compared to many deities, Jesus Christ comes with a fairly standardized image. But, like the childhood game of telephone—in which a message is relayed around a table until it bears little resemblance to the way it started—Jesus, too, is shaped and softened to fit individual and cultural needs. If there is such plasticity surrounding a physical entity like Jesus, one can only imagine how many variations there are in the perception of a far more abstract figure like the father of Jesus.

THE POWER OF GNOMES

When a pastor puts a sign in front of his church saying, "There is only one God and Allah is not His name," he is revealing more than just his opinion. A "my God is better than your God" attitude is probably responsible for more human suffering and death than any other single cause in history with the exception of microscopic pathogens. And like the pathogenic foes that have tormented our species, we have natural selection to blame for the large- and small-scale religious wars we have waged upon ourselves.

The teaching of specific rights and wrongs is hardly the stuff of neutrality. I might believe, despite evidence to the contrary, that an invisible garden gnome controls my destiny and, without fear of him and prayer directed to him, events in my life may turn really sour. Were I to hold such a view, it might be possible to lead a satisfying life and not bring harm or distress to others. The problem arises when I start wearing Gnome Power t-shirts and riding through the countryside killing those who don't share my beliefs. If my Gnome cult were to grow in strength, Gnomers might be able to field an army and afford weapons of mass destruction. I would probably never be as passionate or convinced of my righteousness as when I slaughtered my neighbors who didn't share my Gnomic beliefs. The more of us there were, the less we would question our actions. Certainty is a powerful force. Some would even say "attractive." Citizens often value such certainty in their leaders. From that point of view, one who questions or reevaluates his or her beliefs may be seen as "soft" or indecisive. Perhaps lacking "the courage of his convictions."

There are two ways that religious indoctrination hurts us all. The first is by its divisive effect. You need look no further than the sign in front of that Mississippi church. In extreme cases, when a "convert or die" mentality becomes the order of the day, religion may also provide the means to wage horribly successful holy wars. It is this second point that has been brought to public consciousness by evolutionary biologist Richard Dawkins. That religious belief might not have such a salubrious effect on our species has rarely been a topic for polite discourse. Eighteenth-century philosopher David Hume probably endeared himself to few when he wrote, "The greatest crimes are compatible with a superstitious piety and devotion. . . . Those who undertake the most criminal and dangerous enterprises are commonly the most superstitious."[15] In like manner, Dawkins has argued that whatever benefits religion may once have conferred upon our species, it is time to recognize the harm that also results.

The tragic events of 9/11 have been written about in precisely the xenophobic terms that contributed to those events in the first place. Franklin Graham, son of evangelist Billy Graham, noted publicly that the people who flew planes into buildings weren't Protestants. His message can be summarized in terms even a caveman might grasp: *Protestants good. Muslims bad.* Graham failed to note another possible conclusion: the people who flew planes into buildings weren't atheists.

In a September 14, 2001, editorial in the (UK) *Guardian,* Dawkins attempted to "call attention to the elephant in the room that everybody is too polite—or too devout—to notice: religion." Dawkins was specifically concerned with "the devaluing effect that religion has on human life" by teaching "the dangerous nonsense" that death is not the end. By removing death as an endpoint, Dawkins argues that the possibility of rational discourse between, say, hijacker and victim becomes useless. If we are in a standoff with loaded guns aimed at each other, but only I believe that death is final, there is no longer a level playing field for reconciling our differences. Without equal acceptance of the finality of death, armed conflicts or even threats of war lose their meaning.

Every species of animal life on the planet acts as if it had a "survival instinct." Mice may not hold a deeper understanding of their own life cycle, but even in the absence of such knowledge they behave in precisely the ways they need to in order to maximize their reproductive success. Humans, on the other hand, are capable of abstract understanding of conception, birth, and death. But what has it gained us? We are the only species capable of reading and writing biology books, but we are also the only species who engages in belief systems that can subvert the instinct to survive and reproduce.

SCIENCE AND THE MOVIES

Many people are intimidated by science; they revere it but they also mistrust it. Mainly, they just don't get it. If you tell them that *you're* a scientist, they look kind of oddly at you. You're no longer one of them. It's like telling someone you're a psychologist. I've done that enough times to have a practiced set of skills to deal with the social fallout.

Scientists are often perceived as being odd people. They are called by endearing terms like "pencilneck," "egghead," or "geek." They are seen as social misfits, obsessed with arcane matters and lacking the social skills that might land them a date with the prom queen or one of the cheerleaders. They seem to understand things that most normal people cannot; that alone makes them objects of fear and mistrust. We need scientists to invent things or keep us safe, but we'd rather not be around them.

In *Border Phantom*, a 1936 Republic western, one character says to another, "Those scientific eggs are a screwy lot." His pal replies, "Screwy is right!" Nashville-based songwriter John D. Loudermilk wrote and recorded a satirical song in 1962 called "He's Just a Scientist, That's All."[16] The song decries our fascination with athletes and rock stars, while disregarding the scientists who labor in anonymity to increase understanding and make our lives better.

Despite Loudermilk's enlightened attitude, the simple truth is that average people are fearful of others who are *too smart*. Maybe they have a begrudging respect for them and their accomplishments, but there is also an element of concern. These people may *know* things we don't, and who's to say they won't use those things against us? They can ruin our world with weird things like gene splicing and stem cells and cloning and nanotechnology. God knows (literally) what they're doing because it's a cinch that we don't. Even if they tried to tell us, we probably wouldn't understand them. Somehow, we've got to keep them on a short leash before they turn the whole world into one big immoral, 1950s science fiction mess.

This is why we want our leaders (who are no smarter than we are) to have strong moral values. At least government will keep these crazy scientists from going too far. Former US senator William Proxmire used to be a regular guest on late-night TV shows, where he would announce his "Golden Fleece" Awards, which often targeted publicly funded research about topics the average person neither cared about nor understood. Proxmire took glee in reporting the exotic-sounding titles of NSF or NIH grants in his best populist, know-nothing fashion, saying in essence, "Can you believe the way they waste our tax dollars? Who cares about this stuff other than some silly eggheads?"

You don't have to look far to find where some of that misunderstanding and distrust come from. Hollywood, indeed American entertainment in general, has done a wonderful job of stereotyping and misrepresenting both science and scientists. It isn't just a recent problem. In the 1920s, the great silent film *The Lost World* portrays Professor Challenger as a feisty, cantankerous adventurer who is constantly at war with *real* scientists, portrayed as mild-mannered fops, wearing thick glasses and tsk-tsking him for his transgressions. Just a decade later, the film version of Baron Henry Frankenstein became the prototype of the scientist gone wild— ostracized from his profession for outrageous ideas and for going where God-fearing man was not meant to go. He—indeed most scientists of his ilk—is usually portrayed as highly intelligent and obsessive. His social skills suffer. His fiancée becomes worried, then disenchanted. He is not *himself* anymore. He has lost all per-spective. He is taking his work *too far*.

This combination of too smart and obsessive is a stereotype Hol-lywood has not fully abandoned. It shows up again in the 1940s in a series of "Mad Scientist" movies, often produced by so-called Poverty Row studios and starring Boris Karloff or a down-on-his-luck Bela Lugosi.[17] These characters experimented with preserving their dead wives or restoring their beauty, for which they needed serum extracted from virgins or neighborhood dogs or gorillas. In some cases, they turned themselves into ape-men, skulking around the neighborhood under cover of night, murdering mysteriously. When they were finally caught, someone—either a reporter or a preacher—delivered the canned speech about science "going too far."

The next decade—the 1950s—took the same fear of scientists to nearly comic levels. More often than not, scientists were por-trayed as craggy, old, absentminded men with beautiful daughters who worked as lab assistants. (Just how these social incompetents might have conceived such daughters was never addressed.) The daughters did their utmost to steer daddy through the mundane chores of life, like remembering to eat lunch or pay the bills. The secrets these men transgressed were often nuclear in origin and usually resulted in an enlarged insect or spider (ants and praying mantises and tarantulas come to mind) roaming around the desert on the edge of a large city. The plot usually asked the question, "Has science taken us where no man was meant to go?" The answer was usually yes, which gave the special effects crew enough time with miniatures to delight a whole theater full of screaming kids on a Saturday afternoon.

Modern audiences know these themes and characters as well. They've seen them in films ranging from *Jurassic Park* to *Honey I Shrunk the Kids*. The list is long and the special effects just keep getting better. But in the name of family entertainment, we are also teaching that scientists as well as what they do are both weird and dangerous. *Back to the Future* (Parts I through whatever) may have offered some thrilling adventures, but the Christopher Lloyd char-acter is a certifiable loony tune. Smart, out-of-control, and, most of all, unconventional. Not hemmed in by the sorts of rules and commandments that keep decent folks in their safe, predictable places. We give such scientists high marks for their entertainment value, but in real life we want to cut a wide swath around them. This is unfortunate. The basic attitudes of science confer some immunity to Caveman Logic and offer an antidote to many of its most obvious features. Yet, popular culture seems to delight in disdaining those carriers of the scientific method: the scientists, themselves.

None of this is helped by the fact that the quality of scientific education in North America is appallingly low. This ugly little secret has been getting more and more attention of late as the products of American high schools fall further and further behind their counterparts in Europe and Asia. We are leaders no more. As *Time* magazine asked in its March 6, 2006, cover story, "Is America Flunking Science?" The answer appears to be yes, which is doubly troublesome since these effects often take generations to reverse. There will surely be both intellectual and economic consequences. But documenting the patterns does not address why science seems to be so hard for so many of us. It becomes easier to avoid, even disdain science, when a culture enshrines such negative attitudes. But the roots of the problem were there well before our culture decided to consensually support ignorance. Which is easier to understand: Astronomy or astrology? Science or superstition? Geometry or ghosts?

There may be good reason for that. Science and math are new. For one thing, we are a very new species. For another, we have spent at least 99 percent of our existence on this planet without science and math. They are very new concepts and do not come easily to us. It is much easier for us to grasp astrology, superstition, and spirits. Those kinds of ideas have an extensive natural history. They are part of our Pleistocene thinking. Astronomy, science, and geometry? Not *impossible* concepts for our minds, but certainly difficult. Concepts that require concentration, attention, practice. Imagine yourself trying to get through to a room full of thirteen-year-olds who would almost certainly rather be any place but in your classroom. You've got an hour to reach them. Do you think you've got an equal chance to get them to understand the Pythagorean theorem or a ghost story?

OUT THERE IN TELEVISION LAND

The content of television both reflects and contributes to public perception. From either point of view, its treatment of science (and scientists) is very disturbing. We've come to set the bar pretty low as with series like *In Search Of . . .* and *Unsolved Mysteries*. It's a bit more surprising when venues like the National Geographic Channel also dumb down their fare. Few viewers bother to read the written disclaimers tagged to the beginning or end of shows like *In Search Of. . . .* If they did, they'd see a clear denial of any responsibility to present a balanced view of the subject matter. It's clear that these shows pander to the most unschooled and uncritical elements of the audience, stirring up their "Oh wow!" response and short-changing anything resembling rational alternative explanations.

Somehow we expect more of the National Geographic Channel. NGC is described by its cable and satellite carriers as offering "adventure, exploration, culture, and natural wonders." It is further described as "educational." So what are these "natural wonders" that NGC selects for its audience? Certainly, the universe is full of wondrous things. Will we use the telescope or the microscope? Will we look into the deepest recesses of space or peer into a drop of pond water? No. That stuff is too "sciencey." Here, instead, is a sample of the evening programming running on NGC on a randomly selected weeknight (Monday, June 26, 2006) with start times between 6 PM and midnight. We have consecutive one-hour features on extreme sleepwalking, the Bermuda Triangle, UFOs, ghosts, apemen, more UFOs, and more ghosts. The latter two are presumably reruns of the earlier broadcasts in case you were busy watching reality shows during prime time. You might also want to consider that these "educational" segments are sponsored by Jack Link's beef jerky. A typical thirty-second commercial for this company's product contains scenes of several male friends, who are probably not on the short list for a Rhodes scholarship, tormenting a Bigfoot they have found napping in the woods. You might also consider that advertisers study audience demographics carefully before spending their limited resources. In fairness to NGC, their approach is more balanced than that of many of their competitors. They do not emphasize wonder to the exclusion of skepticism or common sense. But the topics they select for treatment represent the lowest common denominator of interest in the world around us.

Maybe that's *why* they choose these things and why their more measured approach is of some value. But if NGC can enlighten its audience by actually suggesting that there may be simpler explanations for Bigfoot or alien abductions, then why can't they also introduce their audience to some of the more legitimate wonders of the world around them? Just how many times can you dredge up the same tired tales from Roswell, New Mexico, or Loch Ness, Scotland? At some point merely giving these topics any more coverage, even if it offers some semblance of balance, offers them a continued legitimacy they might otherwise lose through attrition.

How about this for a network TV show for next season: Call it *The Skeptic*. Actually, that might be a risky way to start. The word *skeptic* has taken on a negative connotation, like *grinch*. Skeptics are boring people who doubt things that are either holy or fun. So maybe let's call the show *The Quest* or, better yet, name it after its hero. Give him a catchy Anglo-Saxon name like McGlower or something macho like Manning. Anyway, let's give him a business card to display on-screen like Paladin did on the old *Have Gun Will Travel* TV series. The card features just his name and the word *Skeptic*. Then let's cast a young (late-twenties/early-thirties) guy. Make sure he's very sexy and very cool. Give him an assistant who's drop-dead gorgeous. She's smart and savvy and obviously very attracted to him. Let everything emphasize just how cool and with-it and desirable he is as he goes about his business of doubting supernatural events.

Our hero is a professional debunker. Every week someone brings him a new case: some sort of psychic fraud or supernatural charlatan or UFO hoaxer. We begin by witnessing a demonstration of their scam. This should be as effective as possible. In fact, if this were any other show, we might be persuaded to believe that it's legitimate. But here we're not taken in; for the next hour, we're going to think like real skeptics. Because it's cool. Also because all of these agents of the supernatural are portrayed as uncool, physically unattractive, and predatory. They do their job well, but they are cheats, living off the gullibility of uncritical believers. You make their gullibility understandable—after all, most of the audience would have shared these beliefs in the past. But here the gullible target has suffered a recent loss or death of a loved one. He is vulnerable and is targeted by a professional scam artist. The highlight of each weekly episode is watching the good-looking, cool, skeptical hero with the gorgeous girlfriend/assistant debunk the slimy scam artist while the cameras are rolling and everyone is looking. Skepticism is sexy. Debunking is debonair. Critical is cool. The supernatural is silly and associated either with pathetic, uncritical victims or cynical, manipulative con men.

If the show is well cast and well written (as, say, *The X-Files* or *Medium*) it might go a long way toward making critical thinking seem desirable and wide-eyed uncritical acceptance seem foolish. Perhaps these attitudes will spread. As we know, success breeds imitation in the entertainment business. This is not so much about education as it is conditioning. All is fair in the culture wars and it's been a while since the good guys had a victory in their column.

THE DEAD WILL TELL

A film called *The Dead Will Tell* starring Anne Heche and Kathleen Quinlan appeared on the CBS television network at 9 PM on October 24, 2004. The film dealt with a woman who probes the death of the original owner of her antique engagement ring. She believes the woman is trying to "tell her something." This was not written, filmed, or presented on the Trobriand Islands where, we assume, superstition and ignorance are widespread. It was a strictly urban American product. Similarly, one of the major success stories of the 2005 television season was NBC's new entry called *Medium*, in which an ordinary housewife hears and sees the dead and uses these contacts to help the Phoenix district attorney's office.

The series' success may rest more in the excellent weekly performance of its star, Patricia Arquette, as she struggles to come to terms with her not altogether welcome "gift." The series is actually quite well written and acted, so I do not lament its success. But the whole "talking to the dead" thing has become a cottage industry. Hot on the heels of *Medium*, CBS announced a new entry in its fall 2005 schedule called *Ghost Whisperer*. The advertising tag line for the new series was, "Do you believe in ghosts? Because they believe in you." Like *Medium*, the show is based on the adventures of an everyday housewife who acts as a "social worker for the dead," in the words of one reviewer. The appearance of such a show might not be surprising or particularly distressing (after all, networks *do* chase trends) were it not for the fact that we are told that it is based on the life of a "real person." In other words, this isn't entertainment; it's a documentary. Mary Ann Winkowski, a former dog groomer from Ohio and the basis for the CBS show, makes a distinction between spirits who have already "passed over" and those who are still hanging around. It's only the latter group she can exchange information with. It's nice to know there are some ground rules affecting her work. But even with these limitations, there are still enough talkative spirits out there to support a weekly series and a thriving ghostbusting business for Winkowski.

It's hard to know just where all this nonsense started. Plainly, death has never been something most humans took kindly to. Thus, stories about people who "came back" or could communicate with the dead have usually spelled success. Whether sitting around the campfire back in the Pleistocene or reading Victorian novels, there was no surer way to captivate an audience than pushing back the boundaries of death. You'd like to lay it all at the feet of Bruce Willis and his influential box-office hit *The Sixth Sense*, but the trend started long before Willis and his youthful patient who could see dead people. Almost as soon as there were motion pictures, there were films about denying death. The first version of Mary Shelley's Frankenstein legend appeared in a 1911 Edison kinescope called *Life without Soul*. Twenty years later *Frankenstein* became one of the first successful talking films and cemented the career of an English actor named William Henry Pratt, a.k.a. Boris Karloff. The rest, as they say, is history. Film history in this case. And you can include such alternate forms of death-defying characters as *Dracula* (Bela Lugosi, also 1931) and *The Mummy* (Boris again, in 1933). The thread running through these films, other than commercial success, is the unwillingness to accept death as an endpoint. Biology be damned. We can and will live on. We can be resurrected by a powerful bolt of electricity (*Frankenstein*) or a swig of blood (*Dracula*) or tana leaves (Kharis in *The Mummy*). Note that in none of these cases is the resurrected body particularly friendly to the living. The ill-tempered dead also seems to be a theme that refuses to go away, finding its clearest expression in zombie fare like the classic 1968 film *Night of the Living Dead*.

Variants of this theme continue to appear and prosper. Whether on television (*Dead Like Me*) or on the big screen (*Shaun of the Dead*, *White Noise*), it's clear that death is no impediment to movement or communication. Some of these productions are well done and quite entertaining. The problem I have is those cases where there is nothing to suggest that what we are watching is in any way unreasonable. Too often, there is the presumption that the abilities or events we are witnessing may be infrequent, but not *impossible*. The message on shows like *Medium* is, "Not everyone can do this, but it *can* be done." Illusionist James Randi revealed to me that some years ago he was approached by an American TV network that saw some potential in his psychic investigations. "These might make an entertaining weekly series," he was told by a network executive. Randi was asked what percentage of the cases would prove to be real. "None," he replied. At this point negotiations broke down. "You've got to have *some*," was the network's response. Zero percent just wasn't interesting or worth broadcasting because it wouldn't sustain an audience and sell cars or detergent.

This is actually a sad state of affairs. Pseudoscience will usually enjoy greater acceptance and financial reward than either real science in general or the real science that debunks the charlatans. It was unclear to Randi whether the network executive who rejected his show did so because he, himself, was a believer and didn't want to see his cherished worldview held up to public ridicule or whether, simply put, he knew that irrational shlock sells. The latter seems far more likely. The six hundred or so attendees at the annual Randi.org Amazing Meeting held in 2005 were largely of the view that the world holds enough natural wonder without importing supernatural accounts or abilities in order to attract or sustain viewer interest.

A show based on a Randi-like character might initially draw attention. Imagine a weekly TV series in which some paranormal claim is made—Water dowsing? Faith healing? Communication with the dead?—which is then thoroughly investigated and found to be a fraud. What is wrong with that? I've asked this question of many undergraduate students and their answers are surprisingly consistent. Many of them describe such a show as a "bummer." In one's words, "You get all built up for some neat thing and then you see it was just a trick. A fake. Who cares about that?" The second most popular answer is perhaps more disturbing. "Even if you show some medium or faith healer to be a fake, you still end up wondering, 'Yeah, OK. She's a fake. But that doesn't mean it can't be done. There are probably other ones out there who can do this stuff. You just didn't test them.'"

IT TAKES ONE TO CATCH ONE

Successful psychics enjoy tremendous financial rewards and wide popular acclaim. Arguably, they shouldn't. If the public were more astute and less gullible, psychics would be discredited and their shopworn bag of tricks revealed for what they are. Many magicians and professional illusionists are among the most vocal critics of so-called psychics. The reason is obvious.

As Jamy Swiss[18] notes, magicians like him are honest professionals. They forthrightly promise to deceive you. In his view, a professional "psychic" like Uri Geller uses the same tools for dishonest goals. Swiss rightly notes that he and his professional colleagues never pretend to be more than they are. It is one thing to entertain and amaze people by exploiting their lack of observational skills and rampant Caveman Logic. It is quite another to sell these tricks as evidence of the supernatural. Magic tricks or illusions are fun to watch because they violate our expectations. The sense of awe we feel often borders on the physical. But they are magic tricks. Illusions. We should *know* we are in the presence of illusionists and conjurers. No claims should be made for supernatural abilities. Not surprisingly, Swiss points out that a professional magician is the best candidate to detect the subterfuge used by Geller and others like him. "It takes one to catch one."

Imagine how you might feel confronting a colleague who uses the same gimmicks you do, but then deludes his audience by pretending to have spiritual or supernatural abilities. He's just like you: another conjurer, maybe a bit better at it, maybe a bit worse. But unlike you, he's a liar. He pretends to be more than he is and misguides and perhaps exploits people in the process. Outspoken social critic and illusionist Penn Jillette (of Penn and Teller) singles out well-known "psychic" John Edward for some of his disdain. In Jillette's words, "John Edward is an alchemist. He takes grief and turns it into cash." Edward's performance is all the more egregious because his audience often consists of grieving people who are understandably more vulnerable and needy. Edward works his wares using mass media like television and paperback books to supplement his income. Essentially, though, he is no different from smaller-scale mediums who provide (for a fee) séances for grieving loved ones so they might contact their dearly departed.

We need to call into question the behavior on both sides of this offense. Yes, the exploitive medium or psychic who preys on the grieving believer is a parasite or worse. But the belief system of the exploited victims is no less at fault. It is their gullibility that creates a market. Before we justify their actions with a "But they're grieving" defense, consider what they believed *before* they were grieving. In fact, consider the irrational beliefs of those around them who have not lost a loved one. Grief does not suddenly create a whole new set of beliefs. The core irrationality that gets exploited by the John Edwards of this world was well in place before the sad event that brought it into the exploitable range. Uri Geller and John Edward could not make a living if Caveman Logic was not already rampant. And we cannot blame them for *that*.

There is an unfortunate coda to this message. Once they have been discredited, charlatans and the irrational beliefs they exploit do not simply disappear. Author and skeptic Joe Nickell (who has written several *Real-Life X-Files* books) reports that he was one of several "psychic investigators" who caught John Edward cheating on a segment of *Dateline NBC*. According to Nickell, it didn't matter. Nor have James Randi's public debunkings of Uri Geller mattered. People remember Geller as the "psychic spoon bender." They are unlikely to remember his surprisingly frequent public refutations or his futile legal action against Randi. If most Americans remember Geller, it is for his "abilities," not their unmasking.

Nickell has also investigated the Shroud of Turin controversy. His unassailable conclusion is that there is more than enough scientific evidence to show that the shroud was in fact the work of a self-confessed forger in the Middle Ages. But, as Nickell points out, it does not seem to matter how many times the hoax of the shroud is uncovered and publicly reported. It keeps coming back. Neither the public nor the media will let go of it. Every Easter the story resurfaces somewhere and is disproved all over again. It is just too good a myth to let go.

The media are obviously complicit in this. They know a good story when they see one. No one has ever gotten poor banking on naiveté, superstition, or Caveman Logic. Many have gotten rich. It is easier to sell a scam than to debunk one. A haunted house is considered news or, at least, entertainment. Revealing the fact that a haunted house has been faked is neither. At the start of the twenty-first century, the paranormal still has a cachet that skepticism sorely lacks.

CENSORING NIPPLES

Science and politics should never mix. Indeed, science—to do its business according to the rules—must stay clear of all doctrinaire thinking. Here is a familiar example of where it has not.

Lysenko was a Russian biologist who championed the Lamarckian idea that acquired traits could be inherited. This is, of course, wrong. Imagine the Three Blind Mice losing their tails to the farmer's wife, and then producing tailless offspring. However, because a connection was made between this non-Mendelian view of genetics and prevailing Soviet Marxist values, the view received political and economic support. Indeed, Lysenkoism was the official Russian brand of genetics until it was formerly discredited in 1964. The problem is, the rules and findings of science cannot be confined to national borders. It is a universal enterprise and the rest of the scientific universe (i.e., geneticists everywhere else) found Lysenko and his ilk ludicrous.

It is easy to criticize the Lysenko episode and many American and Western European teachers use it as an instructive episode in what happens when science comes under the grip of politics. It is an easy moral tale to share. It does not hurt that the protagonists are somebody else. Better yet, they are a former enemy, whose demise has only confirmed what America believed all along about the "Evil Empire," to quote Ronald Reagan's celebrated meme from the Cold War era.

Americans believe that something like the Lysenko episode could or would never happen *here*. Ask the average American why that is so and the response will be that this is a free country. There are no dictators. There are no threats of imprisonment in frozen gulags or worse to bring uncooperative nonconforming scientists under control.

All of that is probably true. However, the ideological suppression of images or ideas or research can occur in subtler but no less effective ways. One is called *prior restraint*. It is a highly efficient way to censor content without having to publicize the process or involve the legal system. Censorship stays well below public detection and thus avoids civil or legal repercussions.

Some years ago in Ontario, Canada, there was a considerable flap over sexual expression in magazines. When I moved to the province in 1971, it was customary to cover portions of nude pictures, even in mainstream publications like *Playboy* or *Penthouse*, with small black rectangles. Residents of Ontario were thus kept from the crippling psychological effects of seeing images of nipples or pubic hair. These same photos were readily available to any Canadian who could drive across the border and purchase the same magazine in Buffalo, New York, or Detroit, Michigan. These standards were liberalized over the years but for a while the battle to keep Ontario sexually prim was quite successful.

The province spent taxpayer money prosecuting magazine sellers or distributors, not surprisingly losing in court as often as they won. At some point, the censors found an easier way to do their business. They simply had uniformed police officers visit a neighborhood variety store (often run at the time by Asian immigrants) and threaten prosecution if the offending magazines were not removed from display. It worked almost every time. I know of no "mom & pop"–owned variety store that had the time and resources to take on the local police, especially in a country to which they had recently immigrated. They simply complied.

The suppression of research or ideas requires different strategies. Some readers will recall that religious pressure can affect the funding and even the legality of various types of research. The most recent example involves stem cells. However, there is another kind of suppression that occurs well below the radar. Most Americans are aware that there is controversy over the teaching of Darwinian natural selection in public schools. There is fear by some that this information will erode the spiritual values of their children or cause them to question their faith. They ask for religious accounts of biological events to be taught side by side with scientific ones. They argue that this is only fair. It isn't that they want to suppress science altogether, it's just that they want their kids to hear "both sides of the issue."

All of this is old, if disturbing, news. What isn't so well known is the fact that textbooks have also been affected by America's ambivalence about biological science. People wrongly assume that the textbooks used in public science classes will contain the truth, even if some teachers or school districts restrict student exposure to it. Surely the books, they reason, are above this fray. Sadly, this is not the case. Textbooks are typically published by large corporations. These corporations are often publicly traded companies guided by the profit motive. Their writers and editors are aware that a full and undiluted treatment of Darwin is the road to controversy. Controversy does not sell textbooks. In fact, it may cause them to remain unsold.

The adoption of a textbook for the lucrative high school (or university) market is a plum that publishers and their representatives seek. The field is highly competitive. For every science text you've ever seen in a classroom, there were several unsuccessful competitors. Each of those alternatives was a viable candidate that fell short in some way. In the case of university textbook adoptions, the decision is usually made by a single professor teaching the course. There are rarely committees to please and the final choice may be somewhat idiosyncratic. I have seen choices swayed by factors as trivial as seeing a reference to one's own work in the text, having known the author from graduate school days, or liking the book salesman.

Decisions about high school textbooks are usually made by committees and involve larger numbers (and more financial incentives) than the average university adoption. Such committees may be swayed by concerns about public opinions and, like TV programming, are often driven by lowest common denominators. Thus, a book that "plays it safe" even if deficient in many ways is more likely to be chosen than its alternatives that offer better science without pandering to ruffled feathers in the process.

At a recent conference, I discussed the issue with a book rep from one of the large academic publishers. I was stunned by what he confided to me.

"You have no idea how textbooks are dumbed down. Even when we get good scientists or educators to write them, they go through revision by committees who are concerned with politics and the demands of the marketplace. These people know nothing about science. They simply get letters from local school boards who have received threats from local parents or clergy. One thing leads to another and before it's over, the textbook is politically correct. We've got to pull our punches or the book will never sell. We can publish textbooks that remain true to science, but nobody will get to read them. Somebody else's book will get the adoption."

Censorship without tribunal or public awareness is a frightening prospect. In the case of science textbooks it is accomplished without threat of imprisonment or other loss of freedom. Its underlying method—capitalism—is as American as apple pie. You offer the product the market wants and you make money. If you get out of step with your market, you suffer the consequences. Ironically, the entire process is quite Darwinian. Selection currently favors a right-wing, religious conservative approach to teaching biological science. And so those textbooks are proliferating. Pure science books, offering an unapologetic look at Darwinian natural selection, are in danger of becoming extinct.

GOD RUNS FOR OFFICE

Ask most Americans what kind of government they have and they will tell you, "a democracy." By that, they mean the country is governed by the will of the people. Close, but no cigar. Americans may have the vote, but their will does not directly determine the running of the country. The Founding Fathers were very clear about this. They trusted the average American to vote (spare us from a monarchy!), but not to run the country. They were careful to make provisions for a little more expertise. And so, Americans vote for people, presumably more qualified than they, who in turn will run the country. Just how qualified are these candidates? In what way are they superior to the common folk who vote for them?

Selecting our leaders through public elections is further complicated by the fact that a vast number of Americans do not even bother to vote. Voter turnouts in the United States are disgracefully low compared to those of other voting nations. Presumably, the problem does not lie simply with Americans being too lazy to vote. In May 2006, an Alabama singer named Taylor Hicks won the *American Idol* television contest by receiving about 64 million votes. That figure is noteworthy because it is larger than the number of votes ever received by a candidate in a US presidential election up until 2008. Plainly, Americans know how to vote when the issue is something they really care about.

The situation is even further complicated by the fact that American presidential elections are decided not by the popular vote, but by the Electoral College, guaranteeing that a vote in Vermont, for example, is worth less than a vote in Texas. But that is another story. The point is simply that it behooves Americans to look very closely at the leaders they elect because it is the character of these persons, not of the voters themselves, that will determine how the country is run.

Some of our leaders take pride in acting "intuitively." But defaulting to beliefs or decisions that feel "natural" can also be an unmitigated recipe for disaster in the modern world. Allowing what feels "right" or "comfortable" to dictate the terms of international politics is a luxury we can ill afford. But how do we raise the consciousness of those who make critical decisions on our behalf? How do we raise the standard by which an electorate makes its decisions in a democracy?

If we elect superstitious persons whose dependence on unenlightened belief systems shapes their private worldviews, then it should surprise no one that their running of the country will also reflect such thinking. Educated or enlightened voters may be horrified by such a prospect, but it is part of the deal, etched into our Constitution. Is this so much hyperbole? Will our valiant leaders set aside their private superstitions and irrationalities when it comes time to decide America's actions and policies?

Probably not. In fact, it is almost surely the case that a candidate for the US presidency would face certain defeat if he or she did not profess belief in a supernatural controlling deity or did not attend regular (and probably Christian) church services. Thus, statements such as George W. Bush's well-publicized words about God wanting him (Bush) to run for office are viewed with equanimity, if not admiration by the American electorate. As for presidential advisors, here is a sample of the thinking of televangelist James Robison, a close friend and spiritual advisor of former President George W. Bush: "I was driving down the road with my wife one day when I heard God speaking in my mind and my heart. It was not an audible voice, but it was nonetheless real. I heard Him say, *I really like the way you come to me. You don't just come to me with a list of requests and concerns. Instead you crawl up into my arms, lay your head on my shoulder and rest. I like that.*"[19]

One can only hope that Robison's wife was driving at the time. His words are consistent with a long tradition of US presidents invoking the approval of a deity when announcing policy decisions. Even Josiah Bartlett, the fictional US president on television's *The West Wing*, was no exception. Bartlett, more educated and liberal than many real presidents in recent history, regularly ended his public addresses by stating, "God bless you, and God bless America." Moving from television to reality, few wars have been waged without leaders (on both sides) proclaiming that "God is on our side." The antidote to this kind of self-serving pomposity has been a matter of public record for nearly 150 years but is rarely acknowledged. When President Lincoln was asked during the Civil War whether the deity was in line with his policies, Lincoln famously replied, "My concern is not whether God is on our side, (but rather) whether we are on God's side."

The Constitution is supposedly there to protect us from the blurring of church and state, because neither the candidates nor the clergy have much inclination to do so. Rev. Rick Warren, viewed by many as the heir apparent to Billy Graham's role as national spiritual leader, was quite flagrant in attempting to influence the results of US elections. Warren, whose book *The Purpose-Driven Life* sold in excess of 30 million copies, sent a well-publicized message to more than 100,000 preachers, reminding them to emphasize "non-negotiable" issues (such as stem cell research and gay marriage) for Christians to keep in mind when selecting a candidate for political office.

Whether politicians like it or not, the electorate is doing what it can to negate the Constitution and blur the distinction between church and state. The Presidential Prayer Team publishes books and maintains a Web site (www.presidentialprayerteam.org) in order to teach Americans how to pray for their leaders. Once again, we are faced with the puzzle of why God will be more persuaded by the choreographed prayers of the many than the humble, uncoordinated efforts of the few. In any case, books sold by this organization are geared to helping individuals "record the journey of your intercession on behalf of the United States."

The supernatural belief systems lying at the core of American politics go well beyond conventional religion. For example, would most Americans be perturbed to learn that the running of their country at the highest levels was based on astrology? Following the Reagan presidency, it was revealed that virtually nothing of importance, from the president's daily schedule to interactions between the superpowers, had been decided without first consulting an astrologer. Three books have confirmed these events: one by Donald Regan, Reagan's chief of staff; another by Nancy Reagan, whose faith in astrology informed and directed presidential actions; and a third by Joan Quigley, the San Francisco–based astrologer whom Reagan regularly consulted. Mrs. Reagan explained in her book that a background in show business had predisposed her and her husband to an uncritical acceptance of superstition in navigating life's uncertainties.

The question is, had the American electorate been aware of the extent to which the running of their nation had been turned over to such irrational beliefs, would they have protested or taken steps to replace the Reagan presidency? The answer is far from clear. Remember that a large portion of the US population admits holding a belief in astrology. Whether this extends beyond reading daily newspaper astrology columns "for fun" to seeking astrological advice before making life-altering decisions is really the question. The point simply is that the man we elected *did* believe that the fate of Americans and their country was best entrusted to the alignment of celestial bodies, and so that is how our affairs were governed during his presidency. Democracy or not.

The September 17, 2007, issue of *Time* magazine contained a full-page editorial by Michael Kinsley, titled "God as Their Running Mate." Kinsley noted, "Candidates often call him [God] a personal advisor. Voters need to know exactly what that means." Kinsley's focus was on the possible conflict between the orthodoxies and doctrines of one's faith and how adherence to those beliefs might affect performance in elected office. As the June 9, 2008, issue of *Time* made clear, the problem is not uniquely American. The issue featured a cover story about a recently resigned British prime minister; it was titled, "The Faith of Tony Blair."

There is a second cause for concern that does not get addressed often enough to satisfy atheist voters. If candidates are literally engaging in dialogue, and important dialogue at that, with an imaginary being, what does this say about their sanity? If we do not share the view that God exists, much less gets involved in political contests or international affairs, then who is speaking in God's voice during these dialogues? Is this still a private conversation, or do voters have the right to hear what kinds of ideas are floating around the heads of our candidates? Does attributing the dialogue to what may be an imaginary playmate confer some sort of immunity from voter scrutiny?

Chapter 7
CAN IT BE FIXED?

TOYS WON'T SAVE US

As a species, we're always picking up after our mistakes and inventing new sorts of toys. But the real question is whether we can survive the mental equipment we've been blindly depending upon since the Pleistocene Age.

We are a species predisposed to supernatural views of misfortune: when lightning strikes our favorite tree in the backyard, we ask, "What did I do to deserve that?" We are a species that, when faced with the normal effects of disease and decay, turns to a supernatural agent and asks for an exception to be made in our case. We are a species prone to thanking a supernatural agent when fortunate outcomes occur, lest we be seen as ungrateful and risk jinxing the deal. We are a species that sees faces in grilled cheese sandwiches and is prepared to pray to them. We are a species that has trouble supporting a baseball team named the Devil Rays, ultimately resulting in the offending word *devil* being dropped (*angel* fish, good; *devil* ray, bad). We are a species that sometimes shows the sophistication of a Neanderthal when evaluating fragmentary evidence and reaches conclusions about ghosts, "signs," and magical powers in the world around us. We are a species that chooses comfort over reality, especially when that comfort enjoys widespread social support. And we are a species that goes to war to protect our particular delusions against those who do not share them.

I have a colleague who, whenever I raise these issues, humorously says, "Well, we're not going to get anywhere with *this* brain." You can see his point. Natural selection has produced a mind with a very low ceiling. Admittedly, in some respects, it is a spectacular instrument. It certainly has kept our bodies alive and breeding. But in other ways, it has painted us into some unbelievable and potentially deadly corners. Most humans seem incapable or unwilling to get past the haze of Caveman Logic. It's bad enough that we are wrong about so many things, despite the availability of alternative knowledge. What is worse is the genuine peril that surrounds us as the twenty-first century dawns. What *is* the prognosis for our species?

One possibility is that despite the pleading of a small number among us, we will remain mired in superstition and delusion. Our social institutions will continue to support the most flawed parts of our minds. Without wallowing in the details any further, it is clear that this is a bleak picture. But is there a rosier one and can it be achieved? We might sit around and wait for our minds to evolve past their Pleistocene limitations, but this seems foolhardy. For one thing, we are dealing with a *very* slow process and, given the ignitable mixture of superstition and technology in the world today, we just may not have the luxury of waiting. For another, there is no reason to believe that selection pressure will favor the kinds of changes we'd have to make in order to improve. As we have already pointed out, virtually everything that is *wrong* with our minds is tied, one way or another, to something that is quite right. As my grandma (last heard from in chapter 1) might have pointed out in her own less-formal way, taking away the distorted lenses we presently use to see the world is unlikely to improve our reproductive fitness.

TRANSCENDING CAVEMAN LOGIC

"Nature," observed Katharine Hepburn's character in *The African Queen*, "is what we were put in this world to rise above." This famous line—and there are many others like it—is readily interpreted to mean "to rise above our basest nature." In other words, cut out the violence, jealousy, greed, rape, lying, and cheating, and let's get on with what makes us really special.

This is a really bum rap for "nature," which is often blamed for everything that is wrong with us. But to Ms. Hepburn's credit, her statement also includes a rather enlightened premise that is not celebrated widely enough. Namely, that we *can* rise above it. Putting the case in more contemporary terms, our destinies are not carved in stone or etched into our genomes. Her words are a rallying call against biological determinism.

We consider it a badge of accomplishment when we suppress a primitive antisocial impulse. This is the essence of Freudian psychology: our conflict with basic instincts that continue to prod us toward aggression, sexuality, and immediate gratification. But we are better than that. Most of us do not simply hit, rob, or rape whenever the urge crosses our mind. We control those urges, learn to sublimate them, and live peacefully with other members of our species. We pride ourselves on this. We enshrine it in our legal system. We disparage and punish those who do not suppress those primitive impulses we have all experienced. We know you can't simply grab that piece of cake in the bakery window or reach for that woman (or man) whose appearance has just excited you.

Sometimes we describe those who do hit or rob or rape impulsively as "animals." What are we saying? That giving in to primitive impulses is a sign of a "less-evolved" individual or species. We have entered into a social contract and it guarantees in return that our cake, our partners, and our selves will remain safe. Virtually every culture on the planet has learned to control such impulsive behavior under penalty of ostracism or worse.

But why do we draw the line there? There are other, less obvious parts of our "nature" that we might also want to rise above. It isn't just the murder, meanness, and mayhem that we'd like to leave behind. We seem very concerned about protecting our cake and our sex partners, but rather lackadaisical about guarding against the thoughts, feelings, and perceptions that owe their origin to the same early, less-evolved stages of human development. Most of us go blithely reeling into the primitive, error-prone logic of our Stone Age minds. We allow deductive mistakes, misperceptions, and supernatural beliefs—which are no less the remnants of an earlier stage of human evolution—to carry the day. We seem in no hurry to question or discard them.

Every Introductory Psychology textbook on the market today has a chapter on *perception*. Every one of those chapters contains material on *illusions*. We seem to delight in the ways our visual system can be misled by ambiguous sensory information. Our psychology textbooks bask in full-color illustrations of the "Moon Illusion," the "Ponzo Illusion," the "Muller-Lyer Illusion."[1] These reliable malfunctions of our mental hardware seem to cause us no embarrassment. In fact, we're so entranced by them that we make our undergraduates memorize their names and properties.

But we are not equally proud of all our mental malfunctions. Why do we embrace visual distortions but become defensive about flaws in our ability to evaluate information and draw logical conclusions? The underlying dynamics are identical: we have inherited a mental system that thrives on snap judgments and shortcuts. These heuristics serve us in good stead most of the time; however, they can be misapplied or overextended. When that happens, we are handed faulty conclusions and, eventually, erroneous beliefs. The trick is not to depend upon heuristics reflexively, but rather to take the results they provide under review.

When is the last time you heard someone say, "Wow! Given the information I've just received, I'm tempted to drag some supernatural agent into play here. But that seems pretty extreme, so I'm going to have a closer, more careful look at what I've just seen or heard before jumping to any supernatural conclusions."

Like most people, I have experienced the Moon Illusion (the size of the moon appears unnaturally large when it is close to the horizon). I recognize the faulty functioning of this mental module for what it is: the misfiring of something that works very well on most other occasions. I do not argue for the validity of the faulty perception I am experiencing. I do not embrace the company of other persons who also see the moon as impossibly large. I do not seek, at any cost, to find more evidence that the moon actually *is* much larger than we thought. In short, I let it go. I'm proud of my perceptual system. Most of the time, it works admirably well. But sometimes, the very qualities that make it such a streamlined analyzer of the world around me cause it to malfunction. I can live with that. I can even joke about it and teach young professionals in my field how and why such malfunctions occur. The malfunctions may be hardwired, but my acceptance of their results is not. I am not simply willing to accept each and every verdict produced by the ancient, hair-triggered heuristics in my head.

TALKING TO THE INNER CHILD

For this section I am borrowing the language of John Bradshaw and others whose work on "Inner Child" therapy,[2] which became a popular adjunct to psychotherapy in the 1990s and continues to offer a useful metaphor for understanding human behavior.

Assume there's a Holy Trinity of sorts living inside you: an inner child, parent, and adult. Each represents an aspect of your experience and personality that is very much alive in your day-to-day functioning. People sometimes have problems when those three components get out of balance. An overactive inner parent, for example, can result in a repressed or rule-bound individual. An overactive inner child can result in impulsive, shortsighted decisions and a decided lack of maturity. The solution is not to purge the child or the parent altogether, but to heal them and get them back into balance with the whole system. Create a nurturing, understanding parent and a happy, expressive child. The wise adult should be there, too, overseeing the whole show and mediating if necessary.

When that wide-eyed, uncritical inner child of yours sees something amazing and comes running to the inner parent, holding the latest treasured illusion her mind has just produced, the parent can say, "That's wonderful" to little Alice or little Billy or whatever name you have privately given to that excitable, easily impressed, delightfully naive part of yourself. You can let that kind, understanding inner parent who also lives there thank the child for the perceptual illusion he or she has brought "home" with such wide-eyed wonder. "Thank you for doing your job, Billy. Thank you for showing me this thing you've seen or heard. Now we're going to let the adult have a good look at it and see what needs to be done." And ultimately that adult, who is a lot more sophisticated and reality based than the child, will decide that no matter what kind of illusion the child has seen, the Earth really isn't flat. That *isn't* the face of Jesus on a hot cross bun. And your having shouted "I hate you" to your sister didn't cause her to get run over by a car the next day. Those "prayer requests" you make are not being "answered" by a dead ancestor spirit or a personal God who is listening for your voice twenty-four hours a day, waiting to intervene in the fabric of your day-to-day life. A few words of supplication from you will not let you win the lottery or deliver a pony or bring your goldfish back from the dead.

These are all beliefs your inner child may embrace, but they are all wrong. You may cherish that innocent child who lives within you and, indeed, there is much there to cherish. But you do not want her to steer the ship, run the show, or make important decisions in your life.

Perhaps your kind, gentle inner parent can explain to her that it can't possibly work that way. That seeing is not always believing. That there are no magic faces in pizzas or in the clouds. That there are billions of people on Earth, most of whom also want things. Some of those things, like the lottery ticket or the pony, are relatively trivial. Others are not. They involve the pain and suffering of loved ones. They involve life and death. These things, sad as they are, are still part of the natural order of our world. What's the point of having natural laws if they can be broken at the whim of a prayer?

The inner adult should know that living on Earth is both a sad and joyous business. Good things, like sunsets and health and winning lottery tickets, do not require thanks to a supernatural being that you or someone has imagined into existence. The bad things, as sad and painful as they may be, are also part of life on this planet. Asking for exceptions to be made in your case is somewhat arrogant, especially when those requests involve the death and deterioration to which we are all subject. Those inevitabilities are there for the general good. They are not arbitrary. Sure, maybe you'd like to live forever, but as the old parental comeback goes, "What if *everybody* did?" Well, damn near everybody *does* want to. So where does that leave us? Why should God play favorites with you or your child or your puppy? Why not just abolish pain and suffering and death and be done with it? Then *nobody* would have to pray.

If this God you believe in is really as wise as people say he is, then, like your own inner adult, he should be able to sit down with your inner child and say, as kindly as possible,

> I know you're in need. And I know you feel right now that your need is the greatest in the world. But it isn't. And because all things are interconnected, I can't really break the rules and let your gerbil or child or grandmother live. Because if I do, a lot of hamsters or beagles or other grandparents and children are going to die. And they were good pets and people too. And their loved ones are also praying for me to make an exception. So, since I don't want to be arbitrary, I'm going to step back and let it all happen just as it does on this wonderful planet. I'm sorry, little Alice or Billy, that I'm not quite the God you hoped to create, but I'm being very respectful and honest with you. With any luck, your own inner parent or adult can get this to make sense and someday when you grow up, you can be a compassionate, real parent or adult mentor to a real child or friend. And you can explain that everything I've told you is true. Sometimes very difficult, but true.

INCENTIVE TO CHANGE

What incentive is there to change? In baseball terms, will we ever stride to the plate without praying to deities or smearing chicken entrails on our bats? Will we take credit for that crucial base hit rather than attributing it to a higher power? Will we take ownership of our failures as well, rather than attributing them to curses or not enough prayer?

Why should we care about what people believe privately? Because those people vote. Because they band together into groups that wield social power. Because some of them fly airplanes into buildings. Others join armies and feel absolutely justified when they go out to kill opposing armies whose side God is presumably not on. If we are among the relatively few who see things less comfortingly but more realistically, we have got to do everything in our power to educate those around us. This is no easy task. We may be putting our livelihoods and our relationships at risk.

My "not with *this* brain" colleague is fond of pointing out that as a species we have a marvelous track record of repairing our environments and our bodies when necessary. Is it too hot? We invent air-conditioning. Is it too rainy? We put a retractable dome over it. Our eyes don't provide adequate visual information? We invent corrective lenses or laser surgery. Auditory stimuli no longer getting through to you? We invent a hearing aid. Have trouble walking? We reach for a cane, a crutch, a wheelchair, or prosthetic surgery.

There seems no end to compensating for physical problems in our lives. But what of our mental shortfalls? The cliché goes, "If you don't recognize it as a problem, there's no hope of getting it fixed." Tell the folks shaking their fists as they listen to tales of tsunami theology that they have an inaccurate worldview that is in dire need of repair. But don't wait around for them to see the error of their ways. Tell the conferees at an alien abduction gathering that, in all likelihood, the events they are describing originate inside their heads rather than in a universe full of sexually predatory aliens. But, again, don't hold out for much in the way of enlightenment.

Fixing problems *within* our minds is exactly where our minds let us down. Plainly, not all problems can be fixed, but there is a relatively small set of beliefs or mental activity that our society does recognize as needing a fix. As a culture, we agree about certain minimum standards for sanity. Most Western societies would agree that a schizophrenic experiencing florid hallucinations is not OK. That person needs to be isolated to keep him from doing harm to himself or others. Once isolated, there are certain drug regimes that seem to help. We have invented these chemical agents and are willing to make them available to afflicted individuals.

But just how many mental patterns have we identified as pathology? Physical defects are easy to spot and remedy; mental defects are trickier. On balance, most of us would rather have it that way. I would be more optimistic about our species' chances for survival if pseudoscience, organized religion, and a host of other delusions were voluntarily taken off the table. Yet, I would have no hand in prohibiting them. I would much prefer it if my fellow humans opted out of their own accord, preferring to dust off their critical and rational faculties.

The point of mentioning mental illness is to show that on those rare occasions when we agree on what constitutes defective mental functioning, we can do something about it. The problem is that most mental deficits that we agree need fixing are only present in a minority of people. The kind of Caveman Logic we have been discussing in this book involves the majority of humans. By definition, this is going to be tough to remedy. If the world were paranoid schizophrenic and 5 percent of the population saw things in less-threatening terms, what is the likelihood that the problem could be identified and fixed? At present, we find ourselves in a situation in which at least 95 percent of people on the planet believe in some combination of ghosts, alien visitations, communication with the dead, astrology, and an all-powerful deity who screens and answers prayer requests. What incentive is there for this substantial majority to reconsider its beliefs?

In the main, these are good people. They are capable of compassion, decency, generosity, creativity, and hard work. But the list is longer than that and not all of the remaining qualities are admirable. Some of them may be downright dangerous. Not a day goes by when you can't read a story in your local newspaper about those less-admirable qualities at work.

It is true that human nature is a package. Let us embrace what is best about it and work to our fullest to modify what it is not. At least let us be forthright about our deficits. If we choose not to live up to our name *Homo sapiens*, let us do so with our eyes open and for reasons that make sense.

AN ANALOGY FOR YOU ALL

Learning to avoid childlike magical thinking later in life is like learning a second language postpuberty. You can do it, but you'll probably always have an accent. So it is with the mental mistakes and superstitious belief systems we have discussed in this book. Unless you were immunized against them as a child, you will have to work extra hard not to lapse into their effects. It will, in essence, be the mental equivalent of speaking with an accent.

And, speaking of language, here is an analogy. In general, people want to be able to make a distinction between saying "you" in the singular versus plural form. Most languages allow them to do this. In Spanish, for example, the words *usted* and *ustedes* mark the difference. In Hebrew, the distinction is between *ata* and *atem*. In Persian, the word *shoma* means the singular you, and *shomaha* is used for the plural case. In Greek, the distinction is between *esi* and *esis*. In Italian, it's *lei* and *voi*.

Unfortunately, English is not one of those languages that differentiates between the singular and plural form of "you." Since there is no formal solution to the problem, many strategies crop up colloquially. Perhaps the most famous of these is the Southern term *you all* (shortened to *y'all*)—a collective pronoun if there ever was one. It even shows up in the possessive form ("Is that y'all's house?"). In sections of New York such as Brooklyn and the Bronx, the plural term *youse* (often corrupted to *yiz*) handles the task. In parts of Canada, including Ontario and Manitoba, *youse* is also the plural pronoun of choice (e.g., "Would youse like a drink before dinner?"). In western Pennsylvania, the term *you'uns* is used. In Scotland, the variant *youse'uns* has been reported.

In general, a shortfall in the English language seems to go against the grain and has given rise to a host of regional solutions, none of which is officially sanctioned. What is interesting is that in all of these cases the use of an unofficial plural form is tied to socioeconomic status. Educated or professional classes are far less likely to remedy the linguistic problem with a colorful neologism. A former graduate student of mine came from a working-class background and was the first person in his family to attend university.

One day he was complaining to me about faculty policy and commented, "Youse never give the first-year students: . . ." I stopped him and pointed out his use of the language, offering an abbreviated version of my "Lose the Youse" speech. I suggested that, in terms of his success, sounding educated might at times be as important as being educated. He responded by saying, "I can't believe I said that. I didn't even hear it. Everybody I know back home says *youse*. I want to leave that behind. Please point it out to me the next time I do it." To the best of my recollection, he never did, at least around me.

The point of this story and the whole digression into plural pronouns is this: the mind seems to want a plural form of "you" for the sake of communication. When its native language lets it down, the mind will create and/or embrace any reasonable solution. But the activity is strictly optional. The compelling linguistic force that draws us to use "youse," if you will, or some plural form where none exists, can be resisted. The force to alter language is obviously not as powerful as the one that compels many other forms of Caveman Logic. In the case of language, a regional speech pattern can be overcome or avoided altogether by exposure to social incentives for using so-called correct English. That's all it takes. My student was able to will himself out of two decades of socialization by "youse" users in order to sound more like the educated man he was becoming. Avoiding most of the mental mistakes we describe in this book may require more work than that. Many people have been socialized to commit these mistakes. Both the mental errors and the beliefs they lead to feel extremely natural. Worse yet, their *absence* may feel quite unnatural. Nevertheless, it can be done. There are those who do not regularly engage in these mental missteps, and there is no reason to believe that such persons have different cognitive architecture than the rest of us. Moreover, they do not all come from "enlightened" backgrounds. Turning again to my former student, it was clear that he wanted to move beyond where he had been. That simple bit of motivation may be a crucial prerequisite for change.

THE BETTER ANGELS OF OUR NATURE

"The better angels of our nature." What a wonderful phrase. It appears in the final paragraph of Lincoln's first inaugural address in 1861. If Lincoln took it from an earlier source, the reference has escaped my attention. The phrase has been borrowed countless times since, often as part of sermons or commencement addresses. It is plainly inspirational and often appears along with the words "appeal to." Special people or special circumstances are considered appeals to the "better angels of our nature." I have always understood the phrase to mean that under certain conditions we should go beyond what comes easily. Whether in thought or action, we should dig more deeply into the information or—if you will—into ourselves and think or act in a way that is somehow more highly evolved or enlightened. By definition this will not come easily. To some it will come not at all.

It will certainly take more work and it may not always receive much in the way of social support. But despite the difficulty and the lack of consensus, we will somehow know that this path is better: something we can be proud of. Some might describe it as higher or purer. The phrase "better angels" suggests that not all the angels that inspire us are created equal. Some of those alternative angels may be "worse," even if their call is to a well-traveled path that comes more naturally.

Nowhere is it suggested that we must summon the better angels of our nature all the time. But it is the hope of such an appeal that we can rally this extra energy when it really matters. At least we know it is an available option. We know that sometimes it really is OK to decline those default settings or shortcuts with which natural selection has imbued our minds. In other words, using the language of cognitive psychology, it is sometimes OK to use the algorithm and forget the heuristic. It is sometimes OK to think about what we're really seeing and discount or second-guess the conclusion that is forcing its way into our consciousness like a mindless brute. Even though the same brute is doing his work on the minds of our friends and family, we can resist the social pressure and consider the better angels of our nature. Doing what comes naturally, seeing those faces in the clouds, interpreting that quarter on the sidewalk as a "sign" from the universe—those are default Pleistocene settings. They are not our better angels. They are what natural selection, that ruthless efficiency expert, has trip-wired our minds to do.

It would be easier to face the world without that Stone Age mess rattling around in our heads, but we can still express our "better angels." We can acknowledge the default settings in our minds, but not relinquish control to them on a reflexive basis. We have enough cognitive flexibility to act, much of the time, as if we had evolved to a higher level. We may still see the face in the pizza when we look quickly, but we do not have to act on that perceptual impulse. We do not have to form prayer vigils outside the pizzeria. We do not have to beseech the Holy Pepperoni to intervene in our lives and make them better. We do not have to vote for politicians who include Pepperoni references in their campaign speeches. We do not have to fall under the leadership of pizza-prophets and kill those who do not see the same face we do, or perhaps see a different face in a jelly donut.

JUST IMAGINE

We have examined the roots of Caveman Logic, we have looked at its manifestations in our present society, and we have considered strategies for overcoming its worst effects. The simple question remains: Will we succeed?

Not surprisingly, others have addressed this issue. They have examined the superstitious, the irrational, and the dangerously wrongheaded things humans continue to believe and do. Most authors like myself are implicitly optimistic in the sense that they offer suggestions for improvement. If we didn't believe in the possibility of enlightenment and change, we wouldn't spend thousands of hours writing our books. By analogy, I do not believe I am holding a red card in front of a color-blind person, repeatedly shouting, "See it, damn you!" I am not concerned with the absence of an ability, but with its overapplication. I am asking people to be more circumspect in their use of mental tendencies that come far too easily to them.

But optimism isn't the only attitude you'll find. When asked to speculate directly on the irrational aspect of human nature, other psychologists and philosophers have sounded downright pessimistic. David Hume wrote of irrationality, "Though this inclination may at intervals receive a check from sense and learning, it can never be thoroughly extirpated from human nature."[3] Other authors, Carl Sagan[4] among them, decry the fact that we have never been more educated and informed, yet we seem hell-bent for another Dark Age of fear and superstition.

What if Sagan is right? Isn't it a liberal edict that everyone is entitled to his or her belief system? Aren't ignorance and stupidity God-given rights, so to speak? Perhaps, but as such ignorance moves into the mainstream and has implications that threaten all of us, isn't it time to stand up and say so? As neuroscientist and author Sam Harris writes, "Half of the American population believes that the universe is 6,000 years old. They are wrong about this. Declaring them so is not 'irreligious intolerance.' It is intellectual honesty."[5]

Moreover, doesn't such ignorance become more egregious as alternative knowledge becomes more readily available? Few of us would condemn a man in 1308 for professing the superstitious misinformation of his age. But how do we react to persons among us professing those same beliefs seven hundred years later? Or demanding that their beliefs be taught to their children in public institutions? If it is *still* too soon to be sure about what is correct, can we foresee a time in the future when the weight of evidence will be so overwhelming that it will be OK to say, "This is right, and this—although some clung tenaciously to it for a while—is wrong." A time when, other than teaching earlier beliefs as part of the history of human folly, we can simply say no to continuing to offer them equal time in our public institutions?

When Shakespeare wrote, "The fault, dear Brutus, lies not in our stars but in ourselves," he was creating what might have been a mantra to keep us from magical thinking and overactive agency detectors. Unfortunately, although his quotation is still widely known, its sentiments have been just as widely ignored.

Try to imagine a world where 95 percent of the population is voluntarily atheistic. Where rampant belief in supernatural agency is not socially supported. Where the names of supernatural agents are not written on government-issued monetary units. Where political leaders do not invoke the names of deities at the conclusion of speeches or use the blessing of such deities in justifying state-sanctioned wars.

Imagine a world in which natural disasters, accidents, illness, and death are viewed as unfortunate but normal occurrences in a lawful universe, and not as evidence of supernatural vengeance or intervention.

Imagine a world where people routinely accept the fact that some important events lie outside their control. They make no attempt to invent supernatural agents who can be persuaded to intervene on their behalf.

Imagine a world where the large majority of humans lead moral lives because of personal or social codes, not because they fear supernatural retribution.

Imagine a world where one's identity is not so "tribal" that hatred and violence against "out–group" members (on the basis of religion or nationality) can be readily triggered by pandering preachers or politicians.

Imagine a world in which humans accept that they have a finite life span. Although it is longer at present than it has ever been before, it is nevertheless measured in decades, not eternities. That after death, one's body ceases to function and begins to decompose. That while one may be lovingly remembered for past deeds, the days as an active agent, mentally and physically, will be over.

Can you imagine any of this? Certainly, it is a task for the imagination because very little of it is true today. Some of us may be capable of some of these things some of the time, but few of us can do it all routinely. And if you can, you will find little institutional support. That is a shame. I view each of these things as stepping stones toward human improvement. Collectively, they would represent forward movement in the evolution of our species toward behavior and understanding that are truly worthy of our name, *Homo sapiens*. At present, we are a pale imitation of that name.

Certainly, such a world would be very different from the one in which most of us live. Some like Carl Sagan are optimistic enough to believe that with some combination of improved education and social support, humans can be dragged out of the Dark Age into which their present culture seems to be descending. But others are more pessimistic. They question whether we, as a species, are capable of even the six entries listed above. Are they a reachable goal for our species, or are they the sole domain of just a rarified, enlightened few, who are unlikely to succeed in sharing their wisdom with others?

Perhaps someday the majority of humans will not see patterns that are not there or turn to supernatural agents when control seems out of their reach. But that day is not yet on the horizon. Arguably it would require such fundamental changes that we may be looking at a different species, in the same way that *Australopithecus* was a different species of hominin than *Neandertalus*. Someone will have to name this new, less-superstitious, more clear-headed human species. Unfortunately the name *Homo sapiens* will already have been squandered.

This is a pessimistic view, and yet it may be realistic. To the extent that my shopping list of criteria for human improvement seems unimaginable, you may already share this pessimism. Would a change of this magnitude require reeducation or physical change? Could it be accomplished at the level of memes or would selection pressure on cognitive architecture be required for such perceptual and cognitive change? Certainly, it is not as simple as electing new leadership. As deplorable as the present state of affairs may appear to some, it resulted from human choices. Likewise, the emergence of fundamentalist religion as a major factor in world politics in the twenty-first century was not imposed on us by extraterrestrials; it reflects fundamental aspects of human nature. In that sense, there has been little change in the past two thousand years.

This should surprise nobody. Two thousand years is hardly time to alter fundamental things about the nature of a species, unless that species has the life span of a fruit fly. There has been far more technological change in two thousand years than change in our genome. We still go to war with a regularity that makes it clear that fighting and killing "outsiders" is fundamental to our nature. The manner in which we kill each other has evolved technologically, but the fundamental causes or the frequency of the act itself remain invariant. Conflict over territory or resources still triggers battle. Disagreement over supernatural belief systems is still reason to kill. "Death to the infidels!" is essentially the same message whether shouted by a Muslim in 2001 or a Catholic in 1200.

ADDRESSING THE PROBLEM

If there were no solution, it would hardly seem fair to spend an entire book identifying the problem. There *is* a solution. Every mental flaw discussed in this book can be remedied.

We are far from alone in identifying what is wrong with the human mind. In fact, examining the workings of human cognition—with both praise and criticism—has become something of a growth industry in publishing. For example, In *The Demon-Haunted World*, Carl Sagan offers a "Baloney Detection Kit"—a list of twenty common logical errors we use to support our favorite irrational conclusions.[6] These are part of what my students and I often refer to as a "bullshit detector." This book cites other sources similar to Sagan's work. You will find unique insights in each, as well as considerable overlap, both in identifying the problem and suggesting how to fix it.

SUMMARY OF DESIGN FLAWS

Here is a shopping list of mental design flaws you can expect to encounter, not only in most like-minded books on the market, but also when examining your own experience.

1. Events that happen around you are not all under your control. Many have occurred quite apart from anything you did (or thought). If you insist on attempting to control everything, you will end up enmeshed in faulty cause-effect belief systems.

2. Realizing that you cannot control everything is only half the battle. You must then avoid the tendency to imagine causal agents and form "relationships" with these imaginary characters. Lack of control means lack of control. You cannot invent and endear yourself to an imaginary agent whom you hope to influence. This is simply an end run around the lack-of-control dilemma.

3. We have a strong tendency to see structure and patterns where none exist. It is useful to impose order on events, but we often venture too far in this direction. Randomness is a lot more prevalent in our world than we realize. Clouds and pizzas don't have faces in them. You need to work hard to keep that hair-triggered pattern detector under control.

4. Our minds are wired to interpret things we see or hear. Much of what we respond to is fragmentary or incomplete and some of it may have originated *inside* our heads, not outside. Be open to the possibility that the raw material for some of the ghosts or gods or demons you detect resides inside your own mind. It doesn't mean you're crazy. In fact, it takes a sound and disciplined mind to hold off on those easy interpretations.

5. Many types of events occur almost continuously every day. Of necessity, there will be a huge number of coincidences. Most of them will be utterly devoid of meaning. Learn to accept coincidences for what they are. They do not need explaining.

6. Don't be afraid to evaluate your beliefs, especially the most important ones in your life. If all you want is comfort and familiarity, you can disregard this advice. If you are looking for more, remember that scientific evaluation consists of more than accumulating positive cases and ignoring the negative ones. Think of some of your favorite beliefs. Ask yourself what it takes to refute them. Think of some positive evidence you've collected to strengthen these beliefs. If the *opposite* (i.e., negative evidence) had occurred, would you have considered changing those beliefs?

7. Beware of multiple endpoints: Some hypotheses or beliefs are stated so generally that many kinds of events can be taken as evidence. If you allow such vast amounts of cases to be "positive," then confirmation is almost certain to occur. This is a far cry from "science" or "rationality." It's a prime case of Caveman Logic. Don't mistake it for anything else.

8. Don't minimize or fail to consider negative outcomes. They may not be memorable or particularly gratifying, but they are crucial to evaluating many hypotheses and beliefs. At the least, they should remind you that positive cases are actually numerators in fractions and may be less compelling than you believed.

9. Taking (8) above even further, most situations actually lend themselves to a 2×2 matrix. For example: I prayed, I didn't pray. Something good happened, something good didn't happen. Each one of those four cells contains information, although believers and nonbelievers alike tend to be persuaded by evidence from one particular cell. Examination of the full matrix is necessary to evaluate the underlying question.

10. Scientists place a premium on testing a random and representative sample of subjects. In real life, samples are usually very small and highly biased (i.e., nonrandom). Avoid drawing conclusions from such incomplete evidence, even if you happen to like the conclusions.

11. Chance, meaningless coincidences, and lack of control may not describe the world in which we want to live, but it is a good approximation of the one in which we find ourselves. You get two choices: a) acknowledge and accommodate the realities around us, or b) create a delusional cocoon in which to live. If you choose b), you'll have no trouble finding others to live there with you. Again, it's the fundamental choice: reality or comfort.

12. Interactions with Santa Claus can make anyone—from a child to an elderly person—feel good. Enjoy the moment; savor the

Pavlovian conditioned response, the feelings, the thoughts, the memories. But *know* what you are doing. There is a big difference between enjoying Santa Claus and believing there really is a jolly old fat guy living at the North Pole.

Above all, keep this in mind: The basis for each of the tendencies and flaws we have identified is hardwired. Under certain circumstances, the circuits for these flaws may have provided a decided advantage to our ancestors. Those are the conditions that led to the selection of these mental modules in the first place, and which allow them to persist to the present day. It is an axiom in evolutionary psychology that even our finest adaptations can be made to look less than ideal when environmental conditions change. The solution here is not to purge the hardwired heuristic. You probably couldn't even if you wanted to. That heuristic will remain a part of your mental apparatus, and that of your children's children.

What you *can* do is surprisingly straightforward:

1. Recognize the nature of the flaw and the results it is likely to yield.
2. Take conscious steps to counteract these effects.

It may be a cliché, but *forewarned is forearmed.* If you know what to expect of your mind, you can deal with it when it happens. Remember, it may feel very natural as it's happening. But that doesn't make it valid. I can tell you exactly the conditions under which the Moon Illusion and the Muller-Lyer Illusion will occur. I expect them and, true to form, my mind provides the same faulty perceptions it did the last time I was in that situation. And so, forewarned as I am, I am prepared to discount the message and use other perceptual cues to reach a more accurate perception of what's out there. It doesn't matter that six persons may be kneeling by the side of the road, looking at the sky and shouting, "Praise the Moon!" It takes courage to stand alone. Remember, opting into an illusion is a high price to pay for company.

And the next time someone proudly tells you that he's "spiritual" or "patriotic"—two much-vaunted qualities in today's world—

you might consider not falling in line to praise him. Of course, should you convey any disdain toward those qualities, you may find yourself defending your position with your fists.

That reaction is the heart of the matter. Caveman Logic will get you from loving your god or your country to hating someone else's in short order. And once you conclude that your god and country are the best, it becomes harder and harder to tolerate that idiot across the border or in that nearby church. You've just got to make him understand the truth. There are rarely enough "Convert or Die" t-shirts to go around.

You will not eliminate these impulsive, faulty perceptions. But you can make the use of compensatory strategies more "natural" and more likely with each passing event. At first, the process will seem laborious and unnatural. The hardwired perception may seem utterly compelling. But it can be sidestepped in favor of a more reality-based alternative that you can have at the ready. To this end, use the list of twelve design flaws in a prescriptive way. Memorize the list or, at the least, familiarize yourself with it. Anticipate which of those flaws you are likely to be confronted with, given the situation you'll be in. Know what to expect and be ready for it. Understanding the basis for each of these faulty perceptions is to arm yourself against them.

It may be helpful to think of our dependence on Caveman Logic as if it were a substance addiction. In this case, the addiction is shared by most members of the human race, affecting its pursuit of truth and perhaps even its survival. Just as heroin addicts, overeaters, alcoholics, and cigarette smokers tend to socialize with others who share their addiction, so do people whose lifestyle centers around belief in deities, angels, or space aliens.

Viewing Caveman Logic as an addiction raises our awareness of how difficult it can be to turn away from habitual ways of thinking or believing. Recovery from a substance addiction is rarely a smooth or overnight process. It takes effort and persistence to wean oneself away. Occasional relapses, especially partial ones, are normal. We are not suggesting a twelve-step program for Caveman Logic "addicts," but some support along the way, perhaps from a local humanist association or Unitarian church, may be helpful. In her one-woman show, actress Julia Sweeney offers a vivid account of the gradual and painful journey she made from childhood indoctrination in the Catholic church to atheism in her adult life. Sweeney's performance, currently available on DVD (www.julia sweeney.com), is well worth seeing.

Although we can anticipate how our minds will misfire, we cannot always anticipate exactly which environmental triggers we will encounter. Most of us are inundated with fragmentary or confusing information all the time. It is just those conditions that trigger the heuristics whose overapplication often causes us problems. When things are happening fast, take a step back. See the inadequacy of the information for what it is. Suppress the impulse to let the heuristic do all the work. If a lion is chasing you, or an enemy is lurking among your so-called friends, it is probably a good idea to go with your hardwired, evolved circuitry. But in a multitude of other circumstances when the stakes are not quite so high, it is permissible to bring some of your more modern and voluntary brain mechanisms to the table.

The alternative to each of these faulty perceptions and beliefs is easy to describe. If your mind is ready to scream "pattern!" in your ear, the alternative is "nonpattern." Nothing there. No face in the clouds. No Blessed Virgin in the grilled cheese sandwich. Just pure chance or, more to the point, pure cheese. If someone is raving about a "hot hand" by your favorite member of the Boston Celtics or a batting streak by one of the New York Mets, be ready to question it. Ask whether the feel-good display you're both watching really exceeds a chance distribution of hits and misses. When a psychic makes claims for his uncanny accuracy, stop and examine the evidence. Was his "uncanny ability to predict" based on multiple endpoints? What happened to all the negative cases? In fact, confronted with any supernatural or paranormal claim, remember the Randi Foundation and their standing offer. If what you're seeing is real, then you're a million bucks richer. It's a sobering reminder that such claims are probably bogus. Some may reflect outright fraud, but most are just naively evaluated instances of pure chance. Wishful thinking by hungry and untrained minds.

Had it not been for some special moments in your life, that might have been you on your knees, praising the Lord, taking your kids to a creationist theme park, believing that "things happen for a reason," or seeing the face of Jesus in a slice of pizza. You were born just as predisposed to those beliefs and perceptions as you were to learning language. Something went right for you. You obviously worked hard not to indulge Caveman Logic, even while those around you were lining up to embrace it. Maybe you were immunized against it at an early age. But whatever your good fortune, make no mistake about it: you still share those old circuits and predispositions with the vast majority of humanity. If nothing else, that gives you some insight into the problem. You have some idea about the power of Caveman Logic and what it takes to overcome it.

Having read this book or one like it, it is a little harder to claim that yours is an untrained mind. You are now officially infected with the skeptic bug. Your childhood religious training may prompt you to accept naive beliefs or perceptions, but you're going to think twice before acting on them. Like it or not, a more enlightened adult view has moved into your mind. It may be hard to get rid of it. You are stuck with a richer, more accurate awareness of the universe around you.

HERE WE ARE

And so, here we are—a species with some extraordinary mental abilities. In fact, as pure abstract thought and symbolic processing go, there is no species on Earth that comes close to our abilities. As we have noted before, our problem is not with the adequacy of the cognitive mechanisms we have inherited; it is with the inability to turn them off. They work all too well and too frequently.

As we have repeatedly seen, the two biggest offenders are our pattern detectors and our causal agency detectors. If both of these spectacular abilities simply knew when to stop, when *not* to respond or draw conclusions, we would be a more cognitively adroit and reality-based species. Since the cognitive architecture is hardwired, we cannot simply get it to stop working. But we can refuse to accept the verdicts it offers. When the circuit pushes us to see patterns or connections or agents of control, we can say,

"Thanks for the suggestion. I can see why you were triggered. Now I'm going to go back to my real life." I will not call the cops or the local paper to report my "sighting." I understand where this is coming from in me. And I also understand that I do not have to accept it as gospel truth. I choose to remain rational and not give into this trip-wired circuitry. I choose to bring other more cognitively advanced parts of my brain into the act.

Note that we do not want to purge this circuitry altogether. We can recognize the contribution a hair-triggered pattern detector or an agency detector may bring to our lives (and to those of our ancestors). But that does not mean we have to relinquish control to this antique circuitry today. We reserve the right to seek a second opinion from other parts of our brain. Sometimes this will seem like a lonely task. Our friends or family may already be out there pointing to that piece of pizza and genuflecting. We may *want* to join them in order to validate their perception or be validated by our connection to them. This is costly business, but more of us have to take these steps in the evolution of our species.

At the least, we should work to erode the social support that ignorance and irrationality enjoy within our culture. Richard Dawkins and others have argued eloquently against the special immunity that religious belief enjoys from criticism. This is indeed a dangerous state of affairs. But perhaps more important, atheists, humanists, and skeptics must work to establish support networks of their own. Cognitive architecture will not change within our lifetimes, but the allocation of social and political power can. We can work to stigmatize rather than dignify signs of Caveman Logic. We can work to make "skeptical" sound sexy. Rationality is a meme, and there is no reason it cannot be more actively supported and shared in all its forms. Humanists should not feel like outsiders when they express their views at school boards or town hall meetings. Atheists should not feel like pariahs when they band together and speak up at national political rallies. Their viewpoint should not be shunned by network media or relegated to the fringes of publicly supported communication.

At a recent meeting of the Humanist Association of Canada, former Christian evangelist Dan Barker talked about the kind of messages that might have "gotten through to him" when he was under the church's control. Barker's book *Losing Faith in Faith: From Preacher to Atheist*[7] details this phase of his life. He argued that exposure to credible alternatives to delusional beliefs might have made a difference during early stages of his development. Barker has written and performs several antireligious, prohumanist songs. As one conferee jokingly commented, "We need a theme song." Yes, we do. There is no rallying call, no unifying theme or symbol for the increasing number of humanists, skeptics, and atheists.

Many forms of Caveman Logic are embodied in literature, art, and music. Indeed, it is fair to say they are embodied in *great* literature, art, and music. We have no such legacy other than what *Time* magazine called "the roar of atheist books" in its summary of the year 2007. There is more to be written, painted, and composed.

Human history of the past millennium is a halting march away from superstition toward knowledge. We are still far from our goal, but our species is young. Ultimately, this book is about that march, and your part in it. Many of the suggestions in this book will place you, to use a popular idiom, ahead of the curve. That takes not only insight, but also strength of character.

 # ENDNOTES

ACKNOWLEDGMENTS

1. Hank Davis, *Small-Town Heroes: Images of Minor League Baseball* (Lincoln, NE: Bison Books, 2003); Stephen Jay Gould, *Triumph and Tragedy in Mudville: A Lifelong Passion for Baseball* (New York: W. W. Norton, 2003).

INTRODUCTION

1. Jacqueline Salmon, "Most Americans Believe in Higher Power, Poll Finds," *Washington Post*, June 24, 2008.

2. Rob Walker, "Pop-Culture Evolution," *New York Times Magazine*, April 15, 2007, p. 20; James Poniewozik, "It's an Ad. But Is It Art?" *Time*, July 2, 2007, p. 46.

CHAPTER 1

1. Susan Blackmore, *The Meme Machine* (New York: Oxford University Press, 1999), p. 11.

2. Martin Daly, "Natural Selection Doesn't Have Goals, but It's the Reason Organisms Do," *Behavioral and Brain Sciences* 14, no. 2 (1991): 219–20.

3. Steve Connor, "Genetic Breakthrough That Reveals the Differences between Humans," *Independent,* November 23, 2006; Michael D. Lemonick and Andrea Dorfman, "What Makes Us Different?" *Time,* October 9, 2006, pp. 33–39.

4. Stephen S. Hall, "Last of the Neanderthals," *National Geographic* 214, no. 4 (October 2008): 34ff.

5. Timothy H. Goldsmith and William F. Zimmerman, *Biology, Evolution, and Human Nature* (New York: John Wiley and Sons, 2001), p. 283.

6. Michael W. Passer, Ronald E. Smith, Michael L. Atkinson, John B. Mitchell, and Darwin W. Muir, *Psychology: Frontiers and Applications,* 2nd Canadian ed. (Toronto: McGraw-Hill Ryerson, 2005).

7. Carl Sagan, *Contact* (New York: Simon & Schuster, 1985).

8. Steven Pinker, *How the Mind Works* (New York: W. W. Norton, 1997), p. 21.

9. Scott Atran and Ara Norenzayan, "Religion's Evolutionary Landscape: Counterintuition, Commitment, Compassion, Communion," *Behavioral and Brain Sciences* 27, no. 6 (2004): 713–30.

10. Hank Davis and Stephanie Tytus, "Santa Claus and God: A Match Made in Heaven," *Canadian Freethinker* 2, no. 3 (Fall 2008): 8–12.

11. Richard Dawkins, "Life: A Gene-Centric View," *Edge* 234 (January 24, 2008).

12. Thomas Gilovich, *How We Know What Isn't So* (New York: Free Press, 1993).

13. Carl Sagan, *The Demon-Haunted World* (New York: Random House, 1995).

CHAPTER 2

1. Henry Plotkin, *Evolution and Mind* (New York: Penguin, 1997), p. 199.

2. B. F. Skinner, "'Superstition' in the Pigeon," *Journal of Experimental Psychology* 38 (1948): 168–72.

3. Hank Davis and James Hubbard, "An Analysis of Superstitious Behavior in the Rat," *Behaviour* 43 (1973): 1–12.

4. Gerd Gigerenzer and Peter M. Todd, *Simple Heuristics That Make Us Smart* (New York: Oxford University Press, 1999).

5. Paul Bloom and Deena Skolnick Weisberg, "Childhood Origins of Adult Resistance to Science," *Science* 316 (May 18, 2007): 996–97.

6. Seth Asser, paper presented at the Amazing Meeting 3, Las Vegas, January 13–16, 2005, http://www.randi.org.

7. Gabrielle Bauer, "God and Other Mysteries," *Reader's Digest*, Canadian ed., November 2003, pp. 50–59.

8. Susan Blackmore, *The Meme Machine* (New York: Oxford University Press, 1999), cited in Chad M. Lewis, "Investigating Students' Beliefs in the Paranormal," unpublished master's thesis, University of Wisconsin–Stout, Menomonie, May 2002.

9. Lewis, "Investigating Students' Beliefs in the Paranormal."

10. Julian Baggini, "A Woman's Place in Rational Debate," *London Times Educational Supplement*, October 9, 1999.

11. Mike Sofka, Amy Bix, and Beth Wolszon, "Women and Skepticism," Round Earth Society, 2004, http://www.str.com.br/english/res/women.htm.

12. Robert Park, *Voodoo Science* (New York: Oxford University Press, 2000), p. 195.

13. "UK among Most Secular Nations," *BBC News*, February 26, 2004.

14. Jacqueline Salmon, "Most Americans Believe in Higher Power, Poll Finds," *Washington Post*, June 24, 2008.

15. http://www.pollingreport.com/religion/htm.

16. Ibid.

17. Ibid.

18. Cited in Bloom and Skolnick Weisberg, "Childhood Origins of Adult Resistance to Science."

19. http://www.pollingreport.com/religion/htm.

20. Stephen Prothero, *Religious Literacy* (San Francisco: HarperCollins, 2007).

21. David Van Biema, "The Case for Teaching the Bible," *Time*, April 2, 2007, p. 28–34.

22. Gabrielle Bauer, "God and Other Mysteries," *Reader's Digest*, Canadian ed., November 2003, pp. 50–59.

23. Edward J. Larson and Larry Witham, "Leading Scientists Still Reject God," *Nature* 394, no. 6691 (1998): 313.

24. Ron Csillag, "Math + Religion = Trouble," *Toronto Star*, January 29, 2008, http://www.thestar.com/news/article/297564.

25. Larson and Witham, "Leading Scientists Still Reject God."

26. http://www.objectivethought.com/atheism/iqstats.html.

27. Margaret Wente, "Who's Afraid of Darwin? Everyone," *Toronto Globe and Mail*, March 8, 2008.

28. Richard Miller, "From Hobbits to Hobbes: Reducing Students' Belief in the Paranormal," paper read at APA 22nd Annual Convention, Chicago.

29. Daniel Fuselier and Rob Neiss, Letters to *APA Monitor* 34 (February 2003).

30. M. E. P. Seligman, "On the Generality of the Laws of Learning," *Psychological Review* 77 (1970): 406–18.

CHAPTER 3

1. Mark Silk, "Was New Orleans Asking for It?" *Religion in the News* 8, no. 2 (Fall 2005).

2. Carl Sagan, *The Demon-Haunted World* (New York: Random House, 1995)

3. Steven J. C. Gaulin and Donald H. McBurney, *Psychology: An Evolutionary Approach* (Upper Saddle River, NJ: Prentice Hall, 2001).

4. Carl Jung, *Synchronicity: An Acausal Connecting Principle* (Princeton, NJ: Princeton University Press, 1973).

5. Hank Davis, "A Further Penetration into the Deep and Enthralling Mystery of Names," *Journal of Biological Psychology* 20 (1978): 101–104.

6. Jung, *Synchronicity*, p. 15.

7. J. B. Rhine, *Extra-sensory Perception* (Boston: Bruce-Humphries, 1934).

8. Cited in Thomas Gilovich, *How We Know What Isn't So* (New York: Free Press, 1993) pp. 163–66.

9. Todd Zolecki, "Players, Fans Get Attached to Uniform Numbers," *Philadelphia Inquirer*, May 26, 2007.

10. Hank Davis and Andrea Javor, "Religion, Death and Horror Movies: Some Striking Evolutionary Parallels," *Evolution and Cognition* 10, no. 1 (2004): 11–18.

11. http://www.coyoteblog.com/coyote_blog/2008/07/so-lawrence -sum.html.

12. Colin Wilson, *The Occult* (London: Grafton Books, 1979).

13. Richard Dawkins, *A Devil's Chaplain* (New York: Houghton Mifflin, 2003), p. 143.

14. Julian Barnes, *Nothing to Be Frightened Of* (New York: Random House, 2008).

15. "Dionne Warwick Arrested for Pot Possession," http://www.cnn .com, May 13, 2002.

16. http://www.stephanyhurkos.com/peter_biography.htm.

17. Even when the item originates in the outside world (and is thus "real"), there is no guarantee that we will see or hear it accurately. Francis Bacon (1561–1626) called human understanding "a false mirror," inevitably distorted by our own consciousness. Bacon distinguished between species-wide and individual distortions, which he called "Idols of the Tribe" and "Idols of the Cave," respectively. In either case, he argued, there would be a measurable difference between what we perceived and what was really out there. These conclusions still seem sound nearly four hundred years later.

18. M. A. Persinger, "On the Possibility of Directly Accessing Every Human Brain by Electromagnetic Induction of Fundamental Algorithms," *Perceptual and Motor Skills* 80 (1995): 791–99; "Are 'Aliens' All in the Temporal Lobes?" http://www.cfree.org/contact/viewpoints/view005.html.

19. Blaise Pascal, *Pensées* (1670).

20. David Berreby, *Us and Them* (Chicago: University of Chicago Press, 2008)

21. http://www.yamasa.org/japan/english/destinations/aichi/tagata _jinja.html.

22. Amanda Ripley, "Staying Alive," *Time*, May 2, 2005, pp. 39–42.

23. Steven J. C. Gaulin and Donald H. McBurney, *Psychology: An Evolutionary Approach* (Upper Saddle River, NJ: Prentice Hall, 2001).

24. John Teehan, *In the Name of God* (Boston: Wiley-Blackwell, 2009).

25. Steven Pinker, *The Language Instinct* (New York: HarperCollins, 1994).

26. Walter Isaacson, "Einstein & Faith," *Time*, April 16, 2007, p. 34.

CHAPTER 4

1. http://www.sabr.org.

2. Thomas Gilovich, R. Vallone, and Amos Tversky, "The Hot Hand in Basketball: On the Misperception of Random Sequences," *Cognitive Psychology* 17 (1985): 295–314.

3. Thomas Gilovich, *How We Know What Isn't So* (New York: Free Press, 1993).

4. J. E. Alcock, "Science of the Anomalous or Search for the Soul?" *Behavioral and Brain Sciences* 10, no. 4 (1987): 553–65; K. R. Rao and J. Palmer, "The Anomaly of Psi: Recent Research and Criticism," *Behavioral and Brain Sciences* 10, no. 4 (1987): 539–51; Open peer commentary and response, *Behavioral and Brain Sciences* 10, no. 4 (1987): 566–644.

5. Shere Hite, *The Hite Report: A Nationwide Study of Female Sexuality* (New York: Dell, 1976).

CHAPTER 5

1. Frans B. M. de Waal, "Primates: A Natural Heritage of Conflict Resolution," *Science* 289 (2000): 586–90; Matt Ridley, *The Origins of Virtue* (New York: Viking Press, 1996); Marc D. Hauser, *Moral Minds* (New York: HarperCollins, 2006).

2. Dan Barker, *Just Pretend: A Freethought Book for Children* (Madison, WI: FFRF, 2002).

3. Cited in Michael Shermer, "The Political Brain," *Scientific American*, June 26, 2006.

4. http://www.quotationspage.com/quote/27537.html.

5. Pascal Boyer, *Religion Explained* (New York: Basic Books, 2001).

6. Steven Jay Gould, *Triumph and Tragedy in Mudville* (New York: W. W. Norton, 2003).

7. Hank Davis, *The Original Sun Singles, Vol. 1*, liner notes, Bear Family Records, 1994.

8. Peter Guralnick, *Dream Boogie: The Triumph of Sam Cooke* (New York: Little, Brown, 2005).

9. Alice Park, "Battle-Hardened Bacteria," *Time*, June 18, 2007, p. 36.

10. Hank Davis, John Memmott, and Harry M. B. Hurwitz, "Autocontingencies: A Model for Subtle Behavioral Control," *Journal of Experimental Psychology: General* 104 (1975): 169–88.

11. S. Sevigny and R. Ladouceur, "Gamblers' Irrational Thinking about Chance Events: The 'Double Switching' Concept," *International Gambling Studies* 3, no. 2 (2003): 163–70.

12. Daniel Schacter, *The Seven Sins of Memory* (New York: Houghton Mifflin, 2001).

13. James S. Nairne and Josefa N. S. Pandeirada, "Adaptive Memory:

Remembering with a Stone-Age Brain," *Current Directions in Psychological Science* 17, no. 4 (2008): 239–43.

14. Michael Ritchie, *Please Stand By: A Prehistory of Television* (Woodstock, NY: Overlook Press, 1994).

CHAPTER 6

1. Richard Dawkins, *A Devil's Chaplain* (New York: Houghton Mifflin, 2003).

2. Christopher Hitchens, *The Missionary Position: Mother Teresa in Theory and Practice* (London: Verso, 1996).

3. Louis Sahagun, "A Founding Father's View of God," *Los Angeles Times*, July 5, 2008.

4. http://en.wikipedia.org/wiki/Jefferson_Bible.

5. Julian Barnes, *Arthur & George* (New York: Vintage, 2007).

6. Andrew Sullivan, *The Conservative Soul* (New York: Harper-Collins, 2006).

7. Stewart Guthrie, *Faces in the Clouds: A New Theory of Religion* (New York: Oxford University Press, 1993).

8. Chuck Berry, "The Downbound Train," Chess 1615, 1955.

9. Pascal Boyer, *Religion Explained* (New York: Basic Books, 2001).

10. Matthew Alper, *The God Part of the Brain* (New York: Rogue Press, 2004).

11. Dean Hamer, *The God Gene* (New York: Random House, 2004).

12. Jacqueline Salmon, "Most Americans Believe in Higher Power, Poll Finds," *Washington Post* (June 24, 2008).

13. Kat Bergeron, "Church Changes 'God' Sign," *Mississippi Sun Herald*, September 15, 2002.

14. Stephen Prothero, *American Jesus: How the Son of God Became a National Icon* (New York: Farrar, Straus and Giroux, 2003).

15. David Hume, *A Treatise of Human Nature* (New York: Dover Books, 2003 [1740]).

16. John D. Loudermilk, "He's Just a Scientist, That's All," RCA LP 2539.

17. Tom Weaver, *Poverty Row Horrors!* (Jefferson, NC: McFarland and Company, 1993).

18. Jamy Swiss, talk given at the Amazing Meeting 3, Las Vegas, January 13–16, 2005.

19. Edmund D. Cohen, "The Religiosity of George W. Bush," *Free Inquiry* 17, no. 4 (2004): 39.

CHAPTER 7

1. Michael W. Passer, Ronald E. Smith, Michael L. Atkinson, John B. Mitchell, and Darwin W. Muir, *Psychology: Frontiers and Applications*, 2nd Canadian ed. (Toronto: McGraw-Hill Ryerson, 2005).

2. John Bradshaw, *Homecoming: Reclaiming and Championing Your Inner Child* (New York: Bantam Books, 1990).

3. David Hume, *A Treatise of Human Nature* (New York: Dover Books, 2003 [1740]).

4. Carl Sagan, *The Demon-Haunted World* (New York: Random House, 1995).

5. Sam Harris, Letter to the Editor, *New York Times*, December 5, 2006.

6. Sagan, *Demon-Haunted World*, p. 210.

7. Dan Barker, *Losing Faith in Faith: From Preacher to Atheist* (Madison, WI: FFRF, 1992).